Jewish History

An Enthralling Guide from Ancient Kingdoms to Modern Times

© Copyright 2023 - All rights reserved.

The content contained within this book may not be reproduced, duplicated, or transmitted without direct written permission from the author or the publisher.

Under no circumstances will any blame or legal responsibility be held against the publisher, or author, for any damages, reparation, or monetary loss due to the information contained within this book, either directly or indirectly.

Legal Notice:

This book is copyright protected. It is only for personal use. You cannot amend, distribute, sell, use, quote, or paraphrase any part, or the content within this book, without the consent of the author or publisher.

Disclaimer Notice:

Please note the information contained within this document is for educational and entertainment purposes only. All effort has been executed to present accurate, up-to-date, reliable, and complete information. No warranties of any kind are declared or implied. Readers acknowledge that the author is not engaging in the rendering of legal, financial, medical, or professional advice. The content within this book has been derived from various sources. Please consult a licensed professional before attempting any techniques outlined in this book.

By reading this document, the reader agrees that under no circumstances is the author responsible for any losses, direct or indirect, that are incurred as a result of the use of the information contained within this document, including, but not limited to, errors, omissions, or inaccuracies.

Free limited time bonus

Stop for a moment. We have a free bonus set up for you. The problem is this: we forget 90% of everything that we read after 7 days. Crazy fact, right? Here's the solution: we've created a printable, 1-page pdf summary for this book that you're reading now. All you have to do to get your free pdf summary is to go to the following website:

https://livetolearn.lpages.co/enthrallinghistory/

Once you do, it will be intuitive. Enjoy, and thank you!

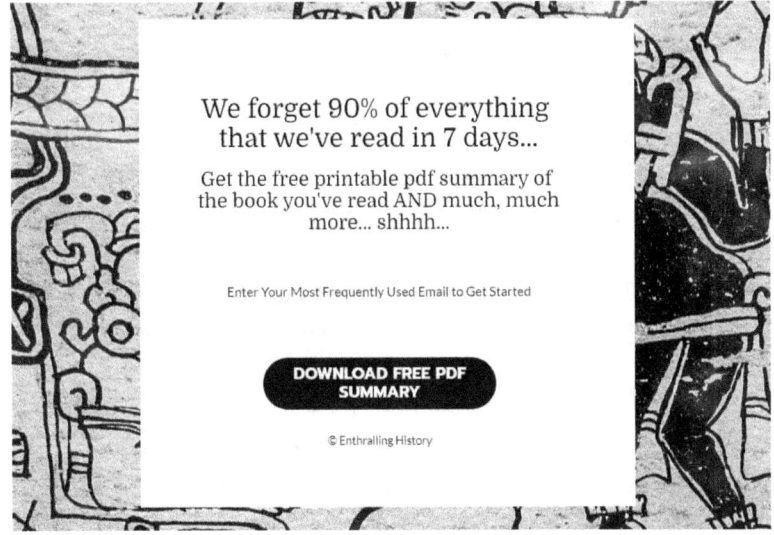

Table of Contents

PART 1: HISTORY OF THE JEWS 1
    INTRODUCTION 2
    CHAPTER 1: WHAT IS JUDAISM? 4
    CHAPTER 2: ANCIENT ISRAEL 14
    CHAPTER 3: THE SECOND TEMPLE PERIOD (540 BCE-135 CE) 25
    CHAPTER 4: BYZANTINE JUDAISM (324-640CE) 35
    CHAPTER 5: MEDIEVAL JUDAISM I: ISLAM AND THE SPANISH GOLDEN AGE 43
    CHAPTER 6: MEDIEVAL JUDAISM II: CRUSADES AND THE MAMLUK PERIOD 51
    CHAPTER 7: THE HOLOCAUST 60
    CHAPTER 8: MODERN ISRAEL 70
    CHAPTER 9: CUSTOMS, TRADITIONS, SYMBOLS, AND ART 81
    CHAPTER 10: FAMOUS JEWS: AN ENTHRALLING COLLECTION 89
    CONCLUSION 99
PART 2: ANCIENT ISRAEL 103
    INTRODUCTION 104
    CHAPTER 1: WHO WERE THE ANCIENT ISRAELITES? 107
    CHAPTER 2: HENOTHEISM AND YAHWISM 113
    CHAPTER 3: THE IRON AGE 121
    CHAPTER 4: BIBLICAL REFERENCES TO ANCIENT ISRAEL 131
    CHAPTER 5: THE KINGDOM OF JUDAH 142
    CHAPTER 6: THE PERSIAN PERIOD 151

CHAPTER 7: THE HELLENISTIC PERIOD (330-50 BCE) 161
CHAPTER 8: THE HASMONEAN DYNASTY (140-37 BCE) 169
CHAPTER 9: THE HERODIAN DYNASTY (37 BCE-100 CE) 181
CONCLUSION 193
HERE'S ANOTHER BOOK BY ENTHRALLING HISTORY THAT
YOU MIGHT LIKE 195
FREE LIMITED TIME BONUS 196
BIBLIOGRAPHY 197

Part 1: History of the Jews

An Enthralling Guide from Ancient Times to the Present

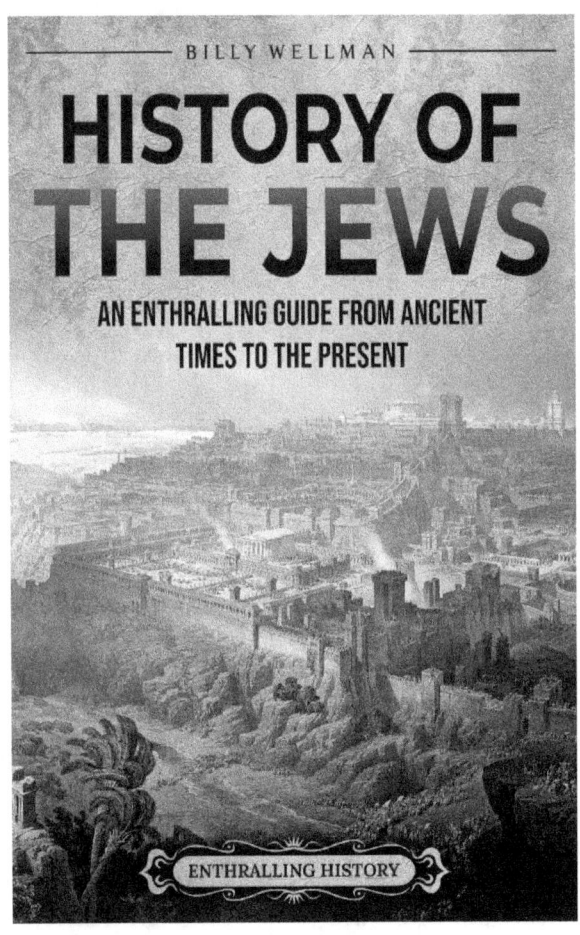

Introduction

The history of the Jews is the story of a people, a nation, and a religion. From a nomadic tribe of seventy people grew a nation that impacted the world on multiple levels. The religion established in the Sinai desert over three millennia ago persists today as Judaism, with about fifteen million followers. The history of the Jews isn't about one country or even one continent. It is global, as more Jews have lived outside Israel than in their ancient homeland for two thousand years. Judaism gave birth to Christianity and influenced Islam; thus, over half of the world's population follows at least some of the teachings of the Jewish Tanakh (Old Testament).

What, exactly, is a Jew? Is being "Jewish" a national identity with a shared history? Is it an ethnic identity with a collective culture? Can one be an atheist and still be a Jew? Can a person follow Judaism but not have an ethnic Jewish background? If one's mother is Jewish, but the father is not, is that person still Jewish? The answer to all these questions is "yes."

It's hard to put "Jewishness" in a box since it is full of schisms, disputes, paradoxes, and evolving history and culture. Yet history, ethnicity, and culture have always connected the Jews. Although many Jews don't go to synagogue or temple, they will gather for the Seder (Passover) meal and attend rites of passage like a bat or bar mitzvah. The Jews have persevered as a minority culture despite attempts to wipe them off the face of the earth. They have adapted to change with "chutzpah," developing ingenuity and innovation.

Today, the State of Israel has close to ten million people, about three-quarters of whom are ethnic Jews, with the rest primarily Arab Palestinians. Almost fifteen million Jews of the diaspora live in the United States, France, Canada, and elsewhere in the world. The Jews have contributed remarkably to the cultures of the lands where they lived and have changed the course of world history. Understanding the history of the Jews is essential to deciphering world history in general and the current political scene in the Middle East.

From the era of the patriarchs to the present day, Jewish history covers almost four thousand years and encircles the earth. This book endeavors to guide readers through the thousands of years of Jewish history, from the Jews' time as nomadic herders to the present day. It explores the patriarchs, the exodus from Egypt, the kingdom of Israel, and its fall. It traces Jewish history through the reign of the Macedonians, the Romans, the Byzantines, and the Islamic caliphates. It will explain why most Jews left their homeland to spread throughout the earth and why many returned in the past two centuries. It will unpack the horrors of the Holocaust and why and how the modern State of Israel was established.

The Jews have always believed that history has a purpose, a belief that has enabled them to maintain dignity and tenacity through unimaginable struggles and persecution. From their history's inception, their religion informed them that "all the families of the earth shall be blessed in you."[1] Let's travel back to ancient Mesopotamia and uncover the history of the enthralling Jewish people.

---

[1] Bereshit (Genesis) 12:3, Torah, *The Complete Tanakh: The Jewish Bible with a Modern English Translation and Rashi's Commentary.*
https://www.chabad.org/library/bible_cdo/aid/63255/jewish/The-Bible-with-Rashi.htm

Chapter 1: What Is Judaism?

Judaism, the religion of the Jewish people, is monotheistic, worshiping only one deity who introduced himself as לִיהוָה (YHVH) or אֱלֹהֵיכֶם (Elohim). Many Jews believe writing out the names of their deity is disrespectful, so they write it as G-d in English. They base this practice on the book of Devarim (Deuteronomy), which says they shouldn't desecrate, destroy, or erase the name of G-d or anything to do with him.[2] If they write out G-d's name and the document is deleted or destroyed, then G-d's name is erased.

Judaism's scripture is the Tanakh, which has the same material as the Old Testament in the Christian Bible (minus the Apocrypha). However, it only has twenty-four books rather than thirty-nine. Samuel, Chronicles, and Kings are each one book instead of two, and all the minor prophets form one book. The Tanakh has three sections: Torah, Nevi'im, and Ketuvim.

The Torah is the five books of Moses (the first five books of the Old Testament). Historically, Jews considered the entire Tanakh divine, yet they reverenced the Torah most highly because their scriptures say the whole nation witnessed its transmission. Moses received it on Mount Sinai while millions of Israelites stood trembling below as the ram's horn blasted, smoke enveloped the mountain, thunder roared, and lightning flashed.[3] The Torah contains the Jewish accounts of the beginning of life,

---

[2] Devarim (Deuteronomy) 12:2-4, Torah, *Tanakh*.

the birth of the Israelite nation, and the laws given by G-d for them to follow.

When all five books of the Torah are handwritten by a specially-trained scribe on a single parchment scroll, this is called *Sefer Torah*. This precious and sacred scroll is kept in a special ornamental chamber in the synagogue called the Torah Ark. It is read in Hebrew using cantillation, a kind of chanting, on Shabbat (the Sabbath), at Monday and Thursday morning prayers, and on special holy days.

The next section of the Tanakh, the Nevi'im, contains the writings of the prophets. However, the books of Eichah (Lamentations) and Daniel are included in the Ketuvim. Some earlier Israelite history is also in the Nevi'im: Yehoshua (Joshua), Shoftim (Judges), Shmuel (Samuel), and Melachim (Kings). The Ketuvim (Writings) has poetic books, such as Tehillim (Psalms) and Mishlei (Proverbs), and historical accounts, such as Ruth and Queen Esther.

Another influential book for Judaism is the Talmud, which contains teachings by rabbis (religious leaders) on Jewish theology and history throughout the years. The Talmud includes the Mishna: oral laws and interpretations of the Torah's laws, completed in written form in the 3rd century of the Common Era. The Talmud's other section is the Gemara, a collection of commentaries by rabbis.

How do today's Jews view Judaism's scriptures? It depends on which sect they follow. The Orthodox Jews believe G-d literally dictated the Torah to Moses, and they do not question that its stories are true and its laws should be followed. They passionately believe in a Messiah who will come from the lineage of King David and usher in an age of righteousness, peace, and justice. They believe G-d will resurrect the dead and create a new heaven and earth.

The Orthodox Jews concur with Rabbi Moses ben Maimon (1134-1204 CE), who wrote the *Mishneh Torah*, a codification of Jewish law from the Torah and Talmud. He said, "I believe with perfect faith that the entire Torah that is now in our possession is the same that was given to Moses, our teacher, peace be upon him."[4]

---

[4] Eli Cohn-Wein, "The Golden Age of Jewish Philosophy," *Sefaria*. https://www.sefaria.org/sheets/327268?lang=bi

Rabbi Moses ben Maimon (Rashi)
https://commons.wikimedia.org/wiki/File:Maimonides-2.jpg

Orthodox Judaism has two sub-groups: the ultra-conservative Haredim (9 percent of Israel's Jewish population) and the Datiim (13 percent of Israel's Jews). Haredi means "trembling," and these Jews are highly devout. The Hasidic Jews of New York City are a sub-group. Like the Haredim in Israel, they live in separate neighborhoods, socialize mainly among themselves, and wear distinctive clothing. The men usually wear a black coat and hat, and the women wear modest dresses and a head scarf or wig. The Datiim are also theologically conservative but don't separate themselves from mainstream society. The men wear a yarmulke (skullcap), and married women cover their hair.

The second sect is Reformed Judaism, known as Hilonim in Israel, where it is followed by 49 percent of the Jews. In 1837, Abraham Geiger declared, "The Talmud must go, the Bible, that collection of mostly so beautiful and exalted human books, as a divine work must also go."[5]

From that point, Reformed Jews denied the divine origin of the Tanakh, considering it to be the work of men. Shortly after, Rabbi Isaac Mayer Wise declared disbelief in a bodily resurrection or a messiah. He omitted the traditional prayers about returning to Jerusalem to rebuild the

---

[5] Walter Jacob, ed., *The Pittsburgh Platform in Retrospect: The Changing World of Reform Judaism* (Pittsburgh: Rodef Shalom Congregation Press, 1985), 104.

temple and eliminated the dietary laws. In 1885, Reformed Jews rejected circumcision as "savage." By 1972, only one in ten Reformed rabbis in the United States believed in G-d in the traditional Jewish sense. They self-identified as agnostic, humanistic, or existentialist.[6] In Israel, 40 percent of the Hilonim Jews do not believe in G-d.

The third sect, Conservative Judaism (known as Masorti in Israel), is the middle ground between the Orthodox and Reformed sects. Conservative Jews were a sub-branch of the Reformed Jews with more moderate ideas of what needed reforming. Zacharias Frankel started with the practices that most Jews had already stopped following, "that the forward progress will seem inconsequential to the average eye."[7]

The Masorti Jews, who make up 29 percent of the Jews in Israel, follow traditional Judaism, believing G-d created the world and made a covenant with the Israelites. They accept the laws of the Torah regarding lifestyle and the Mishnah and Talmudic teachings on the Torah. However, they doubt that G-d literally dictated the Ten Commandments and the rest of the Torah to Moses, although they believe it is a divine teaching of G-d's will. They think they must carefully consider modern science with regard to their religious beliefs. In areas where science and Torah appear to contradict, they interpret religious tradition to comply with scientific facts while recognizing that science is not infallible.

In 1886, Conservative Judaism launched the Jewish Theological Seminary of America in New York City. The seminary permitted driving cars to Shabbat services, previously forbidden because the car's engine "lit a fire," which the Torah forbids on the Sabbath. Actually, the Torah forbids lighting a cooking fire inside the house on the day of rest, and somehow that got applied to all fires.[8]

Within a century, Conservative Jews in the United States had reached the point where they no longer believed in the divine authorship of the Torah, considering its stories mythical. One offshoot, the "Reconstructionists," completely abandoned belief in the supernatural. Another spin-off, the Institute for Traditional Judaism, believes Moses did receive the Torah from G-d at Mount Sinai, but the scrolls were lost

---

[6] Theodore I. Lenin, et al. *Associates, Rabbi and Synagogue in Reform Judaism* (West Harford: Central Conference of American Rabbis, 1972) 98-99.

[7] Michael A. Meyer, *Response to Modernity: A History of the Reform Movement in Judaism* (New York: Oxford University Press, 1988), 85.

[8] Shemot (Exodus) 35:3, Torah, *Tanakh*.

during the Babylonian exile and the temple's destruction. This group believes the Torah we have today is a 6th-century BCE reconstruction of what the Jews of that time considered the original manuscripts.

One thing is clear: Judaism revolves around the Torah, although Jews interpret it differently. Some take it literally, some say it is allegorical, and some say myth. What is in the Torah? This chapter will explore the book of Bereshit (Genesis), and chapter two will review the rest of the Torah. Bereshit tells of creation, the first sin, and the great flood. It introduces the patriarchs who fathered the Israelite tribe, the ancestors of the Jews.

The Torah begins with creation. G-d created day and night and separated the earth's waters from the water in the atmosphere. He formed dry land and plant life. He made the sun to rule the day, the moon to rule the night, and the stars and planets to shed light on the earth. Next, G-d created sea creatures and winged animals. After this, G-d made the animals that walked and crawled on the earth. G-d's final act was creating human beings in his image, male and female. G-d ceased the work of creation on the seventh day, which he made a holy day of rest for human beings.[9]

The Torah account of creation differs markedly from other Mesopotamian origin stories, such as the *Enuma Elish*. In the macabre Babylonian myth, the creator god Apsu and his wife Tiamat, the deity of chaos, created the younger gods. To their annoyance, the young gods kept them awake night and day with riotous singing and dancing, so Apsu decided to destroy them. But the young god Enki launched a pre-emptive strike, killing Apsu. Then Tiamat sent eleven hideous demons to slaughter the young gods. However, Enki's son Marduk conjured up his hurricane powers, blew up his grandmother's body, fileted her like a fish, and created the sky and the earth with the two halves of her body.[10]

The Torah says that G-d planted the Garden of Eden for Adam and Eve, with the Tree of Life and the Tree of Knowledge of Good and Evil standing in the middle. G-d told Adam they could freely eat from any tree except the Tree of Knowledge. But the serpent tempted Eve, telling her that if she ate from the Tree of Knowledge, she would be like the angels, knowing good and evil. Eve ate the fruit and gave it to her husband, who

---

[9] Bereshit (Genesis) 1-2, Torah, *Tanakh*.

[10] *Enuma Elish: The Seven Tablets of Creation*, trans. Leonard William King (London: Luzac, 1902). https://www.sacred-texts.com/ane/enuma.htm

was with her, and he also ate it.

After eating the forbidden fruit, Adam and Eve lost their innocence. G-d cursed the serpent, telling him Eve's descendant would crush his head, although the serpent would bite his heel. He exiled Adam and Eve from the garden lest they eat from the Tree of Life and live forever. From then on, the earth was cursed, work was hard, childbearing was painful, and immortality was lost.[11]

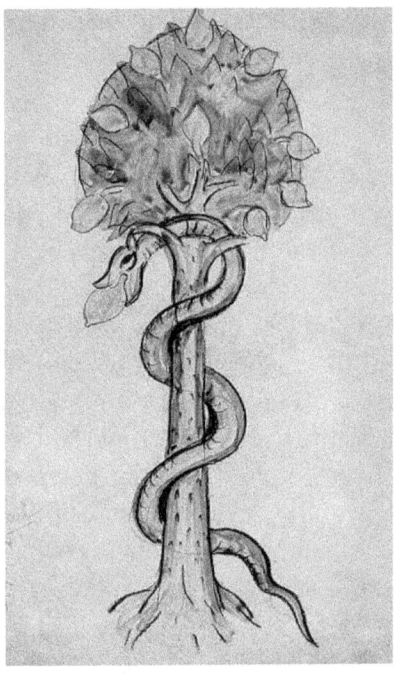

A mural of the serpent in Eden, painted by Chaim ben Yitzchak ha-Levi Segal in the Cold Synagogue in Mogilev, Lithuania (now Belarus) in the 1740s. Belarus authorities destroyed the synagogue in 1938, and this photo and others taken by El Lissitzky are all that remain.
https://commons.wikimedia.org/wiki/File:Cold_synagogue_in_Mogilev_The_Garden_of_Eden_Serpent_by_El_Lissitzky.jpg

Adam and Eve's first son Cain killed his brother Abel, and each generation became increasingly violent and corrupt. G-d decided to blot out human life, but Noah found favor in G-d's eyes. He told Noah to build an ark and bring his family on board, with one pair of all the animals and enough food for the people and animals to eat. Noah was to bring seven pairs of "clean" (sacrificial) animals on the ark. At this point,

---

[11] Bereshit (Genesis) 2:8-3:24.

humans and animals were vegetarian.[12] Noah and his sons built the ark, and the heavens opened. It rained for forty days, and the flood waters rose until they covered the mountains.

After the waters subsided, the ark rested on the mountains of Ararat, on the border between present-day Turkey and Armenia. After his family and the animals left the ark, Noah built an altar and sacrificed some of the clean animals. G-d gave the rainbow as a covenant that he would never again destroy the earth with a flood and permitted humans and some animals to become carnivorous.[13]

The Torah's flood account resembles the Sumerian *Eridu Genesis* and the Akkadian *Epic of Atrahasis*. In the Sumerian and Akkadian versions, the gods were angry at humans and decided to destroy them with a flood, but Enki warned a priest to build an ark and take the animals on it. The ancient Greeks, Chinese, Aztecs, and multiple civilizations worldwide had a similar flood story.

After the flood, the Torah says humans spread out over the earth, and one Semitic family from the lineage of Noah's son Shem settled in the city of Ur in southern Sumer (Iraq). Today, the ruins of Ur sit in a desert wasteland, but in ancient times, it was an incredibly wealthy city close to where the Euphrates River emptied into the Persian Gulf. Global cooling lowered the Gulf levels, and silt from the Euphrates and Tigris rivers moved the Gulf's shoreline about thirty miles away.

The father of this Semitic family in Ur was Terah. Like the Sumerians, he worshiped multiple gods.[14] For some reason, perhaps due to climate change, Terah packed up his family and herds of sheep, goats, and camels and followed the Euphrates north into today's Turkey. They settled in Haran near the border of today's Syria.

G-d called Terah's son Abram to leave his father's house and go to a new land when he was seventy-five years old. G-d told Abram he would make him into a great nation. He would bless Abram, and all the families of the earth would be blessed in Abram. Abram traveled south into the land of Canaan, which G-d said he would give to his descendants. That was problematic, as Abram had no children because his wife Sarai could not conceive. But G-d promised his descendants would be as uncountable

---

[12] Bereshit (Genesis) 1:29-30.

[13] Bereshit (Genesis) 6-9.

[14] Yehoshua (Joshua) 24:2, Nevi'im, *Tanakh*.

as the stars in the sky.

When Abram was ninety-nine years old, G-d changed his name to Abraham (father of a multitude) and Sarai's name to Sarah (princess). Despite Sarah being ninety and infertile even when young, G-d made a covenant that Abraham and Sarah would have a son in one year. Abraham was to be the father of many nations. For his part of the covenant, Abraham and all the males in his camp had to be circumcised. From then on, all baby boys should be circumcised eight days after birth.

As G-d promised, Sarah miraculously conceived and had a baby a year later, when Abraham was one hundred years old. They named him Isaac, meaning laughter. When Isaac was grown, Abraham sent his steward back to Haran, where some of his relatives still lived, to find a wife for Isaac. His steward arrived at the well of Haran with ten camels, extremely nervous about his task. As he saw a group of young women approaching to draw water, he prayed, asking G-d to show him the right woman. If he asked a young woman for water, and she also offered to water his camels, he would know that was the girl for Isaac.[15]

While he was praying, a young woman named Rebecca came with her pitcher, and when he asked her for some water, she immediately gave him a drink. "I will also draw water for your camels," she said, doing just that.

Rebecca Waters the Camels. Painting by Alexandre Cabanel.
Photo modified: zoomed in. Public Domain: https://commons.wikimedia.org/wiki/File:Alexandre_Cabanel_-_Rebecca_et_Eli%C3%A9zer_-_1883.jpg

---

[15] Bereshit (Genesis) 11-24.

When the camels finished drinking, he gave Rebecca a gold nose ring and two gold bracelets. It turned out that she was the granddaughter of Abraham's brother Nahor. The steward negotiated a marriage with Rebecca's brother Laban and her father, Bethuel. They called Rebecca in and asked if she was willing to travel to Canaan to marry Isaac, and she agreed. After gifting the family with treasures, the steward returned to Canaan with Rebecca.

Isaac and Rebecca had twin sons, Esau and Jacob, but Esau was born first, making him the primary heir. Jacob tricked Esau out of his birthright as a young man and stole Isaac's blessing meant for Esau. When Esau vowed to kill Jacob, Rebecca sent Jacob away to her brother Laban in Haran. On his way north to Haran, Jacob dreamed of angels ascending and descending from a ladder reaching heaven. G-d spoke to Jacob, telling him that all the families of earth would be blessed through his descendants, the same thing G-d promised Abraham.

Jacob continued to Haran and encountered his beautiful cousin Rachel at the well, where she had come to water the sheep. Jacob watered the sheep for her, kissed her, and wept, telling her he was her relative. Jacob struck a deal with his uncle Laban that he would work for him for seven years as the bride price for Rachel. After seven years, Laban tricked him and gave Jacob his less attractive daughter Leah. Laban said Jacob could also marry Rachel at the end of the week if he worked another seven years for his father-in-law.[16]

Jacob, who G-d renamed Israel, had twelve sons from his two wives and two concubines, and they became the twelve tribes of Israel. Joseph was his son from his favorite wife, Rachel, and his other sons were jealous of how Israel lavished attention on the boy. One day, his brothers sold Joseph as a slave to Egyptian traders and told their father that a wild animal had attacked and killed Joseph.

Joseph endured slavery and imprisonment in Egypt, but through his gift of dream interpretation, he was finally freed to become the pharaoh's second-in-command. His actions saved Egypt from a horrific drought. When the drought hit Canaan, his brothers came to Egypt for grain and met Joseph, who forgave them for selling him to slave traders. Joseph moved his father and brothers to Egypt, and the Israelites lived there for four centuries.

---

[16] Bereshit (Genesis) 24-29.

Key Takeaways:
- ➢ Judaism is the religion of the Jews
  - o Jews believe in one G-d
  - o The scripture is the Tanakh: Torah (law), Nevi'im (prophets), Ketuvim (writings)
  - o The Talmud interprets the law and has theological commentaries by rabbis
- ➢ Main sects of Judaism
  - o Orthodox: take the Torah at face value
  - o Reformed: believe the Torah and even G-d are myths
  - o Conservative/Masorti: interpret the Torah in line with science
- ➢ What's in the Torah?
  - o Creation and the fall
  - o The great flood
  - o The patriarchs: Abraham, Isaac, Jacob (Israel), and his twelve sons

Chapter 2: Ancient Israel

Seventy Israelites entered Egypt, and two million came out four centuries later. Life in Egypt was good at first. Joseph had interpreted the pharaoh's dream and prophesied that seven years of famine would follow seven years of plenty. During the years of bumper crops, he stored the extra grain so the Egyptians could eat during the famine. They even had enough to sell to the surrounding nations, enriching Egypt. Joseph had saved Egypt and enjoyed the high regard of the pharaoh and the Egyptians.

But a new dynasty came into power in Egypt, as told in the Shemot (Exodus), the second book of the Torah. The new pharaoh knew nothing about Joseph. But he did know that the Israelites' population had exploded, and they now outnumbered the Egyptians. What would keep them from taking over Egypt? He forced the Israelites, also known as Hebrews, into backbreaking work in construction and farming to weaken and reduce their numbers. He also commanded the genocide of all male Israelite infants.

Jochebed, a Hebrew woman from the tribe of Levi, had a baby boy and hid him for three months. Finally, she put him into a basket and floated him down the Nile River, where the pharaoh's daughter found him. The princess adopted him, naming him Moses, and hired Jochebed as his nurse. When Moses grew up, G-d called him to deliver the Israelites from Egypt. But the pharaoh refused to let the enslaved Israelites leave Egypt.[17]

---

[17] Shemot (Exodus) 1-3, Torah, *Tanakh*.

G-d sent ten plagues to Egypt to change the pharaoh's mind. Water turned into blood, then frogs, lice, and flies covered the land. Pestilence, hail, and locusts killed the livestock and grain. Boils afflicted the people, and a deep darkness covered Egypt. Goshen, where the Israelites lived, was spared. Despite the first nine dreadful plagues, the pharaoh refused to let the Hebrews leave Egypt. Then came the final and most terrible plague.

Moses warned the pharaoh that all the firstborn sons in Egypt would die. The pharaoh had ordered the death of all the Israelite male infants, and now it came back to haunt him. But the pharaoh hardened his heart. Meanwhile, G-d instructed the Hebrews to observe the first Passover. Each father must select a one-year-old, unblemished male lamb for his household. At sundown on the fourteenth day of the first month, each family was to kill the lamb and put its blood on the sides and top of their house's doorframe.

They were to roast and eat the lamb that night with unleavened bread and bitter herbs. G-d said he would pass over the houses with blood on the doorframes and spare the people within. The Passover (Seder) would be a permanent festival celebrated each year for seven days to remember G-d's deliverance. That night, the Israelites closed their doors and huddled inside. Because of the blood on the door, the angel of death passed over their homes but killed every firstborn male in Egypt, even in the pharaoh's household.

This time, the pharaoh relented. After 430 years, the entire Israelite population poured out of Egypt, with 600,000 men of military age plus women and children. Assuming the men had at least one wife and two children, more than two million people left Egypt. In addition, a multitude of Egyptians left with the Israelites. Twelve tribes (actually, thirteen) marched out, the descendants of Israel's twelve sons. The tribes were Reuben, Simeon, Judah, Issachar, Zebulun, Benjamin, Dan, Naphtali, Gad, Asher, Ephraim, and Manasseh. Ephraim and Manasseh were Joseph's sons; his descendants got a double portion. The other tribe was Levi, a separate, priestly tribe that lived among the rest of the tribes as religious leaders.

G-d led the Israelites with a pillar of cloud by day and a pillar of fire by night. After they left Egypt, the pharaoh had a change of heart, realizing Egypt had lost its massive slave force. With his vast army, he charged out against the Israelites camped beside the Red Sea. The Israelites panicked and screamed to Moses, "Is it because there are no graves in Egypt that you have taken us to die in the desert?"

But Moses reassured them, "Don't be afraid! Stand firm and see the L-rd's salvation!"[18]

As Moses raised his staff, a strong east wind blew on the sea, splitting it in half. The great multitude crossed over with walls of water on their right and left. Meanwhile, the pillar of fire moved between the Israelite and Egyptian camps, blocking the pharaoh's army as the Israelites crossed over by night. In the morning, the pharaoh saw the Israelites had escaped and followed them into the sea. But the Egyptians' chariot wheels swerved and fell off, and then the waters crashed down, covering the pharaoh's army. Moses's sister, Miriam the prophetess, led the women with their tambourines, singing and dancing.

As they crossed the desert, the Israelites complained that they had no food, and G-d said, "Behold! I am going to rain down for you bread from heaven."[19] The following morning, when the people emerged from their tents, they found the desert covered with thin flakes. The Israelites called it manna, meaning, "What is it?" Moses explained it was bread from G-d. They could bake it into bread or boil it like porridge. Each morning, they should gather enough for their family, but on the sixth day, they should gather twice as much and prepare food for two days so that they could rest on the Sabbath.

Three months after leaving Egypt, the Israelites arrived at the Sinai desert and camped next to the high, jagged Mount Sinai. Smoke enveloped the violently quaking mountain as G-d descended in fire and called to Moses in the thunder to meet him on the summit. And there, G-d gave Moses the Ten Commandments:

1. You shall not have the gods of others in My presence.
2. You shall not make for yourself a graven image. You shall neither prostrate yourself before them nor worship them, for I, the L-rd, your G-d, am a jealous G-d.
3. You shall not take the name of the L-rd, your G-d, in vain.
4. Remember the Sabbath day to sanctify it.
5. Honor your father and your mother in order that your days be lengthened on the land that the L-rd, your G-d, is giving you.

---

[18] Shemot (Exodus) 14:11-13.
[19] Shemot (Exodus) 16:4.

6. You shall not murder.
7. You shall not commit adultery.
8. You shall not steal.
9. You shall not bear false witness against your neighbor.
10. You shall not covet your neighbor's house. You shall not covet your neighbor's wife, his manservant, his maidservant, his ox, his donkey, or whatever belongs to your neighbor.[20]

Moses and the Ten Commandments by Tissot
https://commons.wikimedia.org/wiki/File:Tissot_Moses_and_the_Ten_Commandments.jpg

G-d also gave instructions to build the Mishkan: the tent of worship, which the Israelites carried with them as they traveled, assembling and dissembling it at each stop. In addition to the Ten Commandments, G-d gave other commandments recorded in the Torah, which fall into three broad categories. The most important laws dealt with the people's relationship with G-d, covered in the first four of the Ten Commandments.

---

[20] Shemot (Exodus) 20.

Next were laws about their relationships with each other, which included five through ten of the Ten Commandments. They also had rules relating to health and hygiene. These included the dietary laws, which forbade eating disease-carrying animals. Another law dealt with human waste disposal. They had to go to a designated place outside the camp, dig a hole, and then cover their excrement.[21]

Finally, it was time to enter Canaan and possess the land. The books of Yehoshua (Joshua) and Shoftim (Judges) in the Nevi'im section of the Tanakh tell how the twelve tribes of Israel conquered the cities one by one and divided up the land. They had to contend with the Canaanites, Hittites, and Amorites, who had lived in Canaan in Abraham's day. The Israelites subdued the Canaanites, forcing them to pay tribute but permitting them to live among them. The Philistines, who had settled along the coast while the Israelites were in Egypt, persistently raided their farmland.

The Philistines had adopted the Semitic god Dagan, the grain deity and the father of Baal (Bel), an important god in Mesopotamia and the primary god of the Canaanites. Ashtoreth, the goddess of the sea and fertility, was Baal's wife. The Torah warned the Israelites not to worship these other gods or sacrifice their children to Molek (Molech), an Ammonite god. Abraham abandoned the polytheism of his father to serve one deity only. But in Egypt, some Israelites had strayed into worshiping Egyptian gods. G-d made it clear that they should worship only לִיהוָה (YHVH) to receive his blessing and guidance. If they turned to other gods, they would suffer calamities. The Israelites vowed to follow only G-d but kept straying to Baal and Molek.

When the Israelites first returned to Canaan around 1400 BCE, they were a loose confederation of tribes with no monarch or central administration. Valiant heroes rose to fight their enemies, and their exploits are in the book of Shoftim (Judges) in the Nevi'im. Deborah was a judge who led the tribes of Naphtali and Zebulun against the Canaanites and prevailed. Gideon led three hundred men against the coalition forces of the Amalekites and Midianites with a stunning victory. G-d gave Samson supernatural strength to defeat the Philistines, but he kept getting distracted by beautiful Philistine women, which proved his undoing.

---

[21] Devarim (Deuteronomy) 23:13-15

The book of Shmuel (I & II Samuel) in the Nevi'im records the history of Israel's first two kings, Saul and David. The twelve tribes united into a monarchy around 1020 BCE, and their first king was Saul, the tallest man in Israel. While he was reigning, a boy named David was herding sheep in the fields outside Bethlehem, playing his harp and fighting off bears and lions. Saul led the Israelites in a battle against the Philistines but was stymied when they sent out their champion, a nine-foot-tall giant named Goliath. Everyone was afraid to fight him. When David visited the front lines with food for his older brothers, who were soldiers, he heard Goliath's taunts and told King Saul he would fight the giant.

"You're just a boy!" Saul protested.

David & Goliath by Schindler
https://commons.wikimedia.org/wiki/File:Osmar_Schindler_-_David_und_Goliath.jpg

But David was confident he could kill the giant. He marched out with his slingshot as Goliath laughed. But David retorted, "You come to me with sword, spear, and javelin, and I come to you with the Name of the L-rd of Hosts, the G-d of the armies of Israel which you have taunted."

David ran toward Goliath, killed the giant with the first stone from his sling, and used the giant's sword to cut Goliath's head off.[22] David later became the second king of Israel and conquered Jerusalem, making it Israel's religious and political capital. He brought the holy Ark of the Covenant to Jerusalem, which held the tablets with the Ten Commandments G-d had inscribed at Mount Sinai.

The account of the rest of the kings of Israel and Judah is recorded in Melachim (I & II Kings) in the Nevi'im. King Solomon, David's son, the wisest of men, built the First Temple (Solomon's Temple) in Jerusalem. While everyone else worshiped in the courtyard, only the priests were permitted inside the temple section called Hechal, where the Altar of Incense and Menorah stood. Only the high priest could enter through the curtain into the smaller room called Devir, or Holy of Holies, which held the Ark of the Covenant. One day a year, the high priest entered the Holy of Holies on Yom Kippur, the Day of Atonement, bringing the blood of an unblemished lamb to atone for the nation's sins.

The Kingdom of Israel unraveled immediately after Solomon's death. The Israelites sent delegates to his son, King Rehoboam, asking him to lighten the heavy tax load and enforced labor Solomon had inflicted. Rehoboam's council of elders encouraged him to lighten the load; if so, he would have the lifelong loyalty of the people. But his young friends advised him to take a tough approach. So, Rehoboam told the delegates: "My father made your yoke heavy, and I shall add to your yoke; my father flogged you with whips, and I shall flog you with scorpions."[23]

This harsh reply impelled ten Israelite tribes to split off, forming a divided kingdom. Only the tribes of Judah and Benjamin were left in the southern Kingdom of Judah under Rehoboam, with Jerusalem as its capital. The Kingdom of Israel in the north followed a polytheistic religion until its fall, but the Kingdom of Judah vacillated between the monotheistic worship of YHVH and polytheism.

---

[22] Shmuel I (I Samuel) 17, Nevi'im, *Tanakh*.

[23] Melachim I (I Kings) 12:14, Nevi'im, *Tanakh*.

Divided Kingdom: Israel in the north and Judah in the south
Oldtidens_Israel_&_Judea.svg: FinnWikiNoderivative work: Richardprins, CC BY-SA 3.0
<https://creativecommons.org/licenses/by-sa/3.0>, via Wikimedia Commons;
https://commons.wikimedia.org/wiki/File:Kingdoms_of_Israel_and_Judah_map_830.svg

The two kingdoms coexisted uneasily for the next two centuries, sometimes fighting each other and sometimes allying to fight a common enemy. In 1993, a black basalt stele (stone) was discovered in Tel Dan in northern Israel dating to the 9th century BCE. The Aramaic inscription says that Arameans warred against Israel and Judah, defeating Israel's King Joram, son of Ahab, and King Ahaziah of the "House of David."[24] The Tanakh gives an account of Joram and Ahaziah allied against the Aramean King Hazael. Then Jehu, from David's line, killed both Joram and Ahaziah and usurped Israel's throne, yet was defeated by King Hazael of

---

[24] Nadav Na'aman, "Three Notes on the Aramaic Inscription from Tel Dan," *Israel Exploration Journal* 50, no. 1/2 (2000): 92-104. http://www.jstor.org/stable/27926919.

Aram.[25] Another 9th-century BCE stele found in Dhiban, Jordan, records the victories of King Mesha of Moab over the "House of David."[26]

In the 8th century BCE, the Assyrian Tiglath-Pileser III crushed the Kingdom of Israel. He and his successor, Shalmaneser V, forced the ten tribes into exile in the Assyrian population relocation program. The Israelites resettled in the cities of Halah and Habor (in today's Syria, near Turkey's border) and in the cities of the Medes, probably north of Halah and Habor. The Assyrians relocated some of the Babylonians they had conquered to Samaria in Israel. The Assyrian strategy was that conquered people were less likely to rebel if they were removed from their homeland.

The Kingdom of Judah stumbled along until 609 BCE when Pharoah Necho II of Egypt headed north to assist the Assyrians. The Babylonians had united with the Scythians, Medes, and Persians and were annihilating Assyria. To Necho's annoyance, King Josiah of Judah refused passage through his country, so the pharaoh killed Josiah and annexed Judah as a vassal kingdom. Judah had to pay seventy-five pounds of gold and 7,500 pounds of silver in tribute. After Necho sorted out things in Judah, it was too late to help the Assyrians, whose empire dissolved.

Four years later, the Babylonian crown prince Nebuchadnezzar II destroyed the Egyptian army, making Judah a vassal state to Babylon. The Judaeans had self-rule but had to pay tribute to Babylon. Nebuchadnezzar brought a group of royal Judaean youths to Babylon and trained them in the Chaldean literature to be magi: experts in wisdom, astronomy, astrology, and dream interpretation. Once trained, they served among his advisors. Four of these young Jewish nobles were Daniel, Hananiah, Mishael, and Azariah, who received the Babylonian names Belteshazzar, Shadrach, Meshach, and Abed-nego. Nebuchadnezzar elevated these four young men to high positions.[27]

In 597 BCE, the eighteen-year-old King Jehoiachin of Judah attempted to overthrow Babylonian control. King Nebuchadnezzar marched on Judah, captured Jehoiachin, and imprisoned him for three decades in Babylon. Nebuchadnezzar pilfered the treasures in the temple and palace

---

[25] Melachim II (II Kings) 8-10.

[26] Jean-Philippe Delorme, "בת דוד in the Mesha Stele: A Defense of André Lemaire's Reading and Its Historical Implications," *SBL and AAR New England and Eastern Canada Region Annual Meeting* (Tufts University, Massachusetts, March 22, 2019).

[27] Daniel 1, Ketuvim, *Tanakh*.

and installed Jehoiachin's uncle Zedekiah as the new vassal king. Leaving the humblest people of Judah to tend the land, he took 10,000 Judaean nobility, skilled military men, and craftsmen back to Babylon.

Seven years later, Zedekiah refused to pay tribute to Babylon, resulting in catastrophe. Nebuchadnezzar laid siege to Jerusalem for two years, starving the people inside. King Zedekiah tried to creep out of the city by night but was captured and blinded; the last thing he saw was his sons' execution. This time, Nebuchadnezzar pulverized Jerusalem's walls and palace and burned Solomon's Temple to the ground. The few survivors were marched to Babylon, leaving Jerusalem desolate.

"By the rivers of Babylon, we sat and wept when we remembered Zion. On willows in its midst, we hung our harps. For there, our captors asked us for a song, and our tormentors demanded mirth, 'Sing for us of the song of Zion.' How shall we sing the song of the L-rd on foreign soil? If I forget you, O Jerusalem, may my right hand forget its skill. May my tongue cling to my palate if I do not remember you, if I do not lift Jerusalem as my highest joy."[28]

Key Takeaways:
- Egypt
    - Slavery and genocide
    - G-d calls Moses
    - Plagues and Passover
- Exodus
    - Twelve tribes
    - Crossing the Red Sea
    - Manna
- The Torah Law
    - Relationship with G-d
    - Relationships with each other
    - Health and hygiene
- Taking the land
    - Canaanites and Philistines and their gods
    - Heroes who arose to fight the Israelite's enemies

---

[28] Tehillim (Psalms) 137:1-6, Ketuvim, *Tanakh*.

- Kingdom of Israel
  - David and Goliath
  - Solomon builds the First Temple
- Divided kingdom: Israel and Judah
  - Fall of Israel, Assyrian exile
  - Temple destroyed, the Babylonian exile of Judah

Chapter 3: The Second Temple Period (540 BCE-135 CE)

Tens of thousands of exiles from the tribes of Judah, Benjamin, and Levi now lived in Babylonia.[29] Its capital, Babylon, was probably the largest city in the world, with a population exceeding 200,000. A recent exhibit of ancient tablets sheds light on life for the Jewish exiles: they paid taxes, traded in commodities, and contributed to Babylon's recovering economy.[30] Some were in high positions; for instance, Daniel was Nebuchadnezzar's chief magi and governor of Babylonia.[31]

What happened to the Israelite tribes exiled by the Assyrians in 722 BCE? These "lost tribes" disappeared from the historical record, but most Jews of the Second Temple period believed that the ten tribes would one day return. The 1st-century CE Jewish historian Josephus said an "immense multitude" lived "beyond the Euphrates" in his day.[32]

After Nebuchadnezzar's death, two coup d'états rocked Babylon. The second brought Nabonidus to the throne, who later abandoned his throne for Arabia, leaving his son Belshazzar as regent. While Babylonia crumbled under Belshazzar's incompetent and unpopular rule, Cyrus the

---

[29] Ezra 2, Ketuvim, *Tanakh*.
[30] Luke Baker, "Ancient Tablets Reveal Life of Jews in Nebuchadnezzar's Babylon," *Reuters*,
[31] Daniel 2:48-49.
[32] Flavius Josephus, *The Antiquities of the Jews*, trans. William Whiston (Project Gutenberg EBook), Book XI: Chapter 5. https://www.gutenberg.org/files/2848/2848-h/2848-h.htm

Great's Persian Empire was rapidly swallowing western Asia. When Cyrus approached Babylonia, the Babylonian troops headed north to their border wall, which extended from the Tigris to the Euphrates.

Confident that the two rivers, the troops, and the wall would hold off the Persians, Belshazzar and the rest of Babylon were celebrating the moon god festival. Belshazzar ordered the gold and silver goblets from Jerusalem's temple be brought to his banquet so everyone could drink from them. Suddenly, Belshazzar's face turned white as he saw a disembodied hand inscribing something on the wall. His mother urged him to call for Daniel, "in whom is the spirit of the gods."

Writing on the Wall by Rembrandt
https://commons.wikimedia.org/wiki/File:Belshazzar%E2%80%99s_feast,_by_Rembrandt.jpg

The elderly Daniel entered the banquet hall and informed Belshazzar, "You were weighed on the scales and found wanting. Your kingdom has been broken up and given to Media and Persia."[33]

By this time, Cyrus's army had waded across the Tigris River into Babylonia's northern frontier and marched toward Babylon at lightning speed. While Belshazzar banqueted, the Medes and Persians diverted the Euphrates, crossed over, and crashed through Babylon's Enlil gate. The Babylonians were drunk from the holiday festivities, and with little

---

[33] Daniel 5.

resistance, the Medes and Persians broke into the palace. They killed Belshazzar, and Cyrus the Great entered Babylon as its new king in 539 BCE.[34]

Cyrus permitted the populations displaced by the Assyrians and Babylonians to return to their home countries. Many Jews in high positions remained in Babylon or moved to Persia to serve Cyrus. However, 42,000 left for Jerusalem under the leadership of Judah's Prince Sheshbazzar. Cyrus returned the gold and silver utensils Nebuchadnezzar had taken from Solomon's Temple and ordered the tribes of Judah and Benjamin to rebuild it. The cost would come from the royal treasury and freewill offerings by the Jews.

The Jews resettled in their towns, and on the seventh month, everyone gathered in Jerusalem. The old temple was gone, but in the spot where the altar once stood, the priests built a new altar and reinstated the sacrifices and religious festivals. They purchased cedars from Lebanon to rebuild the temple and laid the new temple's foundation. Joyful shouts rang out, while the older generation remembered the grandeur of Solomon's Temple and wept.[35]

Two hundred years earlier, the Assyrians had exiled some defeated Babylonians to Samaria, thirty-five miles north of Jerusalem. The Babylonian-Samaritans began worshiping the Israelite G-d but continued to worship their own deities. The exiles from Sippara (Akkad) even burned their children in the fire to their gods. When the Jews returned from Babylon, the Samaritans volunteered to help them rebuild the temple. The Judeans refused because they didn't want to get sucked back into polytheism. The Samaritans got offended and started working against the Israelites, sending letters to the Persian kings with accusations against the Jews.

Fearing their adversaries and getting distracted by building their own houses, the Jews stopped building the temple. After the prophets Haggai and Zechariah charged the Jews to finish the temple, they resumed its construction. When this was reported to the new Persian king, Darius I, he ordered a search of the royal archives and found Cyrus's edict to rebuild Jerusalem's temple. Darius ordered the governor of the lands west

---

[34] Herodotus, *Capture of Babylon*, Livius. https://www.livius.org/articles/person/darius-the-great/sources/capture-of-babylon-herodotus/

[35] Ezra 1-3.

of the Euphrates to pay for the temple's rebuilding from the tax revenue and to not interfere with the reconstruction. Finally, the Second Temple was completed in the sixth year of Darius's reign (516 BCE).

Prophets Micah, Haggai, Malachi, and Zechariah by Charles M. Stuart
https://commons.wikimedia.org/wiki/File:The_Prophets_-_Micah,_Haggai,_Malachi,_Zechariah_(The_Story_of_the_Masterpieces).png

The Macedonian king Alexander the Great led a massive Greek coalition force to take on the Persian Empire in 334 BCE. He conquered one city after another, never losing a battle. The Jews in Jerusalem were terrified of Alexander because they had supported Persia when it invaded Greece in the earlier Greco-Persian Wars. According to Josephus and the Talmud, the Samaritans asked Alexander for permission to destroy Jerusalem's temple, and he gave it. So, the Jewish high priest Shimon HaTzaddik (Simon the Just) draped himself in his priestly vestments and went to meet Alexander, walking through the night and arriving at sunrise. When Alexander saw HaTzaddik approaching in the glow of dawn, he stepped down from his chariot and bowed to the high priest. Alexander said he had been having visions of HaTzaddik on the battlefield.[36,37] The

---

[36] Yoma 61 A, *Babylonian Talmud*. The William Davidson Edition. Sefaria. https://www.sefaria.org/texts/Talmud

[37] Josephus, *Antiquities of the Jews*, Book XI, Chapter 8.

Second Temple was spared and became a center of pilgrimage for Jews scattered through North Africa, the Middle East, and the Greek world.

Alexander's unexpected death in 323 BCE thrust his massive new empire into chaos. His generals divided it into separate realms, and the province of Coele-Syria, which included Judea, became part of the Seleucid Empire. The Jews had a measure of self-rule, following the laws of the Torah. Some Jerusalem Jews achieved Greek citizenship after 175 BCE, after the high priest Jason's petition.[38]

The official language for Alexander's former empire was now Koine Greek, which enabled people from Asia, North Africa, and Europe to communicate efficiently. Scholars gathered in intellectual hotspots—especially Alexandria, Egypt—to discuss science, philosophy, and religion. Egypt's Macedonian pharaoh, Ptolemy II, secluded seventy-two Jewish scholars on an island to translate the Tanakh from Hebrew into Greek.

The new Greek version of the Tanakh (Old Testament), which included the Apocrypha books, was known as the Septuagint and placed in the Library of Alexandra. Most Jews no longer spoke Hebrew, but they did know Koine Greek, so the Septuagint soon became used in the synagogues (local places for Jewish worship). Jesus read the Septuagint in Nazareth's synagogue (Luke 4:17-21).

Were the ancient Jews literate? The book of Devarim (Deuteronomy) commanded fathers to diligently teach the Torah to their children and write its verses on their houses' doorposts and gates.[39] Handwriting analysis of tablets in a remote Jewish fort south of Jerusalem indicates widespread literacy in the late 7th century BCE. On these tablets, twelve authors wrote eighteen texts dealing with mundane administrative affairs. The texts reveal that the fort's officers, the quartermaster Eliashib, and his assistant Nahum were all literate.[40] In the Second Temple period, Ezra the Scribe organized a school in Jerusalem for boys who had no father to teach them to read the Torah. And, in 64 CE, the high priest Joshua ben Gamla opened schools in every town for boys.[41]

---

[38] John van Maaren, *The Boundaries of Jewishness in the Southern Levant 200 BCE-132 CE* (Boston: De Gruyter, 2022), 43-108. https://doi.org/10.1515/9783110787450-002

[39] Devarim (Deuteronomy) 6:7-9, Torah, *Tanakh*.

[40] Arie Shaus, et al, "Forensic Document Examination and Algorithmic Handwriting Analysis of Judahite Biblical Period Inscriptions Reveal Significant Literacy Level," *PLOS One* (September 9, 2020). https://doi.org/10.1371/journal.pone.0237962

[41] Bava Batra 21a, *Babylonian Talmud*.

In 246 BCE, Ptolemy III of Egypt wrested Coele-Syria, including Judea, from the Seleucid Empire. In 200 BCE, Antiochus III (the Great) of the Seleucid Empire schemed with Philip V of Macedonia to overthrow Egypt, which was in crisis. The new pharaoh was only six years old, and his family members were clashing over who should be the regent. Antiochus the Great successfully took Coele-Syria back from Egypt, and the Jews threw open the gates of Jerusalem to welcome him. Little did they know the horrors to come.

Rome was a rising power in the region when Antiochus IV Epiphanes usurped the throne from his nephew at Antiochus the Great's death. Antiochus IV wanted to impose a totalitarian Hellenistic (Greek) culture and religion. He sold the high priest position to Menelaus, who was willing to syncretize Judaism with Greek ways. Antiochus dipped into the temple treasury to fund his war against Egypt. Meanwhile, Egypt tried to take back Coele-Syria, but Antiochus Epiphanes successfully quelled its initial effort. He marched on Egypt again in 168 BCE.

But the Roman envoy Popillius blocked his way, holding orders from the Roman Senate. "Leave Egypt immediately, or you will be at war with Rome." The elderly proconsul drew a circle in the sand around Antiochus. "Stay in that circle until you give me an answer for the Senate."

Sputtering in rage, the humiliated Antiochus Epiphanes left Egypt. As he passed through Judea, he took out his pent-up fury on Jerusalem after discovering the Jews had replaced Menelaus with their previous high priest. He slaughtered forty thousand men, women, and children in three days and reinstated Menelaus. When a second revolt broke out, Antiochus outlawed Judaism. He installed a statue of Zeus in the temple and sacrificed a pig, an unclean animal to the Jews.

This outrage triggered the Maccabean Revolt in 167 BCE, led by a priest named Mattathias and his military men called the Maccabees (meaning hammer). They launched guerilla warfare against the Greeks and Hellenized Jews, destroying idols around Judea. Although outnumbered by at least five to one, they defeated the Seleucid army, retook Jerusalem, and purified the temple, rededicating it to G-d. In December 164 BCE, they celebrated the first Festival of Lights (Chanukah or Hannukah).

Judea was now essentially independent of the crumbling Seleucid Empire. The Jewish leaders of the new Hasmonaean dynasty served dual roles of high priest and king. The Hasmonaean dynasty increased its territory five-fold, taking back Galilee and other provinces of the former Kingdom of Israel. But it all fell apart in 67 BCE when Aristobulus II stole the throne and priesthood from his brother, King Hyrcanus. Hyrcanus's advisor, Antipater the Idumean, recommended allying with Aretas III of Arabia and retaking the throne.

Meanwhile, Rome's consul Pompey was in western Asia, conquering the territories of the collapsed Seleucid Empire. He arrived in Judea just as the armies of Hyrcanus and the Arabians were surrounding Jerusalem. Pompey put the Arabians to flight, then broke into the temple and captured Aristobulus. He reinstalled Hyrcanus as high priest but not as king. Shortly after, Julius Caesar appointed Antipater the Idumean as Judea's Roman procurator (governor), although he wasn't ethnically Jewish.

Model of the Second Temple

M.t.lifshits, CC BY-SA 3.0 <https://creativecommons.org/licenses/by-sa/3.0>, via Wikimedia Commons; https://commons.wikimedia.org/wiki/File:Model_of_Jerusalem_in_the_Late_Second_Temple_Period.JPG

In 37 BCE, the Roman Senate made Antipater's son, Herod the Great, the king of Judaea, now Rome's vassal kingdom. The Hasmoneans had enlarged the temple, and Herod refurbished and enlarged it more with Greek-style Corinthian columns. Herod executed the surviving members of the Hasmonean dynasty, including his wife Mariamme and his two sons by her. Herod the Great is the king that the New Testament says killed all the baby boys in Bethlehem in an attempt to kill the infant Jesus (Matthew 2).

The Jewish historian Josephus wrote about Jesus, although some scholars suspect his text may have been edited later:

"Now there was about this time Jesus, a wise man if it be lawful to call him a man; for he was a doer of wonderful works, a teacher of such men as receive the truth with pleasure. He drew over to him both many of the Jews and many of the Gentiles. He was [the] Christ. And when Pilate, at the suggestion of the principal men amongst us, had condemned him to the cross, those that loved him at the first did not forsake him; for he appeared to them alive again the third day; as the divine prophets had foretold these and ten thousand other wonderful things concerning him. And the tribe of Christians, so named from him, are not extinct at this day."[42]

The Second Temple, built by the returned exiles from Babylon, was Judea's center of worship for four centuries. Through this period, the Jews experienced internal conflict between various factions. The Pharisees carefully followed religious rituals, separating themselves from the Hellenistic Jews and others who failed to follow the Torah strictly. The Sadducees allied with the Romans, often buying high positions like high priest. They did not believe in heaven or hell or life after death. The Zealots were fanatical nationalists who wanted to overthrow Roman rule.

In 66 CE, the Jews rioted against their cruel Roman governor Florus, who retaliated by killing 3,600 Jews in Jerusalem, sparking a revolt throughout Judaea led by the Zealots. The Roman emperor sent General Vespasian to quell the uprising, and he brutally crushed the resistance fighters in Judaea's northern regions. Meanwhile, Jerusalem erupted into civil war between the Zealots and other factions. Amid this chaos, Emperor Nero died, and the Senate appointed Vespasian as Rome's new emperor. Vespasian returned to Rome in 69 CE, leaving his son Titus to finish Judaea's subjugation. Titus marched on Jerusalem with eighty thousand men just as thousands of Jews had traveled to the city for Passover.

The Zealots had divided into two warring groups: the extreme and the moderate. The extreme Zealots attacked the moderate Zealots and other worshipers celebrating Passover in the temple courtyard, killing most of the moderates. Outside Jerusalem's walls, Titus launched his attack. Outnumbered four to one, the Jewish factions finally stopped killing each other to face their common enemy.

---

[42] Josephus, *Antiquities of the Jews*, Book XVIII, Chapter 3.

With their battering rams and catapults, the Romans broke down Jerusalem's northern wall after two weeks. As they fought their way toward the center of the city and the temple mount, the Jews dug a tunnel under their siege equipment and burned their catapults and battering rams. Titus built a wall around the unconquered section of the city to starve the Jews. Josephus, who had been captured by the Romans and was serving as a negotiator, wrote:

"Then did the famine widen its progress and devoured the people by whole houses and families; the upper rooms were full of women and children that were dying by famine, and the lanes of the city were full of the dead bodies of the aged; the children also and the young men wandered about the market-places like shadows, all swelled with the famine, and fell down dead, wheresoever their misery seized them."[43]

Titus continued pressing toward the temple, where most of the survivors huddled. His men set it on fire, and for two days, it burned, with many Jews still inside. All that remained of the temple was the retaining wall on the western temple mount. The surviving Jews were enslaved or sent to fight wild animals to entertain the people of Rome.

The diaspora, or dispersion of the Jews, to other regions outside Judaea had begun with the Assyrian and Babylonian exiles. Although thousands of Jews returned from Babylon when freed by Cyrus the Great, many remained in Assyria, Babylon, and Persia. During the Hellenistic age, thousands of Jewish intellectuals migrated to Egypt, where Alexandria was the scientific and philosophical hub. After the fall of Jerusalem in 70 CE, Jews left for places like Egypt, Babylon, or Persia, which already had large Jewish populations. Because they spoke Koine Greek, other Jews migrated throughout the Greek world surrounding the eastern Mediterranean.

Jews had arrived in Rome by the 2nd century BCE. By the end of the 1st century CE, at least two million lived in the Roman Empire as the diaspora spread through southern Europe and northern Africa. As Josephus wrote: "This people has already made its way into every city, and it is not easy to find any place in the habitable world which has not received the nation and in which it has not made its power felt."[44]

---

[43] Flavius Josephus, *The Wars of the Jews*, trans. William Whiston (Project Gutenberg EBook), Book V, Chapter 12. https://www.gutenberg.org/files/2850/2850-h/2850-h.htm
[44] Josephus, *Antiquities of the Jews*. Book XIV, Chapter 7.

Key Takeaways:
- Babylonian and Persian rule
  - Tribes of Judah and Benjamin in Babylon
  - Cyrus the Great overthrows Babylon
- Return to Jerusalem and the Second Temple
  - Cyrus's order to rebuild the temple
  - The Second Temple completed in 516 BCE
- Alexander the Great and the Hellenistic period
  - Tanakh translated into Koine Greek
  - Schools established for boys to learn the Torah
- Maccabean Revolt, Jewish autonomy, Hasmonean dynasty
  - Desecration of the temple
  - Expansion to include most of former Israel
- Roman rule
  - Pompey's conquest
  - Herod's Temple
  - Jesus
  - Revolt and destruction of Jerusalem and temple
- Diaspora movements

Chapter 4: Byzantine Judaism (324-640CE)

Writing down the Mishna, the Oral Law, was forbidden at one time. What is the Oral Law? It is the unwritten law the rabbis believe Moses received from G-d when he received the written Torah. The Mishna helps to interpret the Torah. Why couldn't it be written down? The rabbis explained that a medical student couldn't learn his profession simply by reading textbooks. He must observe a master physician and then have that master guide him through his first surgeries. How could one understand the Mishna simply by reading and not interacting with a master teacher? How would one know how to apply its teachings to the rapidly changing world?

But the rapidly changing world was the problem with learning the Mishna from a master teacher. The Jews were scattered to the four winds, and not everyone had access to a master teacher.

Rabbi Judah HaNasi of Galilee was a close friend of the Roman emperor but knew that the empire's benign treatment of the Jews could change in the blink of an eye. How soon before a new emperor came to power and the Jews were scattered again? So, Rabbi Judah gathered the leading Torah scholars. They spent years analyzing the Oral Law and writing it down with commentaries explaining the teachings. They attempted to resolve disputes among the leading sages on how to interpret the Oral Law. Completed around 200 CE, the Mishna contains instructions on prayer, religious rituals, the Sabbath, special holy days, and how to mourn. It gives regulations on agriculture, marriage and divorce, financial affairs, and court matters.

Around 350 CE, rabbinic scholars completed the Jerusalem Gemara, a collection of discussions by rabbis. They were still reviewing and revising it, but the Romans shut down any scholarly work in Jerusalem. The Gemara, together with the Mishna, formed the Jerusalem Talmud. Many rabbis escaped to Babylon, where Jewish scholars were also developing a written Talmud. The rabbis continued reviewing and expanding the Talmud for decades. At some point in the 400s, they completed the Babylonian Talmud, which is usually considered more authoritative.

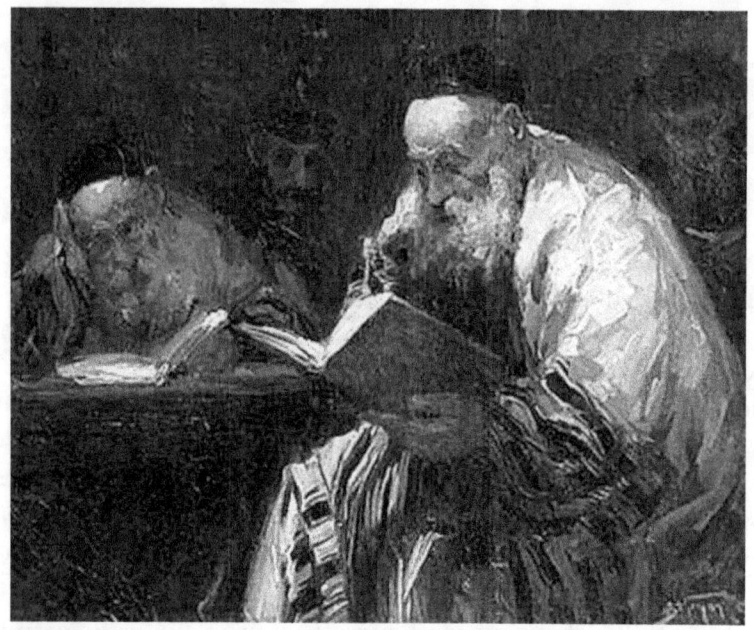

The Talmud Readers by Adolf Behrman, who was killed by the Nazis in 1943 in Poland's Białystok Ghetto
https://commons.wikimedia.org/wiki/File:Adolf_Behrman_-_Talmudysci.jpg

Judaism in the Roman Empire

The necessity of writing down the Mishna underscored the turbulent relationship the Jews had with the Roman Empire. Sometimes they enjoyed favor from the emperor, and sometimes they received cruelty and oppression. It all depended on who the emperor was and how much the Jews were resisting Roman rule. For instance, when Emperor Hadrian rebuilt Jerusalem in 132 CE, he built a temple to Jupiter where the First and Second Temples once stood, sparking a revolt led by Simon bar Kokhba. Hadrian's forces killed 580,000 Jews, enslaved or exiled thousands more, and demolished 1,000 towns. Hadrian outlawed Judaism, forbade circumcision, and burned the Torah. He merged the province of Judaea with Galilee and called it Syria Palaestina.

However, Hadrian's successor, Antoninus Pius, repealed many of Hadrian's harsh policies against the Jews. He permitted them to follow Judaism but not convert others to their religion. Jews were still banned from Jerusalem. In 193 CE, Severus became Rome's military dictator. A North African of Semitic-Phoenician descent, he initiated a new dynasty. During Severus's reign, Jews could hold public office but were still forbidden to convert others to Judaism. Severus's son Caracalla even permitted free Jews to obtain full Roman citizenship. Another Severan emperor, Alexander, allowed the Jews to visit Jerusalem.

Nevertheless, during the Severan dynasty (191-235 CE), the Jews and Christians in the empire suffered sporadic persecution in some of the provinces, albeit not directly from the emperors. The reason was that being a loyal subject of the Roman Empire meant accepting the Roman gods. Since most people within the empire were already polytheistic before being conquered, they simply shrugged and added the Roman gods to their pantheon. Sometimes they renamed their own gods with the names of the chief Roman gods. Yet the Jews and Christians refused to offer sacrifices to any other god or observe pagan religious festivals, which made them seem disloyal to the government.

In 313 CE, Constantine and his co-emperor Licinius passed the Edict of Milan, which protected all religions (including Christianity and Judaism) from persecution. In 315 CE, Constantine passed a law forbidding Jews from stoning a fellow Jew who converted to Christianity. The punishment for disobeying was death in the flames. Constantine also forbade non-Jews from attending synagogue or converting to Judaism.

Influenced by his Christian mother, Constantine studied the Christian faith, although he did not receive baptism until his deathbed. His mother, Helena, drew attention to Jerusalem and Palestine and the location of specific events in the life of Jesus. Helena and Constantine built several cathedrals in Jerusalem as Palestine morphed from an obscure Roman province into a center of pilgrimage. Monasteries for ascetic hermits soon dotted the Judaean landscape.

Judaism in the Byzantine era

In 324 CE, Constantine I became the sole emperor of the Roman Empire. Rome became a backwater and was no longer the capital of the empire. Constantine built his new capital of Constantinople, where Europe meets Asia on the Bosphorus Strait. The Western Roman Empire crumbled over the next two centuries and eventually collapsed, while the Eastern Roman Empire, known today as the Byzantine Empire, flourished.

In 325 CE, Constantine I convened the First Ecumenical Council at Nicaea, which hashed out some Christian doctrinal issues and changed the date of Easter, previously celebrated at Passover. Constantine didn't like a Christian festival connected with a Jewish one.

In 339 CE, Constantine's son Constantius II passed a law dissolving marriages between Jewish men and non-Jewish women employed in the imperial weaving factory. If Jewish men married non-Jewish women in the future, they would be executed. The law forbade Jews from owning non-Jewish slaves, and circumcising an enslaved male brought the death penalty. Theodosius I (347-395 CE) promoted Christian missionary activity among the Jews and forbade Jewish parents from disinheriting their children who converted to Christianity. However, when Christians burned down a synagogue in Callinicum, Syria, in 388 CE, Theodosius ordered the perpetrators punished and forced them to return all stolen property. In 439 CE, Theodosius II forbade building new synagogues, although old synagogues could be repaired and refurbished. If a Jew influenced a Christian to convert to Judaism, he would lose his property and life.[45]

Despite oppression, Judaism grew during the Byzantine period.

---

[45] Jacob Marcus, *The Jew in the Medieval World: A Sourcebook, 315-1791* (New York: Jewish Publication Society, 1938), 3-7.

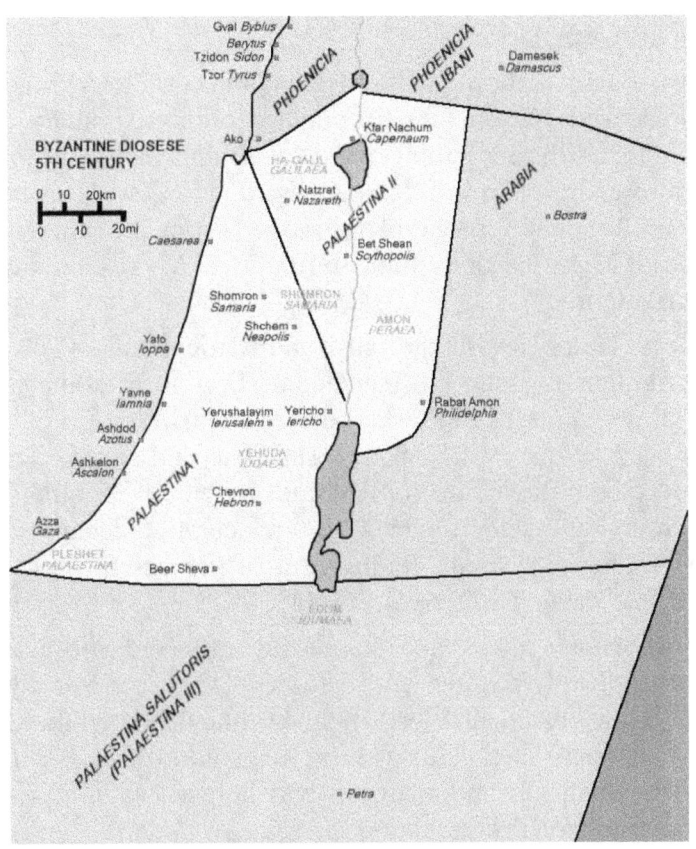

Byzantine Province of Palaestina
*Photo modified: zoomed in. Credit: Haldrik at https://en.wikipedia.org/;
https://commons.wikimedia.org/wiki/File:Israel_Byzantine_5c.jpg*

Judaism's leadership became decentralized in the Byzantine era, focusing on local governance. Jewish communities throughout the empire had their own leadership: scholars chosen from influential and wealthy families. Jewish merchants plied their trade by land and sea, and cloth dyeing became a noted Jewish occupation. The province roughly covering the former kingdoms of Israel and Judah was split in two. Jerusalem was in Palaestina I to the south, and Galilee in the northern Palaestina II.

Palaestina continued as the Jewish cultural center, with significant creative endeavors in Hebrew liturgical poetry. The Jewish poets or *payṭanim,* such as Yose ben Yose, Yannai, and Eleazar ha-Kalir, echoed the ancient psalmists with fervent devotion and a passionate longing for the Messiah. Romanos, a monk who had converted from Judaism to Christianity, employed the payṭanim style in the Byzantine worship liturgy.

Judaism in North Africa

The Jewish people always had a strong connection to Africa, especially Egypt and Ethiopia (Cush). The Torah mentions Abraham and Isaac migrating to Egypt during famines, and Jacob and his sons moved there when Joseph was Egypt's second-in-command. The Jewish prophets, such as Zephaniah, frequently spoke of Ethiopia: "From the other side of the rivers of Cush, My supplicants, the community of My scattered ones, shall bring Me an offering."[46]

The Beta Israel Jewish artisans and agriculturalists of northern Ethiopia's mountains along the Gerzeman River formed the mysterious Kingdom of Semien. How and when they came to Ethiopia is unclear. It must have been before 70 CE, as they still practiced animal sacrifice and knew nothing about the Mishna or Talmud. Isolated from other Jews until the 19th century, they developed a distinct culture. Their ascetic high priests, the *meloksewoch*, are reminiscent of the Essenes sect of the 1st century CE who wrote the Dead Sea Scrolls.

The Beta Israel Jews often conflicted with the mostly Christian Ethiopians in the Byzantine era, although they maintained political autonomy. They eventually lost their farmland when the Ethiopian monarchy only permitted Christians to be landowners. But they were skilled in craftsmanship and masonry and helped build Ethiopia's new capital of Gondor in 1632.[47]

The Maghrebi Jews also lived in North Africa from at least the 1st century CE; however, they maintained contact with Jerusalem and the rest of the Jewish world. Found in Morocco, Algeria, Tunisia, and Libya, some of these Jews were descendants of the 30,000 deported by Titus after the 70 CE fall of Jerusalem. However, a Jewish settlement already existed in Cyrene (in Libya), as the New Testament mentions that the Roman soldiers forced Simon of Cyrene to carry Jesus's cross. The original El Ghriba Synagogue on the island of Djerba in Tunisia was supposedly built with a door and stone from the destroyed temple in Jerusalem. One version of the legend says they were from the Second Temple, but another version insists these relics came from Solomon's Temple, destroyed by Nebuchadnezzar in 586 BCE.

---

[46] Tzefaniah (Zephaniah) 3:10, Nevi'im, *Tanakh*.

[47] Sara Toth Stub, "Letter from Ethiopia: Exploring a Forgotten Jewish Land," *Archaeology*. January/February 2023. https://www.archaeology.org/issues/498-2301/letter-from/11057-ethiopia-beta-israel

Judaism in the Middle East

As mentioned earlier, after Cyrus the Great conquered Babylon, he granted citizenship to the Jews and permission to return to Jerusalem. While tens of thousands returned to their homeland, thousands chose to stay in Babylon. An ancient synagogue in Nehardea on the Euphrates was said to have been built by the exiled King Jehoiachin. After the 70 CE fall of Jerusalem, many Jews left for Babylonia (in today's Iraq), which became the academic center of Judaism. Rabbinical schools flourished, and the kallah (general assembly) met twice a year for scholars to debate theological issues.

The Christianization of the Byzantine Empire led to another exodus of Jews to Babylonia, which was now part of the Persian Sasanian Empire. In 512 CE, Mar Zutra II, the exilarch (leader) of the Jewish community, challenged the Sasanians, who had killed his father and other family members. His four hundred Jewish warriors defeated the Persians of the area, and Mar Zutra established an independent Jewish state in Mahoza on the banks of the Tigris. After seven years, the Persian king Kavadh I defeated Mar Zutra and crucified him.

From 484 to 573 CE, the Samaritans north of Jerusalem launched a series of insurrections against Byzantine rule in Palaestina I (today's southern Israel). Most Jews had left Palaestina I after the Bar Kokhba revolt, except for Caesarea on the northern coast. The Jews were still the majority in Palaestina II in Galilee and Golan, while the Samaritans and Byzantine Christians dominated Palaestina I. The Samaritans had their temple on Mount Gerizim and practiced a hybrid form of Judaism.

The Byzantine emperor Zeno persecuted the Samaritans, trying to force them to convert to Christianity. When they refused, he turned one of their synagogues into a church, and on Mount Gerizim, he built a tomb for his son with a cross on it. In 484 CE, the Samaritans retaliated by storming the cathedral at Neapolis and killing the Christians worshiping inside. Zeno marched on Samaria and quelled the rebellion. He forbade the Samaritans from setting foot on Mount Gerizim and built a church there. Continuing to revolt for almost a century, the Samaritans lost tens of thousands in their struggle against the Byzantine Empire.

In 556 CE, the Jews got involved. With the Samaritans, they attacked the Christians of Caesarea, raiding the churches and killing the governor. The rebellion spread to Bethlehem, where the Samaritan-Jewish coalition burned down the Church of the Nativity. In 572 CE, the Jews joined the

Samaritans again in another insurrection at Mount Carmel. After this, the Byzantines outlawed the Samaritan religion, and the Samaritan population became nearly extinct.

Although they must have likewise suffered the wrath of the Byzantine Empire following the Samaritan revolts, a sizeable Jewish population continued in Caesarea. In 615 CE, Shahrbaraz, shah of the Sassanian Empire, conquered Caesarea, which was now the capital of Palaestina I. The Jews from Palaestina I and II allied with the Persian forces against the Byzantines and took Jerusalem but failed to take Tyre. In 622 CE, the Byzantine emperor Heraclius counterattacked and regained Jerusalem.

Meanwhile, in Arabia, Muhammad was having revelations in a cave and starting a new religion. He died in 632 CE, but his followers continued his quest to spread Islam. In 638 CE, Jerusalem surrendered to the Muslims led by Caliph Umar with a treaty that protected the lives and property of the city's citizens. Heraclius had banned the Jews from entering Jerusalem, but Umar allowed them to return with certain restrictions. For instance, neither Jews nor Christians could hold government offices; Jews could not build new synagogues, and Christians could not erect new churches. But now, the Jews could pray at the Temple Mount and Western Wall (Wailing Wall) in Jerusalem.

Key Takeaways:
- Codification of Mishna and Jerusalem and Babylonian Talmud completed
- The turbulent life of Jews in the Roman Empire
  - Mixed relationship depending on who the emperor was
  - Impact of Constantine and the legalization of Christianity
- The growth of Judaism during the Byzantine period (320-640CE).
  - Initial decline; conversion attempts by Christians
  - Judaism in North Africa
- Jews in the Middle East
  - Babylonia the scholarly center of Judaism
  - Samaritan insurrections and Jewish involvement
  - 615 CE Sassanian invasion
  - 636 CE beginning of Arab rule

Chapter 5: Medieval Judaism I: Islam and the Spanish Golden Age

After the devastating Jewish-Roman wars, a Jewish tribe called the Banu Qurayza moved into western Arabia in the region later called Medina. They introduced the cultivation of date palms, grains, and vineyards, lifting the Jews to a high social standing among the Bedouin Arabs, who were primarily sheep and camel herdsmen. These Jews followed the Torah but intermarried with Arabs and allied with the local Arab tribes in warfare against other tribes. The Arabs called the Banu Qurayza Jews the "kahinan," or priestly tribe. When the Sasanians gained power in Arabia, the Banu Qurayza Jews served as tax collectors for the Persians.

Several other Jewish tribes, including the Banu Qaynuqa and Banu Nadir, also moved into Medina. The Arab tribes around Medina were constantly at war with each other, and the Jewish tribes joined the fray. The prophet Muhammed and his followers migrated to Medina in 622 CE and mediated peace among the tribes with the Constitution of Medina. It assured freedom of religious belief for all who followed the law. The Jews would have equality and not be oppressed or harassed.

Five years later, Muhammed's tribe, the Quraysh from Mecca, who had not accepted Islam, allied with the Banu Nadir Jewish tribe and attacked Medina. In the Battle of the Trench, the Banu Qurayza Jews did not participate in the fighting but gave tools to Muhammed's men to dig a defensive trench. They did negotiate with the Jews fighting with the Meccans, who convinced the Medina Jews that Muhammed would lose the war. However, negotiations between the two Jewish tribes broke down, and the Medina Jews did nothing to support the attacking tribes.

Nevertheless, once the Meccans abandoned the war, Muhammed attacked the Banu Qurayza Jews, offended that they had negotiated with the attackers. About two thousand Jewish men, women, and children surrendered to him. They were invited to convert to Islam and refused. The Muslims beheaded all the Jewish men, enslaved all the women and children, and confiscated their property.

Seizure of the Banu Qurayza by Muhammad Rafi' Bāzil
https://commons.wikimedia.org/wiki/File:Ban%C5%AB_Qurayza.png

After Muhammed died and Caliph Umar came to power, he evicted all Jews from Arabia and confiscated their lands. These Jews migrated to Syria and Babylonia (Iraq). Yet when Umar invaded and conquered Palaestina, the Muslim treatment of Jews was initially benign, especially since the Jews assisted his conquest of Caesarea. The Jews established a rabbinic academy in Galilee at Tiberius. Galilee had attained spiritual supremacy after the 70 CE fall of Jerusalem, and the Sanhedrin (Assembly of Elders) had relocated to Usher in Galilee. The Muslim conquests left Anatolia (western Turkey) as the Byzantine Empire's only Asian territory.

By 686 CE, the Umayyad dynasty ruled North Africa and Syria, which now included Palestine. The Shi'ite Muslims had split off and ruled what is now Iraq and northern Iran. The Kharijites were another splinter group that controlled large areas of Persia (southern Iran) and Arabia. Since only Muslims could serve in the military, all three Muslim groups forced able-bodied non-Muslim males of military age to pay the *jizya* tax. Under Umar's rule, the amount of the tax depended on whether one was wealthy, middle-class, or poor.

Another tax imposed by the Muslims was the *kharaj* tax on the non-Muslim landowners' harvest. Muslim landowners had to pay a 10 percent tithe on their land, which was far less than the *kharaj* tax. By 750 CE, non-Muslims were paying as much as one-third of their harvest in taxes. The crushing *kharaj* taxes forced the land-owning Jews in Babylonia and elsewhere to migrate from rural farms into the cities. This mass migration resulted in most Jews becoming urban dwellers for the next millennia. These urbanized Jews grew wealthy from manufacturing and trade and became increasingly engaged in global affairs and Western philosophy.

Meanwhile, the Muslims in Jerusalem decided on the Temple Mount as their place of prayer. A few Jews could live in Jerusalem once again, but the majority population was still Christian. The Umayyad Caliph Abd al-Malik expanded Jerusalem and rebuilt its walls and roads. On the site where the First and Second Temples once stood, Caliph el-Malik built the Dome of the Rock in 693 CE and the al-Aqsa Mosque in 705 CE. Under Umar II (717-720 CE), Jews were forced to identify themselves by wearing yellow stars, and Christians had to wear blue badges.

In Eastern Europe, a nomadic people known as the Khazars roamed the steppes of today's Russia and Ukraine; they settled along the Danube in the mid-600s as far south as the Black Sea. Around 740 CE, King Bulan and the Khazar nobility converted to Judaism, followed by many of the Khazar population. King Bulan's descendants built synagogues and imported Jewish scholars to teach the Tanakh and Talmud. The Jewish teachers instructed the people to read Hebrew and celebrate Jewish festivals. This Jewish kingdom persisted for five centuries until it fell to Genghis Khan and the Mongols.

Tchufute Kalei, Fortress of the Jews, in the Crimea
*Leah Lipszyc, CC BY-SA 3.0 <https://creativecommons.org/licenses/by-sa/3.0>, via Wikimedia Commons,
https://commons.wikimedia.org/wiki/File:Tchufute_Kalei_tower_near_back_entrance.JPG*

Jews had lived in Western Europe since the Roman era. For instance, the 1st-century apostle Paul mentioned visiting Spain (Romans 15:24). The Jews in France and other Western European states monopolized trade in silk, incense, wine, and spices, but some also owned land and were farmers. Some of the region's legislation was anti-Semitic, such as the third Council of Orleans (538 CE), which restricted Jews from appearing in public from Maundy Thursday to Easter Sunday.

In Western Europe, Charlemagne rose to power as king of the Franks. Eventually, in 800 CE, he united and ruled the Western Roman Empire, which had collapsed three centuries earlier. Charlemagne actively protected the Jews of Western Europe and encouraged the development of Jewish culture. He appointed a Jew as his ambassador to Baghdad. His son Louis the Pius continued his father's benevolent policies and granted privileges to Jewish merchants. At this point, Jews served as the intermediaries between the Christian West and the Islamic East.[48]

The Abbasid Caliphate overthrew the Umayyad dynasty in 750 CE and ruled the eastern Muslim world until conquered by the Mongols in 1258. In 762 CE, the Abbasids established their new capital at Baghdad, about fifty miles north of Babylon. They adopted the Sassanian (Persian) governmental system and promoted the arts and sciences in this "golden

---

[48] Michael G. Minsky, *Agobard and His Relations with the Jews* (Amherst: University of Massachusetts, 1971), 1-18.

age" of Islamic culture.

Most Abbasid caliphs tolerated the Jews, but a few persecuted them with oppressive taxes and strict rules for their clothing and trade. For instance, Caliph al-Mutawakkil (847-861 CE) forced the Jews to wear a yellow hood or patch on their chest or back. Nevertheless, the Jews distinguished themselves under the Abbasid Caliphate as administrators, merchants, physicians, and writers.

Since the Hellenistic age, some Jews had questioned the validity of the oral law (Mishna). Around 767 CE, a Persian Jew named Anan Ben David organized the Karaite sect, which recognizes the Tanakh (Old Testament) as the highest authority for theology and law. The Karaites believe G-d gave Moses only the written Torah, not the oral Mishna. Thus, they do not consider the Talmud to be authoritative. They might consult the Talmud, but ultimately, each person was responsible for deciding how to interpret the Torah.

At this time, tension mounted between Saadia Gaon (882-942 CE), a leading Rabbinic Jewish sage in Babylonia during the Abbasid Caliphate, and Aaron ben Meir, the leading Jewish scholar in Palestine, over changing the dates of Passover and Rosh Hashanah. Saadia won the battle of the calendars, keeping the traditional dates for the festivals and highlighting Babylonian authority in the Jewish world.

Saadia translated the Tanakh (Old Testament) into Arabic, a version still used today. He also wrote a Hebrew grammar book and a dictionary to assist Jews in reading the Torah in Hebrew. Saadia authored his *Book of Beliefs and Opinions* in classic Arabic, defending Judaism and drawing Jews back to the Torah. Yet, he pointed out that the teachings of Aristotle and Plato could rationally fit in with traditional Jewish theology and philosophy.

In 969 CE, the Fatimid Caliphate rose to power in North Africa, Syria, and Palestine (roughly today's Israel). The Fatimid were Shi'ite Muslims, who were more tolerant toward non-Muslims and even appointed Jews and Christians to administrative positions. The Jews in Asia and North Africa now had more religious freedom and positions such as court physician and clerk for the military.

Jews were active in the Fatimid economy and interacted freely with Muslims and Christians. The Jews continued their lucrative roles in textile manufacturing and trade, even supplying the court. They prospered in this era, which lasted until 1171, while continuing to pay the *jizya* tax levied against all non-Muslims. Although they adopted Muslim dress and the Arabic language, the Jews maintained their culture and religious practices. They usually settled legal affairs among themselves following Torah law, rarely taking matters to Muslim courts.

In the Fatimid Caliphate, the Jews elected one of their own as "Head of the Jews," which the caliphate approved and recognized with a letter of appointment. Muhammed had promised this for Jews and Christians, but it had not always happened under other caliphates. The power vested in the Head of the Jews included overseeing legal affairs within the Jewish community and appointing officers under him. He managed religious endowments, supervised tax collection among the Jews, and ensured that the Jewish community observed regulations for non-Muslims. The Jews chose one of their more affluent men, and this leader presided over Jews and Samaritans.[49]

Meanwhile, as the Abbasid dynasty fractured in the 10th century, many Middle Eastern Jews migrated to regions around the Mediterranean. The Umayyad Caliphate had conquered Andalusia (Spain) in 711 CE, and Muslim rule prevailed until the mid-13th century. These Muslim leaders were tolerant of Jews and Christians, opening doors for unprecedented cultural achievement in the Middle Ages. The Jews enjoyed a golden age of splendor in economic, spiritual, and cultural life from 950 to 1150 CE as Spain became the world's largest Jewish community.

Spain's Muslim leadership appointed Jews to administrative posts and encouraged their trade endeavors. Muslim and Jewish scholars surged ahead in astronomy, mathematics, medicine, philosophy, and poetry while the rest of Europe descended into the Dark Ages. Cosmopolitan cities sprang up, with aqueducts, sewers, paved roads, splendid palaces, and breathtaking gardens. The libraries of Cordova, Granada, and Toledo drew science and math scholars.

Spanish Judaism led the Sephardic Jews of North Africa, Palestine, and the Middle East, while the Ashkenazi Jews centered in France, Germany, and Italy. These two groups differed in their prayer service, theology, and pursuit of secular knowledge. The Ashkenazim approached the Talmud analytically; the Sephardim were influenced by Arabic and Western philosophy, believing it helped to understand the Torah. The Sephardim

---

[49] Elinoar Bareket, "The Head of the Jews (Ra'is al-Yahud) in Fatimid Egypt: A Re-Evaluation," *Bulletin of the School of Oriental and African Studies*, University of London 67, no. 2 (2004): 185-6. http://www.jstor.org/stable/4145978.

immersed themselves in the non-Jewish world, while the Ashkenazim avoided secular studies in philosophy, science, and math and gave full attention to the Torah.

In 1027, the poet Samuel ha-Nagid became the prime minister of Granada in southern Spain and led the way for Spanish Jews in literary and political fields. Solomon Ibn Gabirol (1021-1058) was a Jewish poet and philosopher in Spain who penned the *Mekor Chayim* (*Origin of Life*) about the intersection of the earthly and spiritual world. He warned that since G-d is the true source of life, seeking satisfaction in worldly things is idolatry.

Woodcut of Rabbi Solomon ben Isaac (Rashi) by Guillaume de Paris
https://commons.wikimedia.org/wiki/File:Rashi.JPG

Rabbi Solomon ben Isaac (1040-1105), known as Rashi, was a renowned French scholar whose commentaries on the Tanakh and Talmud are still studied today by Jewish children and adults. He meticulously analyzed the meaning of the Hebrew text, paying particular attention to word studies and their literal meaning. Biblical scholars appreciated how he explained complex texts with simplicity and clarity, and his commentary is included in today's editions of the Talmud.

The golden age of the Jews in Spain ended in 1147 when the Almohad Berber Muslims of Morocco attacked the Iberian Peninsula. The Jews had mostly flourished under earlier Muslim leadership in Spain, but the radical Almohads were fanatical about imposing Islam. The Jews and Christians had three choices: convert to Islam, leave the country, or be executed. Most Jews fled to North Africa or to the north of Spain, which was under Christian control.

Meanwhile, affairs in Jerusalem were setting the scene for the Crusades. In 1071, the Fatimid Muslim governor of al-Sham (Syria-Palestine) asked the Turkmens for help fending off Arab Bedouin tribes invading the region. The Turkish Seljuks came down to fight as mercenaries, but then the Fatimids couldn't pay them due to a civil war in their Egyptian heartland. So, the Seljuks switched sides. They fought with the Bedouins, captured Jerusalem, and made it part of the Seljuk Empire. The Sunni Muslim Turks governed Jerusalem until 1098 when the Fatimid warriors retook the city.

Key Takeaways:
- Byzantine Empire loses control to Caliph Umar
  - Migration of Babylonian Jews to the cities due to the *kharaj* land tax
  - Dome of the Rock (693 CE) and the al-Aqsa Mosque (705 CE) built on Temple Mount
  - Jews in the Abbasid Caliphate
    - Anan Ben David and the Karaite sect
    - Saadia Gaon and Babylonian leadership in the Jewish world
- Jewish life in the Fatimid Caliphate
  - More religious freedom and opportunities for economic prosperity
  - Jews chose their leader and mainly followed their own laws
- Golden age of Jewish culture in Spain (950-1150)
  - Jewish scholars forge ahead in science, math, philosophy, and theology
  - Sephardic and Ashkenazi Jews
  - Rashi's commentary
  - Almohad Caliphate outlaws Judaism and Christianity in southern Spain
  - Muslim Seljuk Turks capture Jerusalem in 1071

Chapter 6: Medieval Judaism II: Crusades and the Mamluk Period

The Muslim Seljuk Turks not only captured Jerusalem in 1071 but also the Byzantine emperor Romanos IV Diogenes in Anatolia (western Turkey). The Byzantines had fought fiercely for their territory in western Turkey and suffered a crushing loss. The Turkish Sultan Alp Arslan sent Romanos back to Constantinople after the emperor promised to pay a ransom of 1.5 million gold pieces and give his daughter in marriage to the sultan's son. But Romanos returned home to a coup led by the Doukas family, who blinded their emperor and usurped power.

The Byzantine Empire spent the next few years in the chaos of unstable leadership, in no position to regain its territory in Asia. Nor could they do anything about Jerusalem, which wasn't a priority anyway. Several Muslim caliphates had held Jerusalem for the past four centuries, yet they allowed pilgrims to visit and permitted Christians and Jews to live there with certain restrictions.

The Byzantines wanted all of Anatolia back. Their capital Constantinople sat on the Bosphorus Strait that divided Europe from Asia and formed a channel between the Black Sea and the Aegean. As long as they controlled both sides of the strait, they controlled the lucrative sea trade. But now, the Seljuk Turks held territory just a few miles from the channel, far too close for comfort, and had nearly wiped out the Byzantine army.

Emperor Alexius Comnenus hoped to enlist aid from Western Europe, which was staging a comeback from its cultural and economic Dark Ages. He contacted Pope Urban II for help in driving out the Turks. It had been forty years since the Great Schism divided the Roman Catholic Church from the Eastern Orthodox Church. The pope liked the idea of the two sides fighting together for a common cause in what he hoped would be the first step toward reunification. So, he rebuked Europe's Christian states for fighting each other when they needed to fight together to free Jerusalem. He embellished stories of atrocities the Muslims had committed against Christians in the Holy Land and promised remission of sins for anyone who died fighting the infidel Turks.

In 1095, the Crusaders rallied in France and Germany. Some believed that before marching to Jerusalem to fight the Muslim infidels, they needed to deal with the Jewish infidels at home. Godfrey of Bouillon, one of the leaders of the First Crusade, swore that before leaving, he would avenge Christ's blood by eradicating all Jews in France. Other medieval Europeans recommended that all the Jews either convert or be killed and their property seized.

A 1234 CE illustration of violence against Jews
https://commons.wikimedia.org/wiki/File:Execution_of_Hebrews_by_Pagans.jpg

In the summer of 1095, frenzied mobs of French and German peasants attacked the Jewish communities in the Rhineland, massacring thousands. In Regensburg, Bavaria, a mob rounded up the Jewish community, forcing them into the Danube River in an involuntary baptism. Count Emicho led ten thousand of crusaders through Germany's Rhine Valley the following summer. Despite the Holy Roman Emperor Henry IV's orders to protect the Jews, Emicho's army killed at least 800 Jews in Worms and 1,100 in Mainz who refused Christian baptism.[50]

Meanwhile, waves of professional armies and ordinary citizens marched toward Constantinople on the way to Jerusalem. An estimated 100,000 Crusaders crossed the Bosphorus Strait into Asia, recapturing Nicaea and Edessa in Anatolia and Antioch in Syria. The Crusaders reached Jerusalem in 1099 and laid siege to the city, led by Godfrey of Bouillon. The Christians in Jerusalem had been sent away before the Crusaders arrived, as the Muslims feared they would fight on the Crusaders' side. But the Jews fought alongside the Muslims to defend their ancient city.

A fifty-foot-high defensive wall surrounded Jerusalem, but the Crusaders used two siege towers on wheels, a battering ram, and ladders to scale the wall. The Europeans broke into the city on July 15, 1099, after a five-week siege. The Crusaders dashed through the streets, killing tens of thousands of Muslims and Jews until blood reached the knees of their horses. Many Jews hid in their central synagogue, which the Crusaders burned down over their heads.[51]

---

[50] Iris Shagrir and Netta Amir, "The Persecution of the Jews in the First Crusade: Liturgy, Memory, and Nineteenth-Century Visual Culture," *Speculum* 92, no. 2 (2017): 405–28. http://www.jstor.org/stable/26340194.

[51] H. A. R. Gibb, *The Damascus Chronicle of the Crusades: Extracted and Translated from the Chronicle of Ibn Al-Qalanisi* (Mineola, New York: Dover Publications, 2003), 48.

Crusaders Take Jerusalem 1099, by Émile Signol
Photo zoomed in. Public Domain:
https://commons.wikimedia.org/wiki/File:Taking_of_Jerusalem_by_the_Crusaders,_15th_July_1099.jpg

Other Jews fled to the Temple Mount, where thousands of Muslims had taken refuge in the Dome of the Rock or the Al-Aqsa Mosque. The Crusaders slaughtered ten thousand men, women, and children on the Temple Mount. The stench of corpses filled the city, and the Europeans ordered the survivors to drag the bodies outside the city gates, where they were piled into pyramid-like stacks to be burned. Jerusalem remained in the hands of Christian rulers for almost a century. As historian Salo Baron states:

> "In many ways, 1096 marked a turning point in Jewish history. The trail of blood and smoldering ruins left behind in the Jewish communities from France to Palestine...for the first time brought home to the Jewish people, its foes and friends, the utter instability of the Jewish position in the western world...from the First Crusade on, anti-Jewish persecutions exercised a dangerously contagious appeal, which in periods of great emotional stress degenerated into mass psychosis transcending national boundaries."[52]

---

[52] Salo W. Baron, *A Social and Religious History of the Jews* (New York: Columbia University Press, 1957), Vol. 4:89.

Judah Halevi was a Jewish biblical scholar and poet who lived in Cordoba, Spain, during the First Crusade. He also studied metaphysics, philosophy, and science, but his most outstanding contributions were his nationalistic poems and liturgy for synagogue worship. As his people suffered from violent mobs triggered by the Crusades, his poetry and songs alluded to Zionism: the return of Jews to Israel with Jewish statehood.

In 1144, the Seljuks recaptured Edessa and killed or enslaved the European Christians but spared the Turkish and Syrian Christians. Fears of the Turks retaking Jerusalem sparked the Second Crusade in 1146, fanned by the preaching of Bernard of Clairvaux. A French monk named Radulphe declared that the Jews deserved to die because they were enemies of Christianity, once again spurring violence against the Jews of Germany, Bohemia, and France. Two archbishops gave the Jews shelter in their castles, but a mob stormed one of the castles and killed the Jews in front of the Archbishop of Mainz.

The Second Crusade was a fiasco for the Europeans in the Middle East. King Conrad III of Germany and King Louis VII of France failed to retake Edessa. The Europeans were disorganized, and the Muslim forces were better trained and equipped. Forty years later, Jerusalem fell to Saladin, a Sunni Muslim sultan of Syria and Egypt. Saladin allowed the Jews to resettle in Jerusalem; many moved there from Ashkelon on the coast.

With the Muslims holding Jerusalem again, Pope Leo III called for the Third Crusade, which launched in 1189. This Crusade impacted England's Jews, most of whom had arrived in 1066 from Normandy with William the Conqueror. Once again, the Crusade rhetoric stirred up anti-Semitic actions. For instance, Jews in London were taxed one-quarter of their moveable property in 1188, and the crowds attacked Jews attending Richard the Lionheart's coronation in 1189. In York, a group of Jews hid in Clifford's Tower from a rampaging mob, but over 150 ultimately committed mass suicide as they realized the hopelessness of survival.

The Holy Roman Emperor Frederick I Barbarossa was the first to lead his troops to Asia on the Third Crusade in 1190, but he drowned when crossing a river in Turkey. King Richard the Lionheart of England and King Philip II of France sailed to the Middle East in 1191. They won a battle against Saladin at the northern Israeli city of Acre, where they captured three thousand Muslim prisoners. Saladin also held some

Christian prisoners. The terms of surrender included each side releasing their prisoners, with Saladin agreeing to pay a hefty ransom for his men.

While negotiations continued, Richard and Philip had a falling out, and Philip sailed back to France with his men. Saladin released some of his prisoners but delayed releasing the rest. Richard lost his patience and marched 2,700 of his Muslim prisoners in front of Acre's walls, then cut their heads off. Saladin retaliated by killing the remainder of his English and French prisoners.

Saladin continued to fight Richard for another year around the land of Palestine, but without Philip's French army, Richard could not prevail. Eventually, they made a truce. King Richard got a strip of coastline from Jaffa to Tyre, and Saladin kept Jerusalem. Saladin allowed the Jerusalem Jews to stay and let Christian pilgrims visit Jerusalem's holy sites. In 1210, three hundred rabbis from France and England made *aliyah* (ascent to the Holy Land) and resettled in Palestine.

As in earlier times, some Muslim rulers had forced Jews (and Christians) to wear distinguishing clothing items, such as a yellow star, belt, or hood (Christians wore blue). In 1215, the Roman Catholic Church decreed that Jews had to wear a badge or pointed hat. The theologian Thomas Aquinas even called for the enslavement of all Jews. In 1229, King Henry III taxed the Jews of England 50 percent of their property's value.

Goaded by the Inquisition, on the Sabbath day of March 3, 1240, French officials seized every copy of the Talmud they could find in France. Twenty-four wagon loads hauled the parchments to Paris, where they were burned. In 1254, King Louis IX expelled all Jews from France, and King Edward I did the same in England in 1290. When Germany, Spain, and Italy followed suit, these expulsions created an eastward migration of Jews to Central and Eastern Europe, especially Poland.

Beginning in the 9th century, the Muslims captured teen boys from the Eurasian Steppe, converted them to Islam, and trained them for military service. Known as Mamluks (slaves), these rugged youths had acquired exceptional archery and horsemanship skills before being enslaved. Combined with the Muslim military training, the Mamluks were fierce and indomitable mounted archers, striking fear in anyone fighting against them. The Mamluks played a pivotal role in fighting with Saladin against the Crusaders.

Over time, the Mamluks grew in power despite technically being slaves, attaining high positions in the military. In 1250, the Mamluks took the throne in Egypt in the chaos following the Egyptian sultan's death. Ten years later, they hammered the Mongols swarming northern Palestine and conquered Syria as far north as the Euphrates River. The fourth Mamluk sultan of Egypt was Baybars I. While warring against the Crusaders and Mongols, he also organized the state, reformed its legal system, and enlarged the army. He conquered Acre in 1291, which the Crusaders had held since Richard the Lionheart had captured it a century earlier.

Mamluk warrior
https://commons.wikimedia.org/wiki/File:Mamluke.jpg

Although Christians and Jews were "protected people" under Muslim law, the Mamluks were nervous about the high administrative positions some of them held. Would they be more loyal to the Crusaders or Egypt? The Mamluks began strongly encouraging conversion to Islam, especially among the Coptic Christians who handled taxes and other financial affairs. The Mamluks sometimes swept the Jews into their conversion efforts.

Those who refused to convert lost their positions. Rather than convert, many Egyptian Christians and a few Egyptian Jews left the country.

Riots erupted in Cairo against Christians in 1293, and Sultan Malik al-Ashraf Khalil dismissed all Jews and Christians from administrative positions. In 1301, more riots broke out, this time involving both Jews and Christians, forcing them to convert to Islam and closing all of Cairo's synagogues and churches. Jews had to wear yellow turbans and Christians blue turbans.

Originating in northern Asia, the Black Plague swept the Mediterranean coast from 1347 to 1349. Spreading to Europe, it killed about half the population. The plague and its ramifications plunged Egypt's economy into disarray, inciting more angst against non-Muslims. Rioters grabbed Jews and Christians and threw them into fires if they refused to recite the Shahada (the Muslim creed). The Jews were also suffering financially. They had once enjoyed a middle-class status in Egypt, and some were wealthy. The sultanate itself suffered economically due to the plague and other factors. Now, Jews in higher positions had lost their jobs, and most Jews were struggling through poverty.

In 1442, the Egyptian authorities found what they considered blasphemous writing against Islam in a Jewish synagogue. The name "Muhammed" was faintly inscribed on a raised platform upon which the rabbi would stand to read the scriptures; thus, he was "standing on Muhammed." The Mamluks destroyed the platform, then inspected other synagogues and churches. They discussed cutting off the feet or hands of the rabbis who had stood on Muhammed's name, but the rabbis vehemently denied knowing it was there. Under torture, three rabbis confessed. Two died, and the third converted to Islam.

Inspecting other synagogues and churches revealed that some had built new structures against the Pact of Umar. Others had renovated their interiors following a fire. Despite the Jews and Christians showing certificates of approval from the authorities for the renovations, the Mamluks insisted they were breaking the pact made in 632 in Jerusalem. Many of the Jews and Christians were unaware of the ancient pact, so they were all informed of its contents and warned that any further infractions would result in the destruction of their synagogue or church.[53]

---

[53] Mark R. Cohen, "Jews in the Mamlūk Environment: The Crisis of 1442 (A Geniza Study)," *Bulletin of the School of Oriental and African Studies, University of London* 47, no. 3 (1984): 425-48. http://www.jstor.org/stable/618879.

Although Jews were harassed under Mamluk rule, their plight paled compared to what happened to Jews in Europe. Blaming the Black Plague on Jews poisoning the wells, European mobs destroyed hundreds of Jewish communities. An anti-Semitic campaign in Barcelona, Castille, and Valencia killed thousands of Jews in 1391. Pope Benedict XIII banned the Talmud in 1415, and Jews were forced to live in ghettos throughout Europe.

Key Takeaways:
- The Crusades (1095-1291)
    - Byzantine Empire enlists the pope's aid in expelling Seljuk Turks
    - Crusade rhetoric spurs violence against Jews in France, Bohemia, and Spain
    - Crusaders take Jerusalem in 1099, with horrific atrocities against Jews and Muslims
    - Saladin, sultan of Syria and Egypt, retakes Jerusalem in 1187, allowed Jews to return
    - Third Crusade: Saladin keeps Jerusalem, and Jews are able to remain
- Jewish persecution and exile in Western Europe create an eastern migration
- The Mamluk period (1250-1517)
    - Former slaves who rose to power as Egypt's military force
    - Jews and Christians persecuted, although not as severely as in Western Europe

Chapter 7: The Holocaust

The Nazis' "Final Solution to the Jewish Question" between 1941 and 1945 was the concluding stage in their evolving anti-Semitic policies. The original plan was to segregate the Jews, take their property, and ship them somewhere else, like Madagascar. The "final solution" was the systematic genocide of all Jews in Europe. How did things reach this point? What events and underlying philosophies led to an organized attempt to annihilate the Jewish race?

A century earlier, circumstances were gradually improving for the European Jews as the countries moved toward granting Jews citizenship and civil rights. By the mid-1800s, the Jews in all of Germany except Bavaria had equal rights with the rest of the population, at least on paper. The Jewish lawyer Gabriel Riesser even became vice-president of Germany's National Assembly in 1848.

Yet many Germans equated the Jews with modernity and the leftist Progressive Party, which they believed threatened traditional German values. University professors and clergymen fanned into flame this animosity toward the Jews. In 1878, the court chaplain Adolf Stoecker founded the German Christian Social Party, demanding that all Jews convert to Christianity and calling them "parasites" and a "nation unto themselves."

Kaiser Wilhelm II became Germany's last emperor in 1888 and ruled until his abdication in 1918. He had several personal friends who were Jews and supported the Zionist movement, albeit with racist reasons: he preferred they not live in Germany. Yet, over time, his attitude degenerated into "eliminatory" anti-Semitism. By the end of his life, he called for the extinction of the Jewish race:

> "They keep my people poor and in their clutches. In every small village in Germany sits a dirty Jew, like a spider drawing the people into the web of usury. He lends money to the small farmers on the security of their land and so gradually acquires control of everything. The Jews are the parasites of my empire. The Jewish question is one of the great problems I have to deal with, and yet nothing can be done to cope with it!"[54]

Meanwhile, by 1866, Jews had become Jerusalem's majority population and built a suburb outside the walls to eliminate overcrowding. Following horrific pogroms (organized massacres) in Russia, the First *Aliyah* brought almost 35,000 Jews to Palestine from 1882 to 1903. Their goal was "the political, national, and spiritual resurrection of the Jewish people in Palestine"[55] under the patronage of Baron Edmond de Rothschild of France.

Photo from the 1930s of **Degania**, Israel's first kibbutz

Photo zoomed in. Credit: א דגניה קיבוץ, CC BY-SA 3.0 <https://creativecommons.org/licenses/by-sa/3.0>, via Wikimedia Commons; https://commons.wikimedia.org/wiki/File:Historical_Image_of_Degania_Elementary_School_(9).png

Following Russia's October Revolution led by Vladimir Lenin's Bolshevik Party, Jews fleeing Marxist anti-Semitism formed the Second Aliyah in 1904. In 1906, the Jews founded the first Hebrew high school in

---

[54] John C. G. Rohl, *The Kaiser and His Court: Wilhelm II and the Government of Germany* (Cambridge: Cambridge University Press,1995), 190-212.

[55] "Immigration to Israel: The First Aliyah (1882-1903)," *Jewish Virtual Library* https://www.jewishvirtuallibrary.org/the-first-aliyah-1882-1903

Jaffa and the Bezalel Academy of Art and Design in Jerusalem. In 1909, the Jews built Tel Aviv just outside the port city of Jaffa as a housing estate for Hebrew-speaking Jews. Zionist pioneers established Degania Alef in 1910, the first kibbutz (a farming commune) south of the Sea of Galilee.

World War I raged from 1914 to 1919, with the Allies (France, Italy, Japan, Russia, the United Kingdom, and the United States) pitted against the Central Powers (Austria-Hungary, Bulgaria, Germany, and the Ottoman Empire). Although 100,000 Jews fought for Germany, they were unjustly accused of evading active service. The British seized Palestine from the Ottoman Empire and announced their plan of establishing a "national home for the Jewish people" in the Balfour Declaration of 1917.

From 1919 to 1923, the Third Aliyah of 40,000 young Eastern European Jews increased Palestine's Jewish population to 90,000 pioneers building roads and towns around Palestine. The Fourth Aliyah of 1924 to 1929 brought 82,000 middle-class Jews from Poland, who established factories and small businesses. The European Jews not only built up Palestine's infrastructure and economy but also higher education. The Hebrew University of Jerusalem opened in 1925. When Hitler became Germany's chancellor in 1933, 250,000 German Jewish professionals fled to Palestine in the Fifth Aliyah. They established industrial enterprises and built the Haifa port and oil refineries. Almost a half-million Jews lived in Palestine by 1939.

As a young man, Adolf Hitler nurtured a pathological loathing of Marxists and Jews. He blamed the Jews for Germany's cultural, economic, and political chaos, proclaiming they were corrupting Germany and the "Aryan" race. Just before the end of World War I, he was blinded after being gassed and spent months in recovery, where he gradually regained his eyesight. He spent that time seething about losing the war and fantasizing about rescuing Germany and Austria from the Jews and Bolsheviks (Russian Marxists).

Hitler joined the Workers' Party and became its chairman in 1921. Although of average height and dark-haired, Hitler advanced the ideal image of tall, muscular blonds with blue or green eyes. Hitler gave dramatic and fiery speeches that the "Aryan" Germans were a master race and that the Jews were the cause of Germany's domestic issues. He announced the "Platform of the National-Socialist German Workers' Party," demanding all ethnic Germans unify into one "Reich," or "Greater Germany." Only those of German blood could be citizens; all Jews were explicitly excluded. The platform stated that the Party "fights against the Jewish-materialistic spirit within and around us."[56]

At this point, Hitler talked about removing Jews' privileges and exiling them, not exterminating them. An unsuccessful coup d'état in 1923 landed him in prison for nine months. He used that time to write *Mein Kampf* (*My Struggle*), outlining his ideas about the Aryan race, the Jewish threat, social Darwinism, and his plan of *Lebensraum* (living space)—his concept of conquering all of Europe and deporting non-German people to Siberia so people of German blood could spread out and multiply.

After their humiliating defeat in World War I, which crippled their economy, many Germans were susceptible to Hitler's propaganda. The Great Depression crushed Germany's economy even further, bringing people of all classes, including industrialists and military leaders, into the Nazi Party. By 1932, the Nazis controlled the parliament, and Hitler became Germany's Reich Chancellor in 1933.

Hitler immediately eliminated the Jews, Marxists, and Social Democrats from any political role. Within two months, he established Dachau, Germany's first concentration camp for political prisoners. These prisoners had no indictment or conviction of any crime; the judicial system wasn't followed. This first concentration camp was meant to silence and intimidate anyone considered a threat to the Reich.

Dachau concentration camp after liberation by the US Army on April 29, 1945. A Russian prisoner points to a guard who brutally mistreated prisoners.
https://commons.wikimedia.org/wiki/File:Konzentrationslager_Dachau_1945.webp

---

[56] "The Program of the National-Socialist German Workers' Party, February 24, 1920," *Jewish Virtual Library* https://www.jewishvirtuallibrary.org/platform-of-the-national-socialist-german-workers-rsquo-party

By 1934, Hitler was the unchallenged leader of the "Third Reich"—the third German empire. As he successfully rejuvenated Germany's military and economy, the Germans were so giddy at their comeback that most were unconcerned about the Nuremberg Laws of 1935. These laws stripped Jews of citizenship, which meant Jews lost their jobs in civil service. Even physicians and teachers were forced into unemployment when the hospitals and schools fell under government regulation. The Jews who emigrated had to pay a 90 percent tax on their assets.

In April 1934, Heinrich Himmler took command of the Berlin Gestapo (the secret state police) and the concentration camps. With meticulous methodology, he organized systematic terrorism against the regime's opponents. Himmler and Hitler broadened the criteria for the concentration camps to anyone they deemed inferior. People with hydrocephaly, deformities, Jewish ancestry, and anything else considered "subhuman" were herded into the camps.

On November 9-10, 1938, Hitler coordinated violence against Jews in Kristallnacht: "the night of broken glass." Mobs that included Nazi soldiers and Hitler Youth disguised in civilian clothing plundered and burned Jewish homes, businesses, and synagogues in Germany, Austria, and Czechoslovakia. Firefighters intervened only to preserve neighboring properties. The police arrested 30,000 young male Jews, sending them to the Dachau, Sachsenhausen, and Buchenwald concentration camps.

World War II launched on September 1, 1939, when Hitler invaded Poland. He used *blitzkrieg* tactics: shock assaults with bombers and fighter planes to immobilize military bases, airfields, and communication centers, followed by infantry invasion. Poland fell within a month, then Norway, Denmark, Holland, Belgium, Luxemburg, and France in rapid succession. All of Western Europe except Great Britain fell to the Nazis within nine months.

As the war began, Hitler initiated his T-4 Euthanasia Program, rounding up men, women, and children with psychological illnesses and those mentally and physically disabled. At the killing centers of Bernburg, Brandenburg, Grafeneck, Hadamar, and Hartheim, the Nazis murdered the children with sedatives and the adults by starvation. Later, they began gassing the victims. The Germans also used the concentration camps for forced labor in manufacturing military equipment and artificial rubber. These prisoners lived an average of nine months due to insufficient food, backbreaking work, and overcrowding leading to typhus and other diseases.

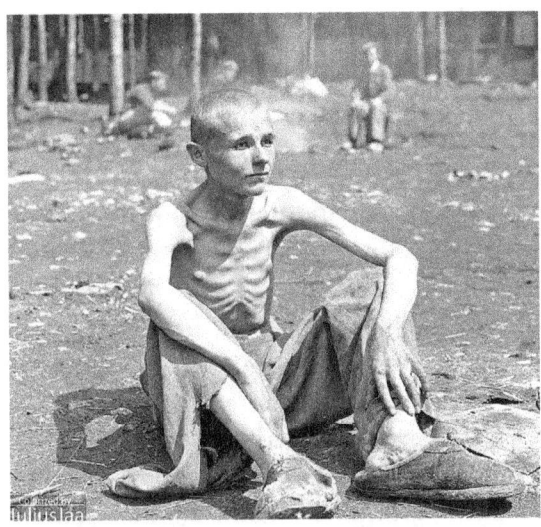

An emaciated teenage boy rescued from the Ebensee concentration camp
Photo zoomed in. Credit: J Malan Heslop, colorized by Julius Jääskeläinen, CC BY 2.0 <https://creativecommons.org/licenses/by/2.0>, via Wikimedia Commons; https://commons.wikimedia.org/wiki/File:Liberated_prisoner_of_the_Ebensee_concentration_camp_in_Austria,_8_May_1945._(45899003575).jpg

On the war front, the British Air Force held off Nazi control of the English Channel, so Hitler turned his military machine against Eastern Europe and North Africa. He took Greece, Yugoslavia, and Crete and invaded the Soviet Union in June 1941. Although Hitler's armies overwhelmed the Communist forces in the Baltic States and Ukraine, he overextended his military. He was unable to conquer Moscow before the deadly Russian winter set in.

In December, the United States joined the war on the side of Britain and the Soviet Union, the Allied powers, which Hitler called "international Jewry." Earlier, the Nazis had planned to exile one million Jews to Nazi-run Madagascar each year for four years. However, the British blockade kept that from happening, so Hitler resorted to his "Final Solution to the Jewish Question," the mass murder of all Jews under Nazi rule.

In Russia, Hitler shot or starved to death over three million POWs: Communists, intellectuals, and Jews. In September 1941, Himmler masterminded the Babi Yar massacre. The Nazis posted notices in Kyiv, instructing all Jews to report to the Babi Yar ravine with warm clothing, documentation, and valuables. Since Babi Yar was close to the train station, the Jews assumed they would be evacuated by train, and over 33,000 gathered in the early morning. To their horror, all the men, women, and children were stripped, forced into the ravine, and shot.

Because of the anguish the German soldiers experienced in shooting women and children, Himmler decided to use "gas vans." Jews, Gypsies, and mentally ill people were herded into the back of sealed trucks, believing they were being transported somewhere. Instead, the engine exhaust was diverted into the back of the truck, killing the people. In 1941, gas "showers" were installed in Poland's Belzec, Sobibor, and Treblinka concentration camps.

As unsuspecting people were unloaded from cattle cars on the trains arriving at the camps, the elderly, children, pregnant women, and anyone too sick or weak to work were divided off. They were told they needed a "disinfecting" shower but instead died from carbon monoxide gas piped into the shower room. Himmler organized the murder of almost 2.7 million Jews, Gypsies, homosexuals, political prisoners, and social misfits at the concentration camps.

At the Auschwitz concentration camp in Poland, Nazi scientists conducted experiments with Zyklon B, a poisonous insecticide and rat killer, on Soviet prisoners of war. Zyklon B became the preferred gassing method at Auschwitz for its swift and efficient action. Five hundred Jews were herded into the "showers" daily to be gassed. On October 10, 1944, the Nazis gassed eight hundred children at Auschwitz.

Hungarian Jews who have just deboarded the train at Auschwitz concentration camp. The healthy are separated out for labor. The old lady in the center front and the lady holding the baby were probably immediately sent to the gas chambers.
https://commons.wikimedia.org/wiki/File:Selection_on_the_ramp_at_Auschwitz-Birkenau,_1944_(Auschwitz_Album)_1b.jpg

When the Jews and other prisoners first arrived at Auschwitz, those who weren't immediately gassed were designated for the labor force. The guards shaved their heads, tattooed their arms with a registration number, and issued striped uniforms. They lived in overcrowded dormitories with tiers of bunks. In the following months, a physician would determine who was still healthy enough to work and who would be sent to the gas chambers. The prisoners who worked at the gas chambers later shared that amid the screams, they could hear the Sh'ma Yisrael: "Hear, oh Israel, the L-rd is our G-d, the L-rd is One."

Those in concentration camps who weren't gassed sometimes faced worse horrors. To keep the Jews from producing more children, physicians irradiated the reproductive systems of men and women or injected chemicals that burned the women's uteruses. Nazi doctors infected prisoners with diseases to test new medications, and some prisoners were frozen to experiment with hyperthermia treatments.

The tide began to turn in 1943 as the Nazis lost North Africa and Sicily to the Allies. The Allies took Italy and Normandy in June 1944, sandwiching the German forces between them and Soviet troops. The Soviet forces liberated the prisoners of the Majdanek concentration camp in Poland that summer, sharing evidence of the slaughters committed there with journalists. The Soviets released six thousand starving prisoners at Auschwitz in January 1945. The Nazis had already left weeks earlier, forcing most of the prisoners on a death march. As the Allied forces continued to liberate the camps, they found unspeakable horrors. Unburied corpses were stacked like firewood. The survivors had lost their body fat and muscle and were skin and bones.

The German army unraveled as its generals seethed under Hitler's distrustful and deranged leadership. A failed assassination attempt on Hitler ended in the generals' gruesome executions, filmed for Hitler's pleasure. As the Allies approached Berlin, Hitler studied his maps and ordered attacks with armies he didn't have. On April 30, 1945, Hitler committed suicide, and the German Third Reich surrendered on May 7, 1945. World War II ended on September 2, 1945, after Japan's surrender.

Two-thirds of the European Jews died in the Holocaust—about six million. Poland had three million Jews in 1933; the Holocaust reduced that number to 45,000. Greece lost 90 percent of its Jewish population. Most survivors emigrated to Palestine, the United States, Australia, or

South Africa. By 1950, over half the world's Jewish population lived in the western hemisphere.

For the Jewish survivors, it was time to pick up the pieces of their shattered lives and forge ahead with the tenacity that carried them through the unimaginable nightmare of the Holocaust. However, anti-Semitism did not die with the Nazi regime. The Jews were still not safe in Europe; over five hundred Jews were killed in Poland in the year after liberation by their former neighbors or roving gangs. Would it ever be possible to live normal lives again? And where would that be?

Women in the Auschwitz barracks
https://commons.wikimedia.org/wiki/File:Women_in_the_barracks_of_Auschwitz.jpg

Key Takeaways:
- Circumstances for Jews in the century before the Holocaust
    - Citizenship and civil rights in most European countries
    - Antisemitic attitudes continue; Jews blamed for economic woes
- Jews resettle in Palestine
    - The majority population in Jerusalem by 1866
    - One-half million Jews settle in Palestine from 1882 to 1933
    - Build Tel Aviv, universities, schools, roads, farms, the first kibbutz
    - 1917 British Balfour Declaration: a "national home for the Jewish people"

- Hitler becomes Germany's Reich Chancellor in 1933
  - Establishes Dachau, Germany's first concentration camp, in 1933
  - Nuremberg Laws of 1935 strip Jews of citizenship
  - In 1938, Hitler coordinates violence against Jews in Kristallnacht
- World War II launches on September 1, 1939, when Hitler invades Poland
  - All of Western Europe except Britain falls to the Nazis in nine months
  - Most Jews forced into concentration camps to work or die
- In 1941, Operation Reinhard initiated to kill all Jews in Europe
  - Babi Yar massacre: 33,000 Jewish men, women, and children shot in Kiev
  - Gas vans and gas chambers kill over one million Jews
  - Eight hundred children gassed in one day at Auschwitz
- Allied forces gain the upper hand in the war in 1944
  - Soviets begin liberating Jews from some of the concentration camps
  - 1945: Hitler commits suicide, Third Reich surrenders, war ends
- Impact of the Holocaust on Jews in Europe
  - Two-thirds of European Jews killed: six million
  - Most survivors emigrate to Palestine, the United States, Australia, or South Africa
  - Antisemitic violence continues to kill Jews in Europe

Chapter 8: Modern Israel

Immediately after WWII, while the Allied administration was still in place, about 250,000 Jews lived in Germany. Some were married to German spouses and had escaped notice during the Nazi regime. Others were children sheltered by kindhearted German neighbors pretending they were their own, saved from being dragged with their parents to concentration camps. A third group was German Jews who had returned from exile.

The fourth and largest group was the thousands of Jews who had survived the "death marches" to Germany from Eastern European concentration camps in the war's final weeks. After "liberation," three-quarters of the Jews in Germany still lived in the overcrowded camps, fighting typhus and typhoid fever while the Allies debated what to do with them. Eighty percent were from Poland; the rest were from Russia, Romania, Hungary, and Czechoslovakia.

When General Patton wanted to transport them back to where they came from, they refused. Their Eastern European communities had been wiped out, and their property confiscated. They had no family, no homes, and no employment there. Pogroms (organized massacres) against Jews were ongoing in Poland, and Jews in the Soviet bloc quickly discovered that Stalin's boast of eliminating anti-Semitism was fiction.[57]

The inmates demanded to be sent to Palestine, where a thriving Jewish

---

[57] Michael Brenner, *After the Holocaust: Rebuilding Jewish Lives in Postwar Germany*, trans. Barbara Harshav. (Princeton: Princeton University Press, 1997), 3-16.

community comprised about 30 percent of the population. Jews throughout Europe echoed the demands of the Jews in Germany. They needed a place of safety to heal and rebuild their lives. They needed to recover the culture that defined them: their religious observances, the Yiddish and Hebrew languages, traditions, music, art, and literature.

The Jews in the "displaced persons" camps initiated a renaissance of Jewish culture, launching newspapers, Jewish schools, and historical committees between 1945 and 1951. They published papers in Yiddish, Hebrew, Polish, German, Hungarian, Lithuanian, and Romanian with printing presses brought into the camps.[58] They shared their stories, angst, and dreams through the written word in their own languages, giving the European Jews a united voice.

Jewish Youth in the Fifth Aliyah to Palestine, February 19, 1934
Zoltan Kluger, Public Domain: https://commons.wikimedia.org/wiki/File:First_Youth-Aliyah_group_walking_to_Ein_Harod.JPG

But was Palestine a viable option for Jewish resettlement? A Jewish remnant had lived there through the Greek, Roman, Christian, and Muslim occupations. And, since the 1880s, Jews had moved back to Palestine in increasing numbers. Other Palestinians had a much longer history in the land. About 70 percent of Palestine's population in 1946 was non-Jewish, primarily Muslim Arabs whose forefathers came in the centuries after Caliph Umar invaded Palestine in 638 CE.

---

[58] Brenner, *After the Holocaust*, 16-19.

Recent genetic studies have revealed that Jews and Palestinians are related, sharing 18 percent of their chromosomes. Both have high repeat numbers of DYS388 alleles and share a single branch in Haplogroup 1. Geneticists believe this link extends back to the Roman era or earlier and think it remarkable that the two groups maintained genetic continuity even though most Jews had lived outside Israel for two thousand years.[59] Some Palestinians report a family history of Jewish ancestors who converted to Islam, while others claim to be descendants of the ancient Canaanites.

Despite their shared ancestry, the Jews and Palestinians were divided by religion and culture. The Palestinians regarded the Jews as recent intruders in their homeland. At the end of WWI in 1918, the Allies had assigned Palestine to Great Britain in the British Mandate of 1920. The mandate incorporated the Balfour Declaration supporting Palestine as a national home for the Jewish people.

The Palestinians demanded independence from British rule and an end to Jewish immigration, as the Jews and Palestinians violently clashed over their claims to the land. The British turned the problem over to the United Nations in 1947. The UN proposed ending the British Mandate for Palestine and establishing separate Palestinian and Jewish states in the land, with Jerusalem under an International Trusteeship.

---

[59] Almut Nebel et al, "High-resolution Y Chromosome Haplotypes of Israeli and Palestinian Arabs Reveal Geographic Substructure and Substantial Overlap with Haplotypes of Jews," *Human Genetics* 107, no. 6 (December 2000): 630–641. doi:10.1007/s004390000426.

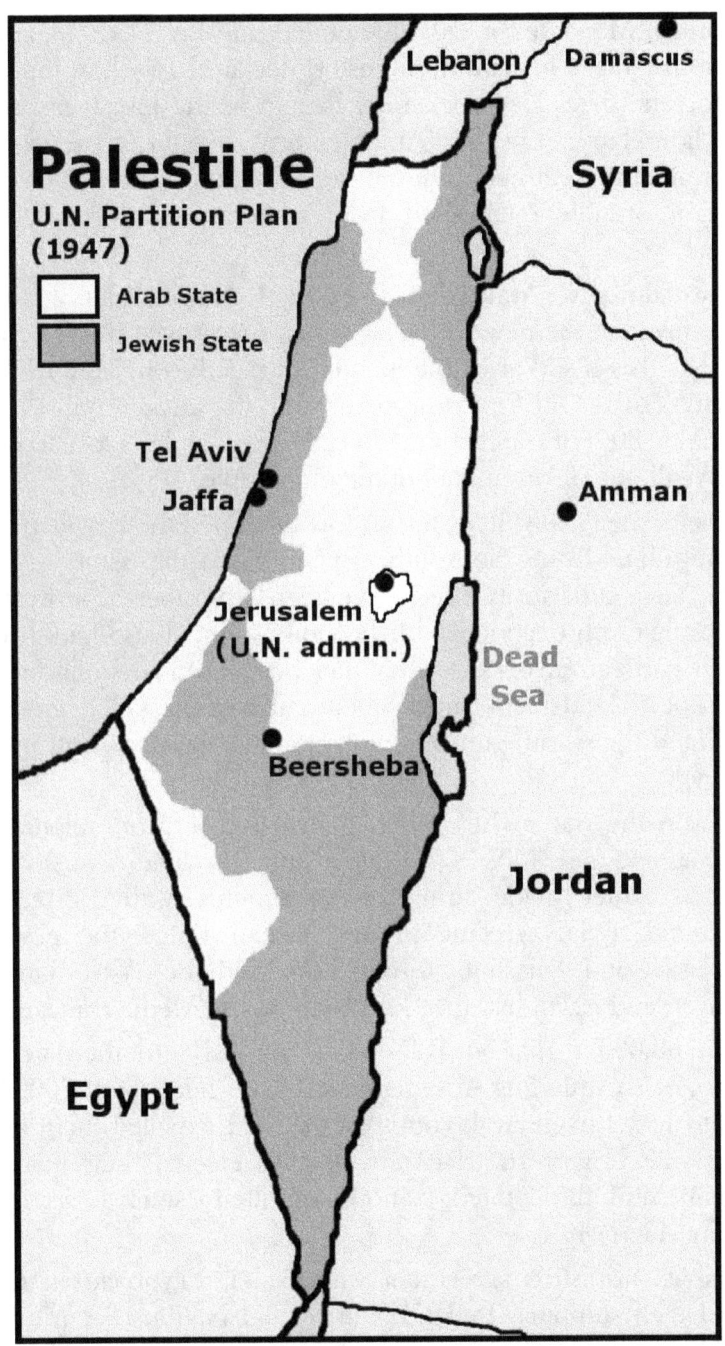

In 1947, the United Nations Partition Plan had the Arabs in the light areas, the Jews in the dark areas, and Jerusalem under UN control.
https://commons.wikimedia.org/wiki/File:UN_Partition_Plan_For_Palestine_1947.png

The British Mandate for Palestine ended on May 14, 1948, and David Ben Gurion, Israel's first prime minister, declared Israel an independent and democratic state. He proclaimed Israel was the Jewish historical and spiritual homeland, but its Arab citizens would have equal and nondiscriminatory treatment. On the same day, the Israel Defense Forces (IDF) were formally established from underground forces already in operation.

The next day, five Arab nations (Egypt, Lebanon, Iraq, Transjordan, and Syria) invaded the new nation of Israel, declaring, "It will be a war of annihilation." Israel's War of Independence raged from May 1948 to July 1949. Jerusalem's "Old City" (the part within the ancient walls) fell to the Arabs on May 30. For the first time in centuries, the Jews lost access to the Western Wall, the only remnant of the old temple.

However, Israel's tiny, fledgling air force stopped the Egyptian armored column invading from the south. By autumn, the Israeli Air Force achieved air superiority as seventeen bombers arrived from Czechoslovakia with experienced fighter pilots. Israel also had three ships the British had seized because they had been used to smuggle refugees from Europe. The Israelis snuck aboard the ships, sailed them to Tel Aviv, outfitted them with guns and anti-aircraft weaponry, and used them against Egypt.

Israel won the war in July 1949. It held the territory allotted by the United Nations and took 60 percent of the land assigned to the Palestinians. Israel made armistice agreements with Egypt, Jordan, Lebanon, and Syria, agreeing to the "Green Line," the new border between Israel and Palestine. Jordan now held the West Bank of the Jordan River, and Egypt had the Gaza Strip on the Mediterranean Sea.

About 700,000 displaced Palestinians moved into the West Bank, Gaza Strip, or surrounding Arab nations. Meanwhile, about 700,000 Jews moved into Israel from Arab countries that had expelled them and from Europe. On February 16, 1949, the Israelis elected their first Knesset (parliament), and the United Nations admitted Israel as its fifty-ninth member in May 1949.

Despite its armistice agreement with Israel, Egypt closed the Suez Canal to Israeli shipping. In 1951, the United Nations Security Council ordered Egypt to reopen the canal, insisting that a blockade was inconsistent with the armistice agreement. Egypt refused, and its foreign minister, Muhammad Salah al-Din, stated: "We shall not be satisfied except by the final obliteration of Israel from the map of the Middle East."

Egypt imported arms from the Soviet Union and sent *fedayeen* terrorists to attack Israel, mainly from Jordan's bases. Jordan bore the brunt of Israel's retaliation, and the Security Council chastised Israel for hostile acts. Egypt then nationalized the Suez Canal Company, which angered France and Britain. France had paid for 52 percent of the canal's construction in 1869, and Great Britain had purchased Egypt's shares in the Suez Canal Company in 1875.

France and Britain secretly plotted with Israel, and Israel invaded the Sinai Peninsula in 1956, advancing within ten miles of the canal. Several days later, Britain and France sent troops into the canal zone, which the United States condemned, considering it a continued act of European colonization.[60] The United Nations ordered Britain, France, and Israel to withdraw their troops from Egypt, and Egypt paid Britain and France for their shares in the Suez Canal Company.

In 1964, the Arab League formed the Palestinian Liberation Organization (PLO), eventually led by Yasser Arafat, who conducted terrorist operations against Israeli citizens. King Hussein of Jordan condemned the attacks for fear of Israeli retaliatory strikes on Jordan. King Hassan II of Morocco warned Israel that the Arab leaders were planning a war on Israel.

Meanwhile, Syria and Jordan were disturbed that Israel was draining water from the Sea of Galilee in its National Water Carrier canal that transported water to Israel's arid south, lowering water levels in the Jordan River that flows out of it and the Dead Sea, where it empties. Syria lay on Galilee's east bank, and Jordan lay on the eastern side of the Jordan River.

Syria began shelling Israeli villages and kibbutzim from the Golan Heights, a plateau towering three thousand feet over the eastern shores of the Sea of Galilee. Israel retaliated by shooting down six Syrian MiG fighters in 1967, so Syria called on Egypt for help. Egyptian forces lined up on Israel's Sinai border while Syrian troops amassed on the Golan Heights. Egypt cut off the Straits of Tiran, which flows from the Gulf of Aqaba at Israel's southern tip into the Red Sea. Losing ship traffic through the Straits of Tiran meant Israel couldn't import oil from Iran. Jordan,

---

[60] "The Suez Crisis, 1956," *Office of the Historian. Foreign Service Institute: United States Department of State.* https://history.state.gov/milestones/1953-1960/suez#:~:text=On%20July%2026%2C%201956%2C%20Egyptian,since%20its%20construction%20in%201869.

Lebanon, Iraq, Algeria, Kuwait, and Sudan allied with Egypt and Syria to wipe Israel off the map.

Using the element of surprise, Israel launched a preemptive strike on Egypt on June 5, 1967, flying almost its entire air force into Egypt and obliterating 180 fighter planes. Israel and Egypt then clashed in tank battles in the searing Sinai desert. Syria retaliated by attacking Tiberias and Megiddo, and Jordan shelled West Jerusalem. Israel's air force attacked the Syrian and Jordanian airfields, destroying half of Syria's air force and twenty Jordanian planes.

Three Israeli battalions headed to Jerusalem to rescue a small Jewish community in mostly-Arab East Jerusalem. They also needed to fend off the shelling attacks on West Jerusalem. The Israelis took the Jordanian command bunker in a brutal battle, but 249 of their 260 soldiers were wounded or killed. The Jordanians also suffered devastating losses.

The Israeli commanders decided to attack Jerusalem by the eastern Lion's Gate. (The only general to ever conquer Jerusalem from the east was King David when it was a Jebusite city.) Most Jordanian troops had evacuated the city, so the Jewish forces reached the Temple Mount unhindered. A rabbi blew the shofar at the Western Wall to celebrate. The Six-Day War ended with Israel gaining Jerusalem, tripling Israel's territory, and capturing the Sinai Peninsula.

But peace did not follow. Within three months, the Arab League formulated the "three no's": no peace, no negotiations, and no recognition of Israel as a nation. Egypt began shelling Israeli forces close to the Suez Canal, starting the War of Attrition. Using Soviet missiles, Egypt sank Israel's destroyer, the *Eilat*, in October 1967.

Israel had a small full-time military and depended on its reserve forces in wartime. (Even today, all able-bodied men serve in active duty for three years and then in the reserves until they are forty. All women do two years of active duty, and unmarried women without children serve in the reserves until they are thirty-eight. Women served in active combat in the War of Independence but, after that, filled non-combat roles until the 21st century.)

Egypt's President Nasser believed Israel could not sustain a lengthy war because its reserve forces would eventually need to return to their jobs. Israel's economy would crumble if the younger men and women were not manning the businesses, factories, and farms. Egypt was in this war for the long haul. The UN tried negotiating peace talks, but Egypt and Jordan refused to come to the table until Israel withdrew from the territory it gained in the Six-Day War.

Golda Meir and Richard Nixon at the White House, September 1969
https://commons.wikimedia.org/wiki/File:Golda_Meir_in_the_white_house_1969.jpg

Israel's new prime minister, Golda Meir, visited the United States, pledging Israel's willingness for armistice talks. President Nixon sent Secretary of State William Rogers to the Middle East to negotiate a ceasefire in 1970. The terms were that Israel would withdraw from the Sinai, Egypt would allow passage through the Strait of Tiran, and the two countries would commit to peace. The first ceasefire agreement fell through, but Rogers finally got Israel and Egypt to agree to an "in place" ceasefire in June 1970, maintaining the status quo regarding territory but ending the three-year war.

The following year, Egypt's new president, Anwar Sadat, hinted he would be open to recognizing Israel as a state if Israel returned the Sinai Peninsula and the Gaza Strip. Golda Meir signaled that Israel was willing to make some withdrawals, but *not* to where it was before the 1967 Six-Day War. In 1973, Sadat threatened to go to war against Israel, but he had been threatening for three years and had never done anything.

But then, Sadat suddenly did—on Yom Kippur, Israel's holiest day of the year. It was also Ramadan, Islam's most sacred festival. On October 6, 1973, Egypt and Syria launched a coordinated surprise assault, beginning the Yom Kippur War. At the Golan Heights, 1,400 Syrian tanks faced off against 180 Israeli tanks. At the Suez Canal, 2,000 Egyptian tanks, 550 Egyptian aircraft, and 600,000 Egyptian soldiers confronted 500 Israeli soldiers with three tanks.

Algeria, Iraq, Jordan, Kuwait, Lebanon, Libya, Morocco, Saudi Arabia, Sudan, and Tunisia supported Egypt and Syria with financing, fighter jets, soldiers, tanks, and radar units. Because the United States, Holland, Great Britain, Japan, and Portugal supported Israel, the Arabs imposed an oil embargo on these nations. Gas prices quadrupled, and President Nixon lowered the U.S. speed limit to fifty-five miles per hour to reduce fuel consumption.

After the Soviet Union transferred eight thousand tons of weapons to the Arabs, Nixon sent tanks, bombs, and helicopters to Israel. This influx enabled the Israeli forces to trounce the Egyptians in the Sinai, cross the Suez Canal, and march toward Cairo. In the north, the Israelis recaptured the Golan Heights and marched toward Syria's capital, Damascus. On October 22, the UN Security Council called for a ceasefire, and Israel complied under pressure from the US. Because President Sadat's initial attack was successful (until the US jumped in with weaponry), he felt that he had "retrieved Arab honor." He signed a peace treaty with Israel in 1979, and Israel returned the Sinai Peninsula to Egypt. Peace with Egypt endures today, over forty years later.

At an agonizingly slow pace, Israel and its Arab neighbors began to make peace. In 1994, the Israel-Jordan Peace Treaty was signed. In 2020, Israel normalized diplomatic ties with Bahrain, Morocco, Sudan, and the United Arab Emirates. In 2022, Israel formed a maritime deal with Lebanon, although the two countries technically remain at war. Syria and Iraq still do not recognize Israel as a legitimate state.

Peace between Israel and the Palestinians continues to be elusive and complicated. In 1993, Israel and the Palestinian Liberation Organization signed the Oslo Accords, giving the Palestinians interim self-government in Jericho and the Gaza Strip. A Palestinian Council was elected in 1995. In 1997, Israel signed the Hebron Protocol, promising to withdraw Israeli troops from Hebron and transfer power to the Palestinians.

In 2006, Hamas (Islamic Resistance Movement) was elected as the head of the Palestinian government. Hamas took the Gaza Strip from Fatah (formerly the Palestinian National Liberation Movement), dividing the Palestinians into the Hamas-led Gaza Strip and the Fatah-led West Bank in 2007. Hamas has refused negotiations with Israel while Fatah has been open. Both Hamas and Fatah want to rebuild a Palestinian state on the old 1967 borders.

What is the political makeup of the current State of Israel? It is a democratic state with freedom of the press and national elections every four years. Israel is a parliamentary republic with three separate governmental branches: the legislative (law-making), the executive (administrative), and the judiciary (judges and courts). The Knesset, or House of Representatives, is the legislative branch with 120 members.

The people of Israel vote for a party, not the individual president or prime minister. Each party receives a number of seats in the Knesset depending on how many votes they get. The Knesset elects Israel's president, who holds a ceremonial role in nominating a member of the Knesset for prime minister after consulting with party members. The candidate for prime minister has twenty-eight days to form a government platform. If the Knesset approves, he becomes prime minister, chief of the executive branch. The modern State of Israel celebrated its seventy-fifth year in 2023.

Key Takeaways:
- Rebuilding Jewish culture and civilization in the wake of the Second World War
  - Returning to former homes not an option: families, houses, and jobs gone
  - Jews in displacement camps launch newspapers and Jewish schools (1945-51)
- Establishment of Israel
  - British ends their control and establishes Jewish and Palestinian states
  - David Ben Gurion becomes prime minister of the new State of Israel in 1948
  - War of Independence May 1948-July 1949
- Conflicts in which Israel has been involved
  - Six-Day War, June 1967
  - War of Attrition with Egypt and Jordan, 1967-1970
  - Yom Kippur War, 1973
- Small steps toward peace in the Middle East
  - Enduring peace with Egypt after the Treaty of 1979
  - Israel makes peace with Jordan in 1994
  - Peace with Bahrain, Morocco, Sudan, and the United Arab Emirates in 2020

- Controversy over Palestine
  - 1993 Oslo Accords gives Palestinians self-government
  - 1997 Hebron Protocol: Israeli troops withdraw from Hebron
  - 2006: Hamas takes over Palestinians in Gaza Strip, Fatah takes over West Bank
- Current State of Israel
  - A democratic state with freedom of the press and national elections every four years
  - A parliamentary republic with legislative, executive, and judiciary branches
  - The legislative branch is the Knesset or House of Representatives, with 120 members
  - Israel's 75th birthday in 2023

Chapter 9: Customs, Traditions, Symbols, and Art

Some Jews are atheists, some are orthodox, and others are somewhere in between, yet the customs and traditions commemorating their shared history tie them together. As Jewish families celebrate Shabbat and the annual festivals, they absorb the essentials of Judaism's distinct culture. New customs, such as bar and bat mitzvahs, have emerged over the centuries and continue to define Judaism.

The Jewish dietary laws are called kosher (*kashrut*), which means "fitness." They are based on the Law of Moses given over three millennia ago in Devarim (Deuteronomy) 14:2-21 and Vayikra (Leviticus) 11. Some Jewish families keep kosher strictly, some only observe it at special times like the Passover (Pesach) week, some don't keep kosher at all, and some follow parts but not all the laws.

G-d permitted the Israelites to eat mammals with split hoofs that chewed cud: cattle, sheep, goats, and deer. Any animal without a divided hoof or that didn't chew its cud was forbidden; the Torah specifically mentions camels, rabbits, rock badgers, bats, and pigs as unclean animals. Jews could eat any marine animal with fins and scales; fish were fine, but not shellfish, eels, or dolphins. They could eat most birds except vultures and birds of prey. Flying insects could not be eaten unless they had leg joints, like grasshoppers or locusts. Crawling creatures like mice and lizards were forbidden. If the Israelites came across a dead animal, they could not eat it. Finally, they could not cook a baby goat in its mother's milk. This enigmatic command is repeated three times in the Torah.[61] Controversies arose over what this command meant. Maimonides (Moses ben Maimon) thought it referred to a pagan sacrificial ritual that the ancient Jews should avoid. In the Talmud, rabbis expanded Moses's law to say no meat of any kind could be cooked or served with dairy products.

Some rabbis forbade cooking meat in the same kitchen as dairy or mandated preparing them on separate countertops using separate dishes. Jews keeping strict kosher are not allowed cheeseburgers and lasagna because they mix meat and dairy. Some kosher Jews wait three hours between eating meat and dairy. Others will not eat yogurt or drink milk at the same table with someone eating meat.

The Torah teaches observing Shabbat (the Sabbath): "[For] six days, work may be performed, but on the seventh day, it is a complete rest day, a holy occasion; you shall not perform any work. It is a Sabbath to the L-rd in all your dwelling places."[62] G-d instituted the Sabbath from the time of creation as a blessed and sanctified day: "And G-d blessed the seventh day, and He hallowed it, for thereon He abstained from all His work that G-d created to do."[63]

Religious Jews keep Shabbat by resting from work from sunset on Friday until sundown on Saturday. On Friday, they clean their homes thoroughly, bathe, and put on nice clothes to celebrate this sacred day. At least eighteen minutes before sunset on Friday, the wife lights candles where the Shabbat meal will be enjoyed. A prayer of sanctification called *kiddush* is pronounced over the wine, and then everyone enjoys a delicious meal. On Saturday morning, faithful Jews attend Shabbat services, often followed by a light luncheon at their synagogue. Stringent observance of Shabbat among Orthodox Jews includes not driving on Saturday, not turning lights on and off, not using electrical appliances, and not cooking.

At Shabbat and most Jewish festivals (other than Passover), many wives (especially Ashkenazi Jews) prepare two loaves of braided challah bread. A small piece of the dough is separated and consecrated to G-d, following the Torah command in Bamidbar (Numbers) 15:20-21. After the wine blessing, everyone washes their hands. Then the head of the household

---

[61] Shemot (Exodus) 23:19, 34:26, Devarim (Deuteronomy) 14:21
[62] Vayikra (Leviticus) 23:3
[63] Bereshit (Genesis) 2:2

pronounces the *Hamotzi*: "Blessed are you L-RD our G-d, King of the Universe, who brings forth bread from the earth." Everyone eats the bread with salt, symbolizing G-d's eternal covenant with Israel.

Coming-of-age ceremonies are common for Jewish adolescent boys (bar mitzvah) and girls (bat mitzvah). This custom began in the Middle Ages. At a certain age, boys were expected to start participating in *mitzvot* (actions) in the synagogue, such as reading the Torah to the assembly or wearing *tefillin* (a leather case with Torah scriptures). Today, the bar and bat mitzvah ceremonies differ depending on whether the synagogue is Orthodox, Conservative, or Reformed. Usually, the boy or girl is called up to the platform to chant a passage from the Torah in Hebrew using cantillation and discuss its meaning. Before this, the young people attend Hebrew school with their rabbi to learn Hebrew, study the Torah, and prepare for their "calling up." Most parents throw elaborate parties after their children's bar and bat mitzvahs.

Jews have seven major annual festivals, although most non-religious Jews only observe Pesach (Passover) and Chanukah (Hanukkah). The Feast of Purim, held in March, remembers Queen Esther, the Jewish wife of a 4th-century Persian king, as told in the book of Esther in the Ketuvim. After the Persian Jews fasted for three days, she interceded with her husband to prevent wicked Haman's machinations to annihilate the Jews in the Persian Empire. Celebrating Purim involves reading the book of Esther at synagogue, and when Haman's name is mentioned, the children twirl graggers (noisemakers) or stamp their feet. Money or food is given to the poor, and people send gifts of food to their friends. The children and adults enjoy a feast and masquerade (demonstrating G-d's intervention behind the scenes).

Queen Esther reveals Haman's diabolical plot
Internet Archive Book Images, No restrictions, via Wikimedia Commons
https://commons.wikimedia.org/wiki/File:The_art_Bible,_comprising_the_Old_and_new_Testaments_-_with_numerous_illustrations_(1896)_(14780507284).jpg

Passover (Pesach) usually falls in April, celebrating G-d delivering the Israelites from enslavement in Egypt. On the first night of the week-long festival, families hold a seder: a special meal commemorating how G-d passed over each house with the lamb's blood on the door. The meal includes four glasses of wine, matzah bread, bitter herbs like horseradish that recall the harsh enslavement, and favorite dishes and delicacies.

A child asks, "Why is this night different from all other nights?" The foods are an object lesson teaching G-d's deliverance. Breaking the crisp matzah reminds the family of the Red Sea split open for the Israelites to walk across. The family thanks G-d for liberating their ancestors and prays for the Final Redemption when the Messiah comes. At the end of the meal, a cup of wine is poured, the door is opened, and the prophet Elijah is invited to join. Then everyone sings the Hallel, songs based on Moses and Miriam's song after crossing the Red Sea.

Shavuot (Pentecost or Feast of Weeks) is a two-day holiday in late May or early June celebrating G-d giving the Torah. Religious Jews observe this festival by reading the Torah all night, lighting candles, attending synagogue where the Ten Commandments are read, and enjoying a meal with dairy products. Shavuot is the festival the Jewish followers of Jesus were celebrating in Acts 2 of the New Testament.

Falling in September, Rosh Hashanah is the Jewish New Year, when Jews believe G-d created Adam and Eve. At the synagogue services, the shofar (ram's horn) is blown one hundred times to honor G-d as King of the Universe while the listeners contemplate how G-d fills all time and space. A wailing blow on the shofar reminds the congregation to reflect on their deeds and repent. The feast includes apples dipped in honey and challah bread with raisins to bring sweetness to the new year. Rosh Hashanah and Yom Kippur are the two Jewish high holidays.

Blowing the shofar near ancient Jerusalem's Western Wall
Amos Ben Gershom / Government Press Office, CC BY-SA 3.0 <https://creativecommons.org/licenses/by-sa/3.0>, via Wikimedia Commons; https://commons.wikimedia.org/wiki/File:Flickr_-_Government_Press_Office_(GPO)_-_The_Wailing_Wall_(cropped).jpg

Yom Kippur comes ten days after Rosh Hashanah and is the Day of Atonement, the holiest day of the Jewish year. G-d ordained this day in the Torah:

> "And [all this] shall be as an eternal statute for you; in the seventh month, on the tenth of the month, you shall afflict yourselves, and you shall not do any work, neither the native nor the stranger who dwells among you. For on this day, He shall effect atonement for you to cleanse you. Before the L-rd, you shall be cleansed from all your sins. It is a Sabbath of rest for you, and you shall afflict yourselves. It is an eternal statute."[64]

---

[64] Vayikra (Leviticus) 16:29-31

Religious Jews "afflict" themselves by fasting from sunset until the following evening after the stars come out. They spend much of the time in introspection at the five services at synagogue, praying for forgiveness. The shofar is blown each morning for forty days before Yom Kippur, and Psalm 27 is recited: "Your presence, O L-rd, I will seek. Do not hide Your presence from me; do not turn Your servant away with anger. You were my help; do not forsake me and do not abandon me, O G-d of my salvation."[65]

Sukkot, or the Feast of Tabernacles, is a week-long holiday five days after Yom Kippur. It celebrates the harvest and G-d's protection of the Israelites when they left Egypt. Observant families erect outside booths covered with tree branches or palm fronds, where they eat their meals for the week. The booths remind them of the Israelites living in tents after leaving Egypt. The outdoor shelters also recall pilgrimages to Jerusalem and the temporary dwellings during the harvest. Each morning, the celebrants take a palm frond, a myrtle branch, a willow branch, and a citron, recite a blessing, and wave them while circling the synagogue.

Hanukkah (Chanukah) is the Festival of Lights celebrated eight days in December to remember the temple's rededication after the Maccabees drove the Greeks out of Judea. Antiochus Epiphanes IV had defiled the temple by sacrificing a pig to an idol of Saturn, and it needed to be purified. The lighting of the eight menorah candles in every household and synagogue reminds Jews of this time when evil forces were eradicated.

On the first night, one candle is lit after singing sacred blessings. On the second night, two are lit, and so on. A favorite food is latke (potato pancakes), and Jews in Israel love *sufganiyot* (jelly-filled doughnuts). Children have fun spinning the dreidel, a game using a four-sided top with Hebrew letters standing for an acrostic: "A great miracle happened there." Children receive gifts of money and give part of this to charity.

The Star of David, two superimposed triangles, represents Judaism and Israel. In the 17th century, it marked Vienna's Jewish quarter and decorated synagogues. The Zionist movement used it in the 19th century, and the Nazis forced Jews to wear it on their clothing. Today, the blue Star of David is centered on Israel's white flag. The Jewish theologian Franz Rosenzweig proposed that the six points represent G-d, man, the world, creation, revelation, and redemption.

---

[65] Tehillim (Psalms) 27:7-9

Star of David on Israel's flag
https://commons.wikimedia.org/wiki/File:Flag_of_Israel_(simplified).svg

Lions and eagles frequently decorate Torah scroll covers or the Torah Ark, where they are stored in the synagogue. The lions are usually next to a crown, representing Judah, the kingly tribe of David and the Messiah. The eagle represents G-d in the Song of Moses:

> "As an eagle awakens its nest, hovering over its fledglings, it spreads its wings, taking them and carrying them on its pinions, the L-rd guided them alone, and there was no alien deity with Him. He made them ride upon the high places of the earth."[66]

Jewish art includes elegant ceremonial objects, or Judaica, used in the synagogues and homes for Shabbat and sacred festivals. Some of these exquisite ritual objects are elaborate menorahs (candleholders), Torah covers, the fringed prayer shawl called a *tallit*, or the decorative pointer for reading the Torah called a *yad*. Another popular art form is Jewish papercuts with religious or mystical meanings that date back to the Middle Ages.

This bowl fragment (300-350 CE) depicts a Torah Ark, menorah, and shofar.
Metropolitan Museum of Art, CC0, via Wikimedia Commons;
https://commons.wikimedia.org/wiki/File:Bowl_Fragments_with_Menorah,_Shofar,_and_Torah_Ark_MET_DP355178.jpg

---

[66] Devarim (Deuteronomy) 32:11-13

Key Takeaways:
- Religion and customs
  - Kosher: Devarim (Deuteronomy) 14:2-21 and Vayikra (Leviticus) 11
  - Shabbat (Sabbath)
  - Challah
  - Bar and Bat Mitzvah
- Festivals
  - Purim: Queen Esther defeats wicked Haman
  - Passover (Pesach): deliverance from the angel of death and Egyptian slavery
  - Shavuot/ Pentecost: celebrates G-d giving the Torah
  - Rosh Hashanah: the Jewish New Year
  - Yom Kippur: Day of Atonement
  - Sukkot: Festival of Booths
  - Hanukkah (Chanukah or Festival of Lights) celebrates the rededication of the temple
- Symbols
  - Star of David: represents Judaism and Israel
  - Lion of Judah
  - Eagle representing G-d from Song of Moses
- Art
  - Religious objects like menorahs and Torah covers
  - Papercuts

Chapter 10: Famous Jews: An Enthralling Collection

The rich and colorful history of Jewish people stretches back almost four thousand years. Some of the most well-known Jews not only contributed to their own culture but positively impacted the world through their faith, literature, scientific breakthroughs, and political acumen. Many suffered dreadfully in the Holocaust and other persecutions, yet their tenacity and courage continue to inspire.

Abraham (circa 20th century BCE)

Abraham was the great-grandfather of the twelve tribes of Israel. He grew up in Ur (in today's southern Iraq) during its third dynasty, the world's largest city of its day with a population of around 65,000. Ur-Nammu, who probably ruled during Abraham's lifetime, erected Ur's great ziggurat tower, built schools to teach cuneiform writing, and wrote the world's first known law code.

Following G-d's call, Abraham traveled to Canaan (today's Israel). G-d promised all the land of Canaan to Abraham's descendants: "And I will give you and your seed after you the land of your sojournings, the entire land of Canaan for an everlasting possession."[67]

Abraham's wife Sarah grew frustrated because she couldn't conceive, so she gave her Egyptian maidservant Hagar to Abraham as his wife.

---

[67] Bereshit (Genesis) 17:8

There was a custom that if a woman's maid became her husband's wife, the child born to the maid was considered the senior wife's child. Hagar gave birth to Ishmael, and the Torah says he settled in the northern Arabian Peninsula as an adult. Today's Muslims consider Ishmael a prophet and the ancestor of Muhammad.

G-d promised Abraham he would be the father of nations (plural). After Sarah died, Abraham married Keturah, and they had six sons: Zimran, Jokshan, Medan, Midian, Ishbak, and Shuah. The Jewish historian Josephus said that Zimran's descendants settled in Arabia, between Mecca and Medina, and Shuah's descendants lived in northern Syria on the Euphrates River. Jokshan's grandson Asshurim may have fathered the Semitic Assyrians of northern Iraq. Midian's descendants lived in northwestern Arabia; Moses's wife, Zipporah, was the daughter of Jethro, a Midianite priest.

Maimonides (1138-1204 CE)

Moshe (Moses) ben Maimon was born in Cordoba, Spain, at the end of the Jewish golden age under the rule of the Muslim taifa states. Descended from King David, he studied the Torah under his father, a judge. The Almohad Caliphate, a Berber Muslim dynasty, conquered Cordoba when Maimonides was around ten, forcing Jews and Christians to convert or leave. Maimonides's family went into exile, and he lived in southern Spain, Palestine, and North Africa for the next decade, studying medicine, philosophy, and Jewish law. He settled in Morocco, married, and had two sons. After relocating to Cairo, Egypt, he completed his commentary on the Mishna in 1168, a condensed overview of the Babylonian Talmud. His most outstanding work was the *Mishneh Torah*, the codification of Jewish law. He wrote *The Guide for the Perplexed*, attempting to reconcile Judaism with Aristotle's philosophy.

Another important work was his formulation of the thirteen fundamental beliefs of the Jewish faith. These core doctrines included the belief in one G-d, who was all-powerful and everywhere at once. Another essential belief was the resurrection from the dead when Moshiach (the Messiah) comes to renew and restore the Davidic dynasty. Maimonides upheld the unchanging teachings of the Torah given to Moses. He taught that those who follow the Torah receive an eternal reward, but the wicked are cut off from perpetual bliss.

While writing the *Mishneh Torah,* Maimonides served for about two years as the Nagid (prince) of the Jews in Egypt. Later, he was the court physician, Sultan Saladin's personal doctor. In addition to his works on theology and philosophy, Maimonides wrote medical treatises, including a guide on antidotes to various poisons and another guide on hygiene and a healthy lifestyle of moderation. He also wrote about conditions such as diabetes, pneumonia, asthma, and hepatitis and served as a physician to Jews, Muslims, and Christians.

Anne Frank (1929-45)

Anne Frank at her school in Amsterdam
https://commons.wikimedia.org/wiki/File:Anne_Frank_lacht_naar_de_schoolfotograaf.jpg

Born to Otto and Edith Frank in Frankfurt, Germany, Anne's Jewish family moved to Amsterdam to escape the rampant anti-Semitism and poor economic situation in Germany. Her father started a company selling spices and pectin, but when she was ten, Germany invaded Poland, beginning World War II. The following year, the Nazis conquered Holland.

When Anne was thirteen, her sixteen-year-old sister Margot received a notice telling her to report to a German labor camp, compelling her family to go into hiding immediately. Her father had been constructing a secret annex in the rear of the 300-year-old building housing his business. It was about 450 square feet on the second and third floors and could only be accessed by an entrance hidden by a revolving bookcase.

In July 1942, Anne and her family moved into the hidden apartment, joined by their neighbor Hermann van Pels, who had helped build the annex, and his wife and son. Her father's employees continued running the business in the front of the house and provided food and other essentials to the families in hiding. In November, a single man, Fritz Pfeffer, joined the two families in their tight secret quarters.

Just before going into hiding, Anne had received a diary for her thirteenth birthday. In her two years in the secret annex, she journaled about events, the people she lived with, and her fears and dreams. In August 1944, the police raided the building, discovered the secret hideout, and arrested Anne and the others. But after the police left, her father's employee found Anne's diary and kept it.

The Nazis transported Anne's family to the Auschwitz concentration camp in Poland. Three months later, they transferred the teenage Anne and Margot to the Bergen-Belsen concentration camp in Germany. The war was ending, but time was running out for Anne and Margot. Living in near-starvation conditions, they contracted typhus and died in February 1945, only three months before Germany surrendered.

Anne's father, Otto, was the only survivor of the eight people who had hidden in the secret annex. He returned to Amsterdam, where his former employee gave him Anne's diary. Moved by his adolescent daughter's account of life in hiding, he published it. The journal was eventually translated into seventy languages, and the secret annex became a museum. Anne's tragic story raised worldwide awareness of the Holocaust's horrors.

Albert Einstein (1879-1955)

Albert Einstein was born in Germany in 1879 to non-religious Jewish parents. He nurtured a curiosity about the Jewish faith as a child and supported the Zionist movement as an adult. Although unquestionably bright, Einstein did not speak in sentences until he was five. Disliking his German secondary school's rigid, pedantic teaching methods, he dropped out but later completed a Swiss secondary school. He graduated from the Swiss Federal Institute of Technology in Zurich despite frequently skipping classes.

In 1902, Einstein found employment in a Swiss patent office, examining patent applications in the mechanical field while pursuing doctoral studies at the University of Berlin. He described 1905 as his "annus mirabilis" (miracle year), publishing his treatise on the photoelectric effect, which won the Nobel Prize in 1920. In 1905, Einstein also published "On the Electrodynamics of Moving Bodies," the beginnings of his theory of relativity, which he completed in 1915. His formula $E=MC^2$ suggested that minuscule particles of matter could generate massive amounts of energy, paving the way for atomic power. His theory that mass causes space to curve was proven by measurements during the 1919 solar eclipse. Einstein continued to work at the patent office until receiving a professorship at the German University in Prague in 1911.

Albert Einstein
Comet Photo AG (Zürich), CC BY-SA 4.0 <https://creativecommons.org/licenses/by-sa/4.0>, via Wikimedia Commons; https://commons.wikimedia.org/wiki/File:Einstein_Com_M19-0053-0001.jpg

When Hitler became Germany's chancellor in 1933, the German press relentlessly attacked Einstein, and the Nazis publicly burned his scientific works and confiscated his bank accounts. He left for the United States later that year, where he served at the Institute for Advanced Study in Princeton, New Jersey. He continued to work on quantum theory, the origins of the universe, and other pursuits until he died in 1955.

Although Einstein was not religious, he saw G-d in the harmony and precision of the universe, saying, "Everyone who is seriously involved in the pursuit of science becomes convinced that a spirit is manifest in the laws of the Universe—a spirit vastly superior to that of man, and one in the face of which we with our modest powers must feel humble."

Regarding his Jewish heritage, Einstein remarked, "The pursuit of knowledge for its own sake, an almost fanatical love of justice, and the desire for personal independence—these are the features of the Jewish tradition which make me thank my stars that I belong to."[68]

David Ben-Gurion: (1886-1973)

David Ben-Gurion was the primary founder of the modern State of Israel and its first prime minister. He was born David Yosef Gruen in 1886 in Plonsk, Poland, to a family committed to the Zionist movement. At age fourteen, he led a Zionist youth group where everyone spoke Hebrew. He immigrated to Palestine when he was twenty and quickly joined the Jewish Social Democratic Workers' Party, which aspired to the political independence of the Jews of Palestine. In 1909, he began writing for the party's newspaper *Ha'ahdut* and took the name Ben-Gurion.

After World War I broke out, the Ottoman Empire deported Ben-Gurion to Egypt in 1915 because of his Zionist activities. Shortly after, he left for a speaking tour in the United States, where he befriended influential Jewish-American leaders and met and married Paula Monbesz, a Russian-born fellow Zionist. The Ottoman Empire had ruled Palestine for four centuries, but in 1917, British troops captured Jerusalem. Ben-Gurion returned to Palestine and became the general secretary of the Zionist Labor Federation, rising to leadership of the Jews of Palestine.

When World War II began, Ben-Gurion advocated supporting the British war effort despite the 1939 White Paper declaring Britain's advocacy for a single Palestinian state with Arab majority rule. He also opposed the terrorist tactics of the Jewish underground freedom fighters.

---

[68]"Einstein's Deeply Held Political Beliefs," American Museum of Natural History. https://www.amnh.org/exhibitions/einstein/global-citizen#:~:text=Although%20Einstein%20did%20not%20observe,that%20I%20belong%20to%20it.%22

In 1942, he called for a swift founding of a Jewish state at the Zionist conference in New York. As the United Nations wrestled with the claims of Arabs and Jews to Palestine, Ben-Gurion began formulating plans for a democratic government.

On May 14, 1948, the People's Council declared the State of Israel and named Ben-Gurion its first prime minister and defense minister while people danced in the streets of Jerusalem. Following the War of Independence, Ben-Gurion developed the new state's institutions and managed the immigration of hundreds of thousands of Jews from Europe and Arab lands. He oversaw the building of new towns and cities around Israel.

Ben-Gurion retired from politics in 1953 to live on a kibbutz but returned to the position of defense minister in 1955 and was reelected as prime minister later that year. He spearheaded the 1956 invasion of the Sinai Peninsula and continued as prime minister until 1963. He again retired in 1970 and lived the rest of his life on a kibbutz in the Negev Desert, passing away in 1973.

Elie Wiesel (1928-2016)

Eliezer Wiesel was born to an Orthodox Jewish family in 1928 in Transylvania, Romania. In 1944, the German Nazis occupied his village, forcing the Jews to wear yellow stars and closing his parents' grocery store and other Jewish businesses. The family's Christian maid Maria begged them to come to her village in the mountains, where she had prepared a hideaway. Elie's father refused, unaware of the horrors that awaited them.

In early June 1944, when Elie was fifteen, the Nazis rounded up his family and forced them into a cattle car filled with eighty people. The train carried them to Auschwitz in Poland, where Elie and his father were camp laborers. The Nazis sent his mother and younger sister, Sarah, directly to the gas chambers. Elie and his father did not know whether his older sisters, Hilda and Bea, were dead or alive. In January 1945, the Nazis evacuated Auschwitz, forcing the inmates on a ten-day death march. Already starving, 14,000 prisoners died on the way.

The surviving six thousand prisoners were herded into freight cars and carried to Buchenwald concentration camp in Germany, but Elie's father died just after they arrived. In April, the guards began systematically shooting thousands of Jews and were preparing to evacuate the rest of the camp. However, as the Allied forces closed in, the Nazis fled, leaving the prisoners behind. US troops marched in on April 19, 1945, liberating the emaciated prisoners.

In this photo taken at Buchenwald Concentration Camp when the Allies arrived, Elie Wiesel is in the second row, the seventh prisoner from the left.
https://commons.wikimedia.org/wiki/File:Buchenwald_Slave_Laborers_Liberation.jpg

    The Allies sent Elie and other underaged liberated prisoners to France. His older sisters had survived, and they all found each other two years later. Elie studied liberal arts at Sorbonne University but struggled with his faith, agonizing over G-d's seeming indifference to the suffering in the war. He found it cathartic to write down his experiences, and his book *Night* told of the horrors at Auschwitz and Buchenwald.

    Elie wrote many more novels and memoirs along the same themes and became a human rights activist for Jews and other groups persecuted because of their race or religion. He advocated for the victims of South African apartheid and the Khmer Rouge atrocities in Cambodia. At President Carter's request, he led the United States Holocaust Memorial Council for six years. In 1986, he received the Nobel Peace Prize for his humanitarian efforts. He died in his home in Manhattan in 2016.

Benjamin Netanyahu (born 1949)

    Benjamin (Bibi) Netanyahu is Israel's longest-serving prime minister, leading the nation for over fifteen years in three separate tenures. He was born in Tel Aviv in October 1949, three months after Israel won its War of Independence. His mother was born in Palestine, and his father was from Poland but immigrated to Palestine with his family when he was ten. Netanyahu spent most of his childhood in Jerusalem and part of his teen years in the United States when his father taught history at Dropsie College in Philadelphia.

Netanyahu returned to Israel at eighteen for his mandatory military service in Israel's Defense Forces (the IDF), fighting in its special forces. In the War of Attrition, he was shot in the shoulder during Operation Gift while freeing Jewish hostages from a hijacked airline in Beirut. He studied at MIT in Boston for his bachelor of science in architecture, returned to Israel to fight in the Yom Kippur War, then returned to MIT for his master of science in Management Studies.

Israel appointed Netanyahu as its ambassador to the United Nations in 1984. After serving four years, he returned to Israel and was elected to the Knesset from the right-wing Likud Party and appointed Deputy Minister of Foreign Affairs. He represented Israel in media interviews during the 1991 Gulf War.

Netanyahu won Israel's first direct elections for prime minister in 1996 and served until 1999. He became prime minister again in 2009, serving until 2021. Netanyahu clashed with US President Obama over his insistence that Israel stop building settlements in East Jerusalem and the West Bank. Netanyahu supported a demilitarized Palestinian state formed through direct negotiations between the Palestinians and Israel. He served in an interim capacity following the 2019 election debacle when neither party won a majority vote.

In March 2021, the fourth election in two years, Netanyahu's party won the most votes but not enough to form a government. His opponents formed a coalition government, ending Netanyahu's twelve-year tenure, but that government collapsed one year later. An increasing number of Israeli youths identified as right-wing, impacting Israel's political scene. By 2021, about 80 percent of Israel's population supported the right. In December 2022, Netanyahu was again sworn in as prime minister, with the most nationalistic and religiously conservative cabinet in Israel's history.

Key Takeaways:
- Abraham (circa 20th century BCE)
  - G-d promised Canaan (Israel) to his descendants as an eternal possession
  - Abraham fathered Ishmael, Isaac, Zimran, Jokshan, Medan, Midian, Ishbak, and Shuah. They settled in Canaan, northern Arabia, Syria, and east of Canaan.

- Maimonides (1138-1204 CE)
  - Wrote a commentary on the Oral Torah, the Mishneh Torah, The Guide for the Perplexed, and Thirteen Principles of the Jewish Faith
  - Served as the court physician and wrote medical treatises
- Anne Frank (1929-45)
  - After the Nazis took Holland, her family hid in a secret annex for two years
  - Eventually arrested and sent to a concentration camp, where she died
  - Her father published her diary, raising awareness of the Holocaust
- Albert Einstein (1879-1955)
  - Developed the theory of relativity
  - Received a Nobel Prize for his treatise on the photoelectric effect in 1930
  - Believed G-d could be seen in the laws of the universe
- David Ben-Gurion: (1886-1973)
  - Avid Zionist who led Jews in Palestine before independence
  - Became the first prime minister of the new State of Israel and minister of defense
- Elie Wiesel (1928-2016)
  - Teen survivor of Auschwitz and Buchenwald concentration camps
  - Author and humanitarian activist for oppressed people
  - Received Nobel Peace Prize in 1986
- Benjamin Netanyahu (born 1949)
  - Born in Tel Aviv, raised in Jerusalem and the United States
  - Israel's longest-serving prime minister: over fifteen years in three separate tenures

Conclusion

Judaism and the Jewish people have radically impacted world history for thousands of years. With their stellar contribution to the sciences, humanities, and economics, Jews continue to play an illustrious role on the world stage.

Judaism gave birth to Christianity, the world's largest religion today. Jesus and his initial group of disciples were all Jewish, and they continued to worship in Jerusalem's temple, attend synagogue throughout the Jewish diaspora, and observe the traditional feasts. Jesus explicitly supported the entire Tanakh: "Don't think that I came to destroy the law or the prophets. I didn't come to destroy, but to fulfill."[69]

The Apostle Paul, who studied under Gamaliel the Elder, built his teachings around the Tanakh. The Jewish writers of the New Testament quoted directly from the Tanakh 283 times and referred to it over 1,000 times. The Christian Church adopted the entire Tanakh into the biblical canon. Christianity initially spread through the Jewish diaspora communities around the Mediterranean.

Judaism also heavily impacted Islam, the world's second-largest religion, which adopted the belief in one G-d. Muslims believe Abraham, Ishmael, Moses, Job, Joseph, and David were prophets who brought divine revelation. The Quran refers to Adam's creation, Noah and the flood, Abraham's covenant, and Moses receiving God's revelation on Mount Sinai. Christianity and Islam also follow Judaism's teaching of

---

[69] Matthew 5:17, *World English Bible*.

Shabbat, or a day of rest (although in Christianity it is Sunday, and in Islam it is Friday).

In modern history, Jews have been incredibly successful. The Nobel Prizes recognize the Jewish contributions to medicine, the sciences, literature, economics, and peace: despite comprising less than 1 percent of the world's population, 22 percent of Nobel laureates have been Jews.

In medicine, Gertrude Elion developed a treatment for childhood leukemia, and Bruce Beutler continues his brilliant research in immunity and inflammation. Ralph Steinman discovered dendritic cells and launched the first clinical trial of a cell-targeted HIV vaccine. Paul Ehrlich discovered a cure for syphilis, and Rosalind Franklin pioneered work on the molecular structure of viruses and DNA. Otto Loewi's research demonstrated that chemicals relay nerve signals to organs. The neurobiologist Rita Levi-Montalcini discovered nerve growth factor. Albert Einstein, Niels Bohr, Wolfgang Pauli, and John von Neumann (a genius savant) made staggering contributions to mathematics, physics, economics, and computer science. Alexandre Friedmann developed the Big Bang Theory. Claude Levi-Strauss made strides in structural anthropology and sociology.

In technology, Siegfried Marcus made the first gasoline-fueled vehicle in 1864, and Paul Zoll developed the cardiac pacemaker and defibrillator. Gordon Gould invented the laser, and Isidor Isaac Rabi developed nuclear magnetic resonance used in MRIs. Zhores Alferov developed semiconductor heterostructures and furthered technology in solar cells and LEDs. Israeli entrepreneur Dov Moran invented the USB memory stick. Bob Kahn gave us the internet by developing IP (Internet Protocol) and TCP (Transmission Control Protocol) that empower communication between computers. Mark Zuckerberg, Dustin Moskovitz, and Eduardo Saverin invented Facebook in a Harvard dorm room.

In commerce, Levi Strauss, a Bavarian immigrant to San Francisco, invented blue jeans in the 1880s to meet the needs of miners in the gold rush. Jewish entrepreneur Emil Jellinek financed the development of the Daimler-Mercedes (later Mercedes-Benz), the fastest car in the races in Nice, France. Charles Lazarus founded Toys "R" Us in 1959. Jewish fashion and cosmetic enterprises include Calvin Klein, Donna Karan, Estée Lauder, Fabergé, Gap, Max Factor, Ralph Lauren, and Revlon. In the food and beverage industry, Howard Schultz launched Starbucks. Reuben and Rose Mattus invented Häagen-Dazs ice cream, giving it a

Danish-sounding name because of the Danes' kind treatment of Jews in World War II. Entrepreneur William Rosenberg founded Dunkin' Donuts.

Paul Rosenberg and Solomon Guggenheim furthered the world art market with their art collections, the Guggenheim Museum, and Rosenberg's financial assistance to Picasso. Paul Rosenberg and his wife fled France in 1940 when the Nazis invaded, leaving behind two thousand priceless pieces, which the Nazis sent to Germany. He was able to reclaim or repurchase some of the art after the war. Paul's brother Léonce, also an art collector and dealer, stayed in France but went into hiding and lost his entire inventory.

Authors such as science fiction writer Isaac Asimov and novelists Franz Kafka and Marcel Proust have graced the world of modern literature. Film directors like Steven Spielberg and Woody Allen have captured the imaginations of millions of viewers. Felix Mendelssohn's compositions, Johann Strauss's waltzes, and Leonard Bernstein's conducting have left a mark on classical music.

Well-known Jewish pop music artists include Neil Diamond and his high school classmate Barbra Streisand, who sang together in their school's choral club. Another Jewish classmate at their Erasmus Hall High School in Brooklyn was Bobby Fischer, the world chess champion. (Half of the world's top chess grandmasters between 1851 and 2000 were Jews.) Simon Garfunkel was a cantor in his synagogue and met his future music partner Paul Simon (also a Jew) in sixth grade in Queens. Bob Dylan was originally Robert Zimmerman from a Russian Jewish family who settled in Minnesota. Billy Joel's Jewish father, a classical pianist, escaped the Nazi regime in Germany as a child.

Today, the world's Jewish population is 15.3 million, with about 7 million living in Israel, 6 million in the United States, and the rest in France, Canada, the United Kingdom, or scattered over the globe. Despite staggering odds, the modern State of Israel was born three years after the end of the "Shoah" (Holocaust). Its neighbors vowed to wipe it off the Middle Eastern map, but Israel's military prowess and political acumen held strong.

Yet Israel hasn't only survived. It has thrived economically as the world's "start-up nation," with more new businesses per capita than any other country. Its per capita Gross Domestic Product is in the top twenty in the world, ahead of much of Europe, Japan, and Canada. It is a beacon of prosperity, utilizes world-class technology, and has a vibrant, albeit contentious, democracy. Around the world, Jewish history has revealed a people who are indomitable high achievers, skilled in adapting to innumerable challenges.

Part 2: Ancient Israel

An Enthralling Guide to Jewish Kingdoms and the Israelites

Introduction

The history of ancient Israel is a fascinating subject that has intrigued scholars, theologians, and enthusiasts for centuries. Israel was a small but influential state located in the eastern Mediterranean region that existed from around 1200 BCE until its destruction by the Babylonian Empire in 586 BCE. It continued to exist under the rule of various empires, including the Persians, the Greeks, and the Romans. The region and its people boast a rich and interesting history that is marked by great religious significance, which continues to influence present-day society and the world.

Beginning in the Bronze Age, the region occupied by the Israelites boasted a more diverse ethnic identity since it was occupied by various peoples and tribes. The story of the Israelites did not begin until the Iron Age when they began to emerge as distinct people with an identifiable culture, tradition, and identity. They began to form their own kingdom, which occurred with the movement of the Israelites from Sinai to Canaan, where they established their own rule under King Saul, though it was Joshua who led the Israelites to the land promised to them by Yahweh.

The period that immediately followed was filled with great prosperity for the Israelites. Under King Solomon, the region was able to extend its influence beyond its borders, becoming a center of culture, trade, and religious learning. However, following the death of Solomon, the kingdom split into two: the Kingdom of Israel in the north and the Kingdom of Judah in the south. While both these regions would eventually fall to foreign invaders, they did much damage to themselves through persistent internecine conflicts.

Despite its relatively short existence, ancient Israel has left an indelible mark on world history. The biblical traditions and stories that emerged from this period have influenced not only Judaism but also Christianity and Islam and have had a significant impact on Western culture and civilization. The story of ancient Israel is of great interest to historians and archaeologists, who have been studying the region and its people for many decades.

Perhaps most significantly, the Israelites created a monotheistic religion, which was unheard of in the ancient Near East besides Zoroastrianism (some debate whether this religion fits the definition of a monotheistic religion, though). Most religions practiced at the time were polytheistic, so the worship of a single god challenged a widely accepted worldview. The Hebrew Bible, also known as the Old Testament, is a collection of sacred texts that tells the story of the Israelites and their relationship with God. These texts contain historical accounts, poetry, wisdom, and prophetic writings that have inspired generations of believers.

Archaeologists have long attempted to establish historical evidence for the story narrated in the Bible. The study of ancient Israel is also important for understanding the broader history of the eastern Mediterranean region. The Israelites were part of a larger cultural and economic network that included the Phoenicians, the Assyrians, the Babylonians, and the Persians. The region was a crossroads of trade and cultural exchange, and its history is characterized by a series of conquests, migrations, and interactions between different groups.

This book on ancient Israel aims to provide a comprehensive overview of the history, culture, and religion of this fascinating period. It explores the major events, personalities, and themes that shaped ancient Israel and its legacy. It also examines the historical and archaeological evidence that has been uncovered in recent years, shedding new light on the lives and beliefs of the Israelites.

Offering a comprehensive overview of the religious history of the Israelites, this book follows their journey through the Iron Age, when the people first began to gain an identity of their own. It continues through to the Babylonian exile, when the Israelites were forced out of their homes, to the Persian period, when they were liberated. The emergence of the Greeks in the region is also discussed, as well as the religious role and significance of the Israelites. The final topic of the book is the Herodian dynasty and its fall to the Romans, marking the end of the Israelite region as it was then known.

Chapter 1: Who Were the Ancient Israelites?

Between the 12th and 6th centuries BCE, the Near East region was occupied by a group of people known as the Israelites. This Semitic-speaking group of twelve tribes was believed to be the descendants of Abraham, moving from Mesopotamia to Canaan around the 2nd millennium BCE. As such, their culture, religion, and way of life are believed to have emerged from the Canaanite tradition, although they would go on to develop their own distinct ethnic and cultural identity.

At the time, Canaan was a culturally diverse region populated by various tribes. These included the Canaanites, the Jebusites, and the Philistines. The first recorded mention of the Israelites comes from an unlikely account of an Egyptian victory over the Libyans during the reign of Pharaoh Merneptah. This mention appears misplaced, as it makes them seem as if they were an established political power rather than a nomadic people. This has led to the speculation that the Israelites might have been part of the Libyan coalition.

The Religious History of the Israelites

The Israelites held great religious significance, as they believed themselves to be the chosen people of God. Although there are extra-biblical mentions of the Israelites, historians still rely on biblical accounts to help navigate the history of the ancient Israelites. The biblical accounts narrate the ancestry of the Israelites, who descended from Abraham. He followed God's command to leave his homeland of Ur and move to

Canaan. The religious history and journey of the Israelites can be found in the Hebrew Bible. However, since historical facts mix with legends and religious teachings, it can be hard to determine the sequence of events.

Between the 10th and 7th centuries, the Israelites practiced a religion that was considered largely polytheistic in nature. It was actually closer to henotheism, meaning that while they worshiped several deities, their primary worship revolved around a single god. Yahweh was the primary deity of worship for the Judeans and the Israelites.

The Israelites performed acts of worship in temples and synagogues and observed animal sacrificial rituals, which were a central aspect of tribal life. Canaan was believed to be the homeland God had appointed for the Israelites, marking their special position in his eyes and enforcing a duty of subservience and worship on them.

History from the Bible

The biblical narrative found in the Torah traces the Israelites' origin to Jacob, whose family was forced to flee to Egypt because of a famine. After around four hundred years, Jacob's descendants had grown to include over 600,000 men, a number that alarmed the pharaoh of Egypt. As a precautionary measure against possible threats, he enslaved the Israelites and ordered any newborn son to be killed at birth.

A woman from the tribe of Levi hid her son and sent him down the Nile in a basket, where he was rescued by an Egyptian woman, which some accounts narrate as the daughter of the pharaoh. As an adult, he fled to Midian after killing an Egyptian slave master who was beating an Israelite. At the age of eighty, this man, who was named Moses, was called on by Yahweh to go to Mount Sinai and was told to lead the people of Israel out of Egypt.

However, the pharaoh refused to free the Israelites. In response, Yahweh struck the Egyptians with a series of calamities, including plague and famine, which resulted in the pharaoh relenting and banishing the Israelites from Egypt. As they began their journey, which is typically referred to as the Exodus, the pharaoh changed his mind and had his armies follow the Israelites as they came to the Red Sea. There, Moses performed a miracle, parting the sea to allow his people to cross. The pharaoh's armies drowned.

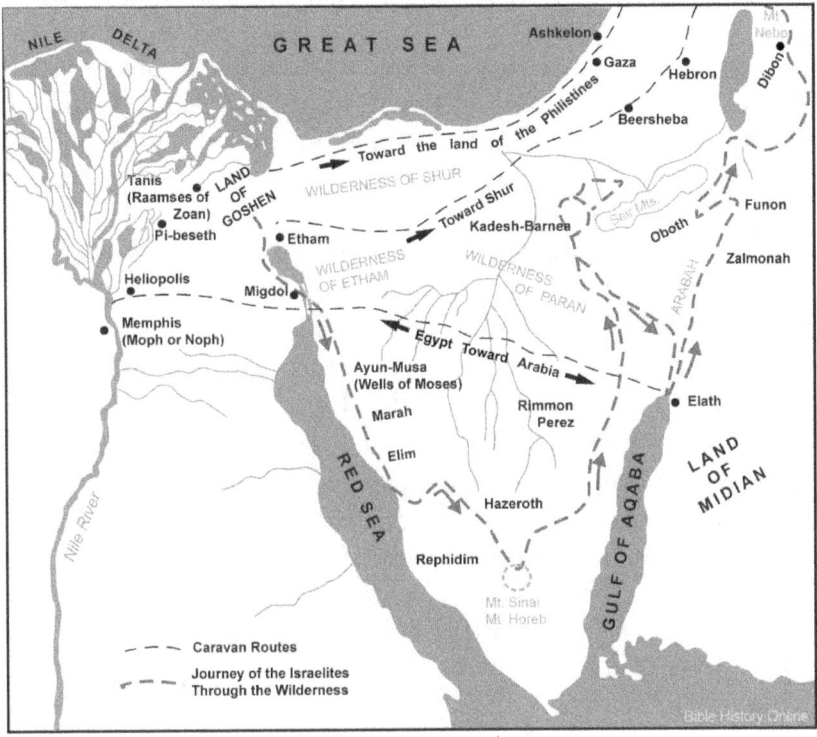

Israelites' Exodus from Egypt to Canaan.
https://bible-history.com/maps/route-exodus; *Publication use is permitted with a link going to Bible History Online:* https://bible-history.com/

The twelve tribes of Israel (Judah, Levi, Reuben, Simeon, Naphtali, Dan, Gad, Asher, Issachar, Zebulun, Joseph, and Benjamin) were then led to Mount Sinai, where Yahweh revealed the Ten Commandments, which Moses recorded along with the Torah. The twelve tribes agreed to be the chosen people of Yahweh and follow the Ten Commandments. However, they refused to march on and conquer the land of Canaan as ordered by Yahweh. As a result, the Israelites were condemned to exile and death in Sinai.

According to tradition, forty years later, a new generation led by Joshua entered Canaan and was allocated parts of this land. Yahweh appointed Saul king of the Israelites, followed by his son Eshbaal, who was then replaced by David. Under his and his son Solomon's rule, the Israelites established a monarchy and the First Temple of Jerusalem. Following Solomon's death, the kingdom was divided in two.

The tale that follows narrates the downfall of the two kingdoms. In the north, the Israelites forgot to worship God, instead permitting the worship of many deities. Thus, they lost Yahweh's favor. The Israelites were later conquered by foreigners and scattered across the lands. In the south, among the Judeans, some remained true to Yahweh, but some allowed the worship of other gods. They also fell to foreign rule, as they were taken into captivity by the Babylonians.

Yet they were not entirely forgotten. Their salvation came in the form of Cyrus the Great, the founder of the Achaemenid Empire. He conquered the Babylonians and allowed the Judeans to return to their homeland. Cyrus even helped them reconstruct their temple. However, the region remained part of the Persian Empire until the empire fell to Alexander the Great in 331 BCE.

Following the death of Alexander, the region was held by Ptolemy I, one of Alexander's generals. It was then held by the Seleucid Empire until the region was taken by Rome around 63 BCE. Unrest in the region continued, with the Jews revolting against suppression and foreign rule until the Bar Kokhba Revolt, which happened between the years 132 and 136. The Jews were defeated, and Jerusalem was renamed Syria Palaestina.

This is ancient Israelite history in a nutshell, but we will be exploring this history in more depth throughout the book. We will also provide historical evidence alongside the biblical narrative where applicable. But now that we have a basic idea of Israelite history, let's take a look at their traditions and the etymology of the name before diving further into the past.

Henotheism to Monotheism

The emergence of a monotheistic form of worship from henotheistic practices began with the Babylonian exile of the Israelites. During the exile, to maintain a sense of identity, the Israelites began to identify more with their religion, dedicating themselves more to living their lives in accordance with the Ten Commandments.

After the liberation of the Jews by the Persian Empire and their subsequent return to Jerusalem, they maintained this practice as a source of religious identity and unity that kept them together during captivity. Hence, Jewish practices abandoned the more henotheistic practices for a monotheistic form of worship.

Cultural Identity

The Israelite identity emerged from their religious history and dictated all aspects of life. For instance, knowledge and education were considered central to society. Much of it was based on the study and understanding of the Torah, which children were taught to read and write. Other than the sacred place it held as God's text, it also held great value as a gift of wisdom from God.

The legal system within Israelite society also stemmed from religion. The Ten Commandments were the rules by which a devout Hebrew or Israelite, as they were called following the conquest of Canaan, was to lead their life. The Torah provided an ethical framework that outlined just and fair behavior as members of society. These laws allowed for the protection of the weak and vulnerable and placed an emphasis on compassion and mercy.

Much of the Israelite experience was marked by oppression. While archaeological evidence does not support the idea that the Egyptians placed the Israelites in slavery, the Israelites faced subjugation throughout their history, with the region and the people being conquered by many different empires and rulers. They were often the subject of oppression because of their religious practice.

One of the most significant challenges faced by the Israelites was the Babylonian captivity when they were removed from their homes and forced into exile. Cyrus the Great's actions in freeing the Jews earned him a mention in the Bible.

The Etymology of the Word "Israelite"

The term "Israelite" is not of biblical origin but is first recorded among the inscriptions of Merneptah. The inscription itself talks about the destruction of "Israel." Since no such land existed at the time, the term is believed to have referred to a people group, perhaps the Israelite tribes that offered armed support to the Lydians in their conflict with Egypt.

In the biblical narrative, the name "Israel" was given to Jacob, who wrestled with God. The term comes from *yisra* ("to struggle with") and *el* ("god"). The Hebrew Bible uses the term "Israelites" to refer to the twelve tribes of Israel, and while this term is often used interchangeably with "Hebrew" and "Jew," this usage is not always appropriate. To be specific, the term "Israelites" refers to the immediate descendants of Jacob and those who converted to the faith. "Hebrews" refer to the descendants who lived in Canaan, and "Jews" refer to those emerging from the Israelite tribe of Judah and later formed the Kingdom of Judah.

While the monarchy lasted, the term "Israelite" was used to denote the people of that land and later to those belonging to Judah in light of the Babylonian exile of the Israelites. The term "Israel," which refers to the region and the ethnic group identified by their worship of Yahweh, emerged from the word "Israelite."

Archaeological efforts to find evidence confirming the movements of the Israelites, as narrated by the Bible, have turned up very little. The enslavement of the Israelites by the Egyptians, for example, is heavily discussed in the Bible but is not conclusively supported by archaeological evidence. The archaeological evidence suggests that the Israelites might have branched out into Canaan instead of taking the region by force, with their monotheistic religion slowly replacing the preexisting polytheism of Canaan.

Whatever may be the true facts, ancient Israelite history has had a profound impact on many aspects of society and religion in the present day. When the Israelites prospered, they gained great influence and saw success in the social and economic spheres. Beginning in the Iron Age, the Israelites began to emerge as a distinct people group in the Near East, and that is where we will start our next topic of discussion.

Chapter 2: Henotheism and Yahwism

Religious ideology and practice form an integral part of the way a society is organized. The understanding of ancient religious practice provides insight into the way regions were organized and the part religion played in people's lives.

Henotheism

Henotheistic worship emerged in Israelite thought between the 10th and 7th centuries BCE, slowly evolving from outright polytheism. Henotheism involves the worship of a single, supreme deity, but it does not preclude the existence and worship of other gods. While the worship of Yahweh was central to Israelite belief, it did not exclude the worship of other gods.

The term henotheism emerged from the works of Friedrich Schelling, who coined the German term *henotheismus*, meaning "one theism (god)." Henotheism often goes hand in hand with the concept of equitheism, the idea of the existence of multiple gods, all of whom are equal. Henotheistic belief is centered around the acceptance of the existence of numerous gods of equal divinity. However, there is one deity that reigns above all others and is the main focal point of the religion.

Since henotheism holds the worship of one god above others, many historians prefer the term monolatrism, a religion where one god is central without denying the existence or worship of other gods. Henotheism may refer to the transitional period between polytheism and monotheism.

Greco-Roman Cultures

One example of henotheistic practices can be found in Greek and Roman cultures. Both cultures evolved from polytheistic beliefs to henotheistic worship. While the ancient Greek culture had many gods and deities, each of whom had distinct roles and personalities, different cities had patron gods that were held in higher esteem than others. The patron god for Athens was Athena, and Poseidon was the patron god of Corinth. The gods were all important, but most Greeks didn't worship the gods equally.

The supreme god did not always remain the same. In the case of Zeus, for example, Uranus acted as the supreme deity before him until he was overthrown by his son, Cronus. Zeus would overthrow Cronus, who had become tyrannical and swallowed his other children in an attempt to maintain supreme power. Zeus, the god of the sky and thunder, thus became the supreme deity of the Greeks.

While Roman culture was already structured based on a henotheistic setup, the assimilation of Greek facets during Rome's takeover of Greek in 146 BCE certainly helped it develop along the same lines. Roman gods held specialized duties, with Saturn being responsible for sowing and Ceres for the growth of grain. However, Jupiter helped supremacy over the other gods.

When the Romans entered Greek territory, and the two cultures began to mix, the Romans began to identify their gods with the Greek deities, and many Greek myths made their way into Roman culture and religious practice. The henotheistic way of life continued in the region until the arrival of Christianity.

Zoroastrianism

Zoroastrianism was the principal religion of the Achaemenid dynasty, as it was observed by the Persian rulers. While the religion was never imposed on Persian subjects, it is safe to assume that its existence and practice had some impact on them. The Zoroastrian religion held Ahura Mazda as the supreme god, but it did not disregard the presence of other deities.

Ahura Mazda was the being that signified goodness. He also had *yazatas* or good agents, such as Anahita and Mithra, which were responsible for providing for various aspects of life. They were held in high regard as well and were worshiped by the Persians in the pre-Islamic period.

Zoroastrian beliefs, which predate the emergence of Judaism, likely influenced Israelite beliefs in a number of ways. Most significantly, it can be seen in the concept of a struggle between good and evil and the concept of heaven and hell. In Zoroastrianism, the latter was a place of cleansing before meeting with the creator and was adopted as such in Judaism. Hell, as a place of eternal damnation, emerged later in Christian beliefs.

Hinduism

Hinduism offers one of the best examples of henotheism. Its scriptures, the Vedas, relate the worship of many gods, leading to the religion being seen as polytheistic in nature by many. However, despite the presence of many gods, one is held supreme, although a different section of the Vedas refers to different gods as being supreme, such as, for example, Agni, the god of fire, or Vac, the god of speech.

Similar to the Greek tradition, the Hindu gods underwent a power struggle, with the supreme god of the celestial waters, Varuna, being overthrown by Indra, who was supplanted by Vishnu and Shiva until they, too, were overthrown. The mixture of monotheism, monolatrism, polytheism, and even atheism within the Hindu tradition led to the appropriate classification of henotheism with an ever-evolving theistic framework.

Christianity

While Christianity is largely considered to be monotheistic, many of its characteristics, particularly among certain denominations, suggest that henotheism may be a more suitable categorization. Some religious experts attribute these categorizations to the Holy Trinity in Christian belief, which states God is the culmination of three equal beings with a single substance. Some early Christian groups made distinct differences in their worship, praising a supreme God and viewing Jesus as only an apparition of a perfect man.

Other Christian denominations, such as the Mormons, see three distinct beings where God rules supreme. The existence of other gods and goddesses is also implied in Mormon scripture, addressing a Heavenly "Mother" in addition to the "Heavenly Father." Despite this, Mormon worship revolves around one true God. Although the Church of Latter-day Saints does not consider itself henotheistic, some have suggested that the term may apply to them.

Some branches of Christianity also place a lot of importance on saints, praying to them instead of directly to God. Sometimes, these saints, such as Mother Mary, are attributed with supernatural powers, making them appear as deities, suggesting a henotheistic component.

Although people have made arguments that Christianity could be considered henotheistic in nature at times, it must be stressed that most people (even those outside of the religion) see it as being monotheistic.

Canaanite, Israelite, and Judean Beliefs

Many of the religions of the Iron Age were henotheistic in nature. In Canaanite practice, for example, the chief deities, El and Asherah, were believed to have seventy sons between them, all of whom ruled over regions of the earth and were, therefore, worshiped as gods.

The henotheistic nature of the Israelite tradition is a matter of contention since it was intended to be a monotheistic religion according to the Ten Commandments. However, evidence suggests the coexistence and worship of Yahweh and Asherah.

Religious beliefs from the Canaanite culture and the Israelite culture mixed to such an extent that the Canaanite god El became synonymous with Yahweh, leading some historians to believe they may have been the same god all along. Another factor that supports this theory is the existence of numerous remains of temples found in the Kingdom of Israel, including one altar depicting a bronze bull symbolizing Bull-El that predates the mention of Yahweh in the 12th century BCE.

The Israelite religion did not become truly monotheistic until the Babylonian captivity, when the Israelites began to strongly identify with their cultural heritage and create a separation between themselves and those around them.

Those who returned to Judah from the Babylonian exile were descendants of the people of Judah who had originally been exiled. As such, they had never lived in Judah prior to their return; however, they still considered themselves true Israelites. After securing positions of authority in Judah through Persian connections, the returnees began to institute their religion, which differed significantly from the principles of Yahwism. A new concept of priesthood began, a written scripture was produced, and written law became a primary focus. In a bid to protect their purity, the Judeans prohibited intercultural marriage.

Yahwism: The Ancient Israelite Religion

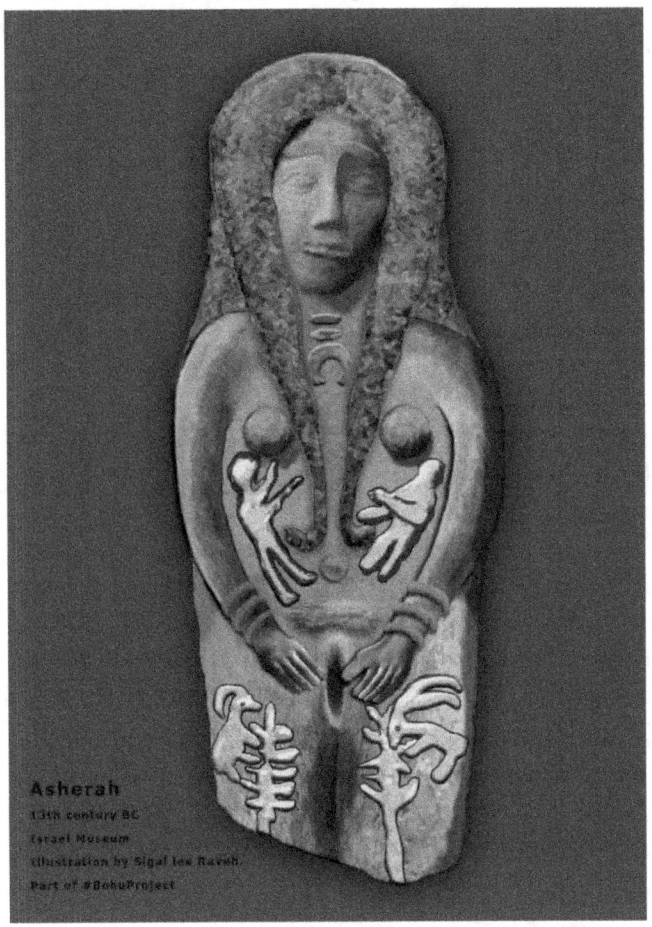

Asherah.
Sigal Lea Raveh, CC BY-SA 4.0 <https://creativecommons.org/licenses/by-sa/4.0>, via Wikimedia Commons; https://commons.wikimedia.org/wiki/File:Asherah_13th_century_BC_Israel_Museum.jpg

Considerable religious overlap can be seen when studying the religion of the ancient Israelites. Not only does the religion draw inspiration from earlier religions and those of surrounding regions, but it also underwent a metamorphosis itself, emerging from monotheistic underpinnings (the Ten Commandments) to a decidedly polytheistic and henotheistic framework. Religions, both new and old, had a great influence on the way Yahwism developed.

The term Yahwism stems from the worship of Yahweh, the central god of worship among the Kingdoms of Israel and Judah. While we know the history of the religion shows it as a monotheistic belief, with worship reserved only for Yahweh, the religion took on polytheistic themes. While Yahweh was the primary god worshiped by the Israelites, he was not the only one. He ruled alongside Asherah, the Canaanite goddess who was seen as the mother goddess. She was associated with sacred trees in the Canaanite and the Israelite religion. Indeed, in many places, the Canaanite goddess remained the supreme deity, followed by a cohort of secondary gods, each of whom had their own sets of prophets and devoted followers.

Yahwism involved many religious festivals, sacrifices, and rituals and played a role in resolving legal disputes. While some accounts suggest the Temple of Jerusalem was the sole temple for the worship of Yahweh, this was not the case; many others existed throughout the two kingdoms, with the king as the head of religion. His role was reflected in a ceremony, over which he presided, where Yahweh was enthroned in the Temple of Jerusalem.

As Yahwism evolved, it began to return to its monotheistic roots. This change occurred between the 10th century BCE and the 7th century BCE, becoming more widespread with the Babylonian exile when the ancient Israelites struggled to stay true to their roots and reject the influence of the surrounding culture. By the end of the 4th century BCE, Yahwism had evolved into Judaism and later led to the development and rise of Samaritanism, the largely monotheistic religion practiced by the Samaritans.

Beliefs of Yahwism

Yahwism is rarely categorized as monotheistic, with most historians seeing it as a polytheistic or henotheistic religion at best. Yahweh's temples also included statues of the goddess Asherah, indicating the high regard in which she was held. A series of second-tier gods and goddesses followed Yahweh and Asherah, such as Bal and Astarte, who had their own sets of priests.

Some accounts suggest that a third tier might also have existed, with this level of deities being specialist figures with specific and defined roles, such as Nehushtan, the god of snakebite cures. The fourth tier would have involved divine beings with a status slightly lower than that of gods. They acted as messengers to the deities. These beings would go on to be categorized as angels in Judaism, a distinct classification from a god.

Worship in Yahwism

Worship in the Yahwist tradition involved sacrifices, rituals, festivals, and vow-making, much like other Semitic religions. Existing largely as a rural region, Yahwist traditions coincided with major events that marked the Israelite way of life, which also later became entrenched into Israelite mythology, although their cultural relevance was not entirely lost. These were the events:

- **Passover**, with the birthing of the lambs, which was associated with the Exodus;
- **Shavuot**, with the cereal harvest season and the practice of implementing laws at Sinai;
- **Sukkot**, with the fruit harvest seasons and the wilderness wanderings when the Israelites were freed from slavery under the Egyptians.

In essence, these festivals were all intended to celebrate the blessings of Yahweh on the Israelites, their salvation, and their appointment as his chosen people. While prayer did not play a major role early on, sacrifices did. Before the Temple of Jerusalem had been destroyed, animal sacrifices were performed on its altar, and blood from the sacrifice was sprinkled around it. The sacrifices also became a symbol of atonement and purity but not until the end of the Babylonian exile when a monotheistic religious identity became more central to the Israelites.

The role of prophets and priests was extremely significant in the practice of Yahwism since they acted as messengers of Yahweh. Talismans and teraphims, small objects depicting deities, were noticeable components of worship among the Israelites, and worship itself was concentrated in high places like Mount Zion.

Yahwism's Evolution into Judaism

After the descendants of the exiled returned to Judah after the fall of Babylon, they found that life had continued while they had lived in suffering. While some accounts suggest that the exiled returned to Judah in vast numbers following the Persian conquest of Babylon, the truth is that only a small number returned home. While they had created their own identity in a foreign land, the returnees had no connection to Judah, having lived their whole lives in Babylon.

Those who had been exiled included the Judean elite, and their Persian connections helped them establish their version of society and religion. The religion of the returnees might not have been entirely monotheistic, but it would later take on such characteristics once Judaism was developed and the Torah became more widely accepted.

Chapter 3: The Iron Age

Natural disasters like earthquakes and droughts toward the end of the Bronze Age spurred mass migrations, pushing people to seek more sustainable lands. More significantly, the introduction of a new metal, iron, led to significant changes in the organization of life. Warfare changed, and the Bronze Age ended with the beginning of the Iron Age around 1200 BCE.

The end of the Bronze Age also marked the collapse of many civilizations, leading to the movement of nomadic tribes toward the mountainous regions along both sides of the Jordan River in Canaan. Around this time, the Sea Peoples invaded many countries along the Mediterranean, which is mentioned in Egyptian tablets. These tablets also referred to the Israelites.

Israelite Settlements

Iron Age settlements in the Kingdom of Israel and the Kingdom of Judah.
Oldtidens_Israel_&_Judea.svg: FinnWikiNoderivative work: Richardprins, CC BY-SA 3.0 <https://creativecommons.org/licenses/by-sa/3.0>, via Wikimedia Commons; https://commons.wikimedia.org/wiki/File:Kingdoms_of_Israel_and_Judah_map_830.svg

Early nomadic settlements in the region existed more as temporary encampments than permanent housing and consisted of a series of stone houses surrounding a yard-like space where livestock was kept. As the settlements grew and evolved, occupying greater spaces and needing more resources, they moved toward establishing more permanent housing. Archaeological evidence from these sites shows sheep and goat remains, as well as more cattle bones the longer the settlement occupied the region. Israelite settlements also had a noticeable absence of pig bones, reflecting the formation of their separate religious identity.

In the beginning, as the tribes migrated to Canaan, they numbered just about forty-five thousand people based on archaeological evidence, a far cry from the number of people during the establishment of the Kingdoms of Israel and Judah. The Iron Age saw the development and evolution of settlements, especially when the city of Shiloh (modern-day Khirbet Seilun) became a religious and political hub for the Israelite tribes. Their growing economic, political, social, and religious influence led to an independent Israelite state, which culminated in the formation of a unified kingdom under King Saul.

Before the establishment of a kingdom, the twelve tribes settled in separate groups in their allotted lands. When they felt threatened by neighboring civilizations, in particular, the Philistines, the tribes realized the need for a unified front. The call arose for a ruler, and Saul was appointed king of Israel.

A Timeline of the Iron Age

The Iron Age extends from the 12th century BCE to the early 6th century BCE. The phase did not progress as a single period but has instead been split into two distinct chronological eras.

- Iron Age I: 1200–950 BCE
- Iron Age II: 950–586 BCE

The first period of the Iron Age was marked by the decline of the Canaanite civilization as it had previously existed, a shift spurred by the end of the Bronze Age. The movements of new civilizations and tribes into the region introduced new cultures and ways of life to Canaan due to the arrival of the Israelites, the Philistines, who came from the Aegean region, and the Sea Peoples from the western Mediterranean.

The second half of the Iron Age began as the Israelites established the United Monarchy under King Saul, with the dynasty continuing until the kingdom split into Israel and Judah. Several other kingdoms emerged during this time, including Assyria and Babylon, which established their own empires in the region. The end of the second half of the Iron Age was followed by the Neo-Babylonian era, which marked the Babylonian attack on the Israelites. But let's start at the beginning.

Iron Age I

As the Bronze Age neared its end, Canaan became a rapidly deteriorating region. Much of the region had been abandoned, with settlements moving to more developed areas. The remaining cities that still retained some people shrank significantly in size. At the time of the Israelites' arrival, the entire region likely did not number more than 100,000 people. Most of this remaining population was concentrated along coastal plains or communication routes. The area the Israelites would later occupy was hilly and removed from open routes; therefore, the area was sparsely populated at the time.

As Canaan deteriorated, so did its cultural and political systems. Any system that existed was abandoned near the end of the Bronze Age since the region became so sparsely populated. The movement of civilizations into the region, such as the Israelites, the Philistines, and the Phoenicians, redeveloped these systems. However, during the Bronze Age, the region struggled with a heavy Egyptian political influence due to Egyptian wars and incursions, which led to much unrest and conflict.

These new civilizations, including the Israelites, began to settle in Canaan, and the social makeup of the region changed. The number of villages in Canaan grew exponentially, going from twenty-five to over three hundred by the end of the first half of the Iron Age. While the density of these villages was greater in the north, where the Israelites are believed to have encamped, no archaeological evidence has been uncovered that could definitively point to Israelite residence in this area. While some historians are attempting to reach such conclusions based on the animal remains or pottery styles unearthed at these sites, it is hard to state with any certainty that Israelite tribes did settle in this region of Canaan.

However, attempts to determine ethnic identity have established some patterns that are consistently found in areas believed to have been occupied by the Israelites. Some common factors that have been identified are the lack of pig bones, pottery with more significant decorative designs than others found in the Canaan region, the practice of circumcision, and a period marked with prohibitive practices, the influence of religion, and the importance of family and genealogy.

Aspects of Israelite society uncovered through archaeological excavations suggest the tribes lived in village centers with small populations, with barely over three hundred to four hundred people belonging to each village. The tribes sustained themselves through farming and herding. Although the tribes lived off of limited resources, they were self-sustaining, and economic trade between them was prevalent. Accounts also suggest the village tribes were led by appointed chieftains who provided leadership and security to the unwalled villages.

Iron Age II

The Hebrew Bible indicates the formation of the United Monarchy as early as the 11th century BCE, which developed under the rule of Saul, David, and Solomon. When this united kingdom split, it gave the cities of Shechem and Samaria, which had been part of the settlements of ten of the twelve tribes in the north, to the Kingdom of Israel. The remaining two tribes, along with Jerusalem and the Jewish Temple in the Kingdom of Judah, were established to the south. While sufficient archaeological evidence has been discovered indicating the existence of the United Monarchy, historians are divided on its dating, although many agree that the separate states of Israel and Judah existed by the 9th century BCE at the latest.

During the first two centuries of the Iron Age II, a population and settlement expansion occurred in the region. The unified kingdom made Samaria its capital, existing in relative peace and experiencing economic prosperity. Sometime between the 11th and 10th centuries BCE, Israel transformed from a settlement of nomadic tribes to an independent state and was often engaged in territorial disputes with neighboring nations, such as the Egyptians.

Judah's emergence as an independent entity occurred later and initially consisted of only small unguarded settlements. During the reign of Hezekiah, in the 8th century BCE, Judah grew to become a great power; meanwhile, Israel was falling to foreign attacks. However, before this period, Israel was the more prosperous of the two, with improved infrastructure and great urban development. Judah's economy was less developed and much smaller. It did not achieve a more advanced or dominant status until the 7th century, possibly as an Assyrian vassal state.

Much of Judah's development can be attributed to the efforts of King Josiah in the mid-7th century. Religious reforms were introduced, with Josiah attempting to centralize worship in the Temple in Jerusalem, extinguishing other forms of worship within Judah. Josiah sought a truly monotheistic religion with the worship of Yahweh. While a new temple was constructed in Judah, sites of other religious worship were destroyed.

Some historians suggest this may have been, at least in part, a political move, with the Judeans seeking to establish harmony with the Babylonians by imitating their style of temple worship since Babylonia was the central power of the region at the time. These efforts proved futile, as Judah was invaded under Babylonian King Nebuchadnezzar II at the beginning of the 6th century BCE. This invasion led to the destruction of the First Temple (the Temple in Jerusalem) and the forced mass deportation of the Judeans in a period known as the Babylonian exile or the Babylonian captivity.

During this period of forced exile, the Judeans attempted to maintain their religious and cultural identity, despite being far away from home and living in slavery. Only after they were freed by Cyrus the Great during his conquest of Babylon were the Judeans able to return home. They immediately turned their attention toward the restoration of the destroyed temple and the construction of a new one.

Campaign of Shoshenq I

Archaeological evidence has shown the true extent of Egyptian Pharaoh Shoshenq I's invasion of the eastern Mediterranean region. Between the years 930 and 925 BCE, he invaded the Levant, capturing many cities and conquering settlements in the process. Rather than annex the Levant, Shoshenq I chose to enforce exile on its people, bringing them under Egyptian dominion. While the reasoning behind this move remains uncertain, historians suggest this might have been to derail the force of a unified state under Israelite rule, which Shoshenq I likely perceived as a threat.

Details of Shoshenq I's campaign against Israel vary, depending on whether you look at archaeological evidence or biblical accounts. For instance, the account of the campaign in the Bible refers to Jerusalem as the primary target. However, the recovered triumphal relief of Shoshenq I indicates the campaign was largely concentrated in the lands that were part of the Kingdom of Israel.

The Book of Kings narrates the arrival of Shoshenq I and recounts his success in taking the treasures from the palace and the Temple of Jerusalem for himself. The Kingdom of Israel might have been brought to Shoshenq I's attention during the reign of Solomon, at least based on biblical accounts.

This might have occurred when Solomon attempted to put Jeroboam, an administrator, to death on account of treason. However, Jeroboam fled to Egypt, where he was granted asylum in Shoshenq's court. Following the death of Solomon, Jeroboam returned to Israel, where he managed to force the assembly to reject Rehoboam, the son and successor to Solomon, instead instating himself as king.

Other accounts suggest a political bond existed between Egypt and Israel because of Solomon's marriage to the pharaoh's daughter, though it must be noted that no archaeological evidence has been discovered indicating such an alliance. However, harboring fugitives of Israel appears to have been an Egyptian policy that caused havoc in the region, as the Egyptian treaty with Israel existed only with David and Solomon. Egypt also supported the split of Israel from Judah, which was a political move since the split made Israel weaker compared to the might of Egypt.

The split of the monarchy provided Egypt with a lucrative opportunity to take control of the region. Some evidence suggests the destruction of Israel by the Egyptians might have been greatly exaggerated. However, it is true that after the kingship of Jeroboam, Israel became a vassal state to the Egyptians and lost much of its power.

The Assyrian Invasion

Shalmaneser III.
*Osama Shukir Muhammed Amin FRCP(Glasg), CC BY-SA 4.0
<https://creativecommons.org/licenses/by-sa/4.0>, via Wikimedia Commons;
https://commons.wikimedia.org/wiki/File:Shalmaneser_III,_detail,_North_Face,_East_End,_Throne_Dais_of_Shalmaneser_III_from_Nimrud,_Iraq.jpg*

Assyrian power began to rise in the Near East in the 21st century BCE, although it would rise and fall several times as the centuries passed. By the mid-8th century BCE, the Neo-Assyrian Empire had conquered much of the Middle East. Because of its formidable kings, the nation was able to increase its power and establish itself as an empire through the expansion of its borders, going on to rule parts or all of Babylonia, Armenia, Media, Judah, Syria, Phoenicia, Sumeria, Elam, and Egypt. Assyrian warfare was the apex of efficiency and complexity, and the Assyrians were also known for their savagery in war. Their reputation brought fear into the hearts of their enemies.

The Battle of Qarqar

In 853 BCE, Shalmaneser III and his Assyrian army fought against an allied force of eleven kings led by the kings of Damascus and Israel at Qarqar. The other allies included Arabia, Ammon, Usnatu, Arwad, and Hamath.

Shalmaneser's account of the battle relates that he inflicted close to fourteen thousand casualties, resulting in a definitive victory for the Assyrians. However, such accounts are often unreliable, as rulers tend to exaggerate their victories and the results of battles. The Battle of Qarqar's only known account comes from the Kurkh Stela, the Assyrian stela narrating Shalmaneser's rule. Whether a victory was indeed achieved, the Assyrians did not conquer any more lands in the region until the years following 840 BCE.

The Destruction of Israel

At the time of Assyria's march against Israel, the empire was at the height of its power. Its reputation for brutality and savagery was well known. Meanwhile, Israelite society had strayed away from its religious principles and forgotten the monotheistic worship of Yahweh. As a result, the Israelites were repeatedly warned by the Prophet Isaiah of the doom that awaited them if they did not repent.

Around 738 BCE, the Assyrians received tribute from Syria and Samaria, the Israelite capital. Four years later, a rebellion in Damascus spurred an Assyrian invasion, which also led to the loss of some Israelite territories in the north. The revolt of Israelite King Hoshea against the Assyrians led to the siege of Samaria around 722 BCE by Shalmaneser V, which went on for three years. During this time, Shalmaneser died, and Sargon II took the throne in his place. The credit for the siege varies, as Sargon claimed to have conquered Samaria, yet historians believe Shalmaneser had managed to do so before his death and that Sargon took credit for it. However, it is possible that Sargon recaptured the city after a brief rebellion. Regardless, the siege of Samaria was successful, and following the fall of the city, Israel was destroyed. Its inhabitants were shipped off to Assyria in captivity and were resettled in various lands, resulting in the loss of the ten tribes of Israel.

The Babylonian Invasion

The fall of the Kingdom of Israel to the Neo-Assyrians had consequences for the neighboring Kingdom of Judah as well, as it became a vassal state to the Neo-Assyrian Empire. The Assyrians abandoned any campaigns against Judah in favor of accepting the tribute the Judeans offered. Campaigns against the Judeans by the Babylonians later led to Judah becoming a Neo-Babylonian vassal state. However, unrest in the region continued, leading to the Babylonian invasion in 586 BCE. While historical accounts fail to provide sufficient information, biblical accounts suggest Judah was besieged by the Babylonians between 589 and 586 BCE. The invasion resulted in the destruction of the First Temple and the exile of the people of Judah. It was also during this time that the Yahwism religion morphed into the monotheistic religion of Judaism.

As a Babylonian vassal, Judah suffered greatly in terms of population and economy. During this time, its defenses were greatly weakened, so regions like Negev, Shephelah, and Hebron were lost to invasions from neighboring countries. Jerusalem, which had been the capital of a prosperous Judah, shrunk considerably in size, and Mizpah in the northern part of the Judean Kingdom was appointed the capital of Yehud, the name for the Babylonian province of Judah. To shift the religious significance of Jerusalem and the power of Judah, a new temple was constructed at Bethel in the province of Benjamin by those who had been left behind, replacing the one destroyed in Jerusalem.

The Babylonian invasion of Judah sought to establish Babylonian dominance over the region and cripple its religious infrastructure. The most significant attempt in doing so was challenging the belief that Jerusalem was the promised land Yahweh had set aside for the Israelites, his chosen people. The fall of the region to foreign invaders introduced a religious crisis of sorts, forcing kings, scribes, and prophets to conceptualize their understanding of their faith.

However, the monotheism of their religion evolved, focusing more on concepts of individual responsibility and universalism. There was also a greater emphasis on individual purity and holiness. The exile of the Judeans also had the effect of fostering a greater sense of religious identity among its people, setting them apart from the Babylonians with whom they were forced to live. The Judeans continued to observe their religion, marking their separation from other groups by observing the Sabbath and continuing the practice of circumcision in secret.

Conflicting archaeological evidence suggests different accounts of the social structure of Neo-Babylonian Judah. Some historians suggest that much of Judah's population was allowed to remain in their homeland, with life continuing like it had before or even better since they were rewarded with the lands of those who had been deported to Babylonia. Many of those who were deported owned lands or held influence over the people. Other accounts suggest that Judah was almost completely depopulated following the Babylonian invasion, with nearly fourteen thousand to eighteen thousand people being exiled, leaving barely 10 percent of the original population behind.

Chapter 4: Biblical References to Ancient Israel

Israel's religious history as the holy land means it has great biblical significance. The land of Israel forms the foundation of the Bible and the Judean and Christian faiths, so it holds great importance for many. As such, it is essential to understand the way the Bible references and discusses this holy land, its people, and their way of living.

Many tales of ancient Israel can be found in biblical texts, particularly with regard to its kings. Their rule is narrated almost entirely within biblical references, as little to no outside sources exist that narrate information relating to the kings of the United Monarchy. Thus, these biblical references are an important historical testimonial to the state of the monarchy and the Golden Age of Israel.

The United Monarchy

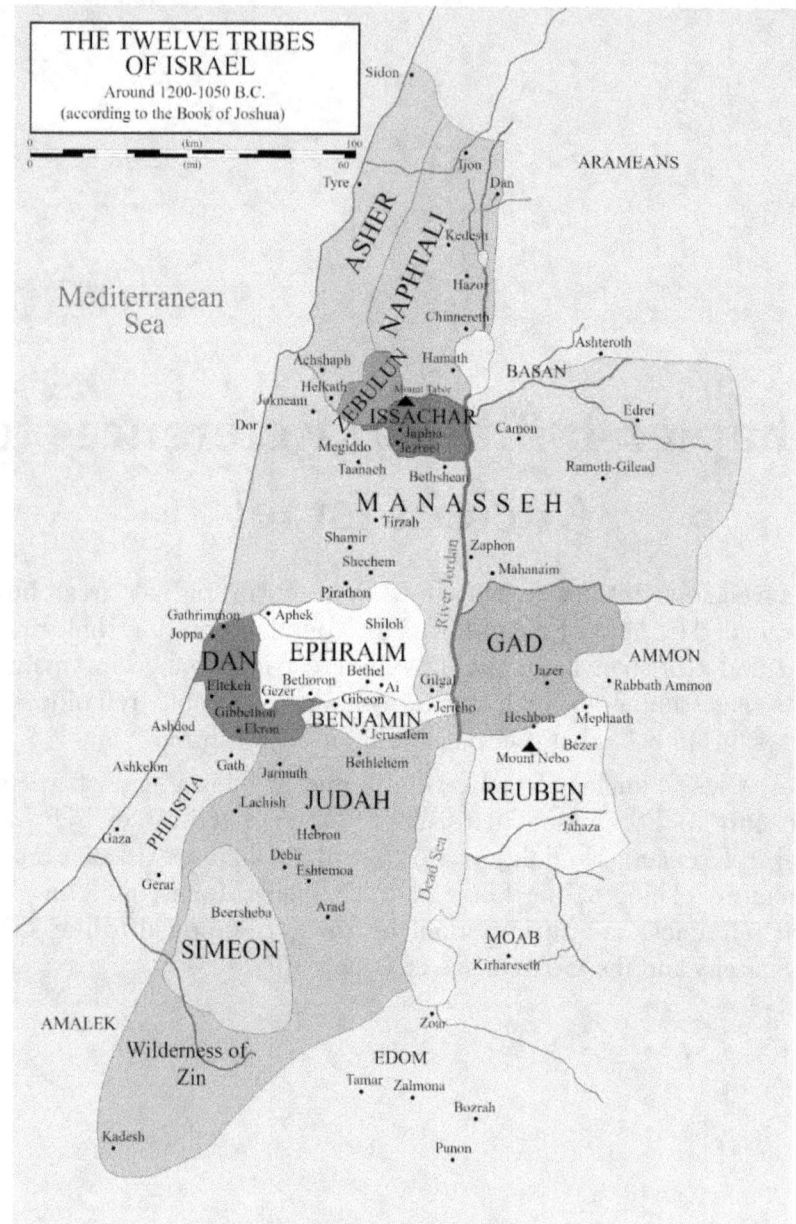

The twelve tribes of Israel.
12 tribus de Israel.svg: Translated by Kordas12 staemme israels heb.svg: by user:סי״12 staemme israels.png: by user;Janzderivative work Richardprins, CC BY-SA 3.0 <http://creativecommons.org/licenses/by-sa/3.0/>, via Wikimedia Commons; https://commons.wikimedia.org/wiki/File:12_Tribes_of_Israel_Map.svg

The story of Israel, as narrated by the Old Testament, starts with the covenant made at Mount Sinai following the freedom of the Israelite people from Egyptian slavery. Israelites were given the opportunity to accept God (Yahweh) and to live as his chosen people. If they accepted, he would lead them to the promised land. The Ten Commandments were then revealed to the people, along with the statutes offered by God that came to be known as the Book of the Covenant.

The teachings of the Ten Commandments are narrated in the Book of Exodus. The Ten Commandments forbid the worship of other gods, idols, or images and to take the Lord's name in vain. They also command the honor of one's parents and forbid theft, killing, adultery, greed, and lying.

Despite the Israelites' promises to adhere to the Ten Commandments, they were unable to stay true to their word. Instead of following God's commands, they were plagued by disbelief, disobedience, and the influence of the people around them. This disobedience is cited as the reason why the Israelites were not led to the promised land right away, entering Canaan around 1250 BCE.

For the next several hundred years, Israel existed as a civilization without a king, guided instead by prophets who had been sent by God to teach his people the right way to live. Eventually, the people of Israel requested a king from the Prophet Samuel. They wanted someone to pass judgment and rule the lands like their neighbors. This request is narrated in the Book of Samuel when the prophet asked God to heed the people's desires. Samuel was then directed to appoint Saul as king.

Reign of Saul

The kingship of Saul, which began in the late 11th century BCE, is largely considered the period when the scattered Israelite and Judean civilizations were united under a single rule. The accounts of his rule come largely from the Hebrew Bible, which speaks of his anointment by Samuel. Saul came from the Gibeah region, which was also the epicenter of his rule, and hailed from the tribe of Benjamin.

Accounts of Saul's rule and the length of his reign vary. Some biblical accounts suggest he only ruled for two years, but historians agree that his rule must have spanned between twenty to twenty-two years if he existed in the first place (there is no firm proof that the early Israelite kings existed, which is something that we will talk about later; the estimated years of Saul's rule come from other historical events that coincided with his reign). The New Testament suggests he ruled for forty years.

Three accounts of Saul's appointment as king are related in successive chapters of the Book of Samuel. One account suggests he was privately anointed by Samuel while he was out looking for his father's donkeys near Ramah. The second account narrates Samuel's attempt to find a king following the rising movement to establish a monarchy in Israel. Reportedly, Samuel gathered people by a tribe, settling on the Benjamin tribe, and then by a clan, choosing the Matri, from among whom Saul was selected. A third account speaks of Saul leading an army against the Ammonites, who had laid siege to Jabesh-Gilead in northwest Jordan. Returning victorious, the Israelites gathered in Gilgal and crowned Saul king.

Following this victory, Saul led many more military campaigns, which the Bible suggests all resulted in victories. This includes campaigns against Aram Rehob, the Edomites, the Moabites, the Ammonites, the Amalekites, the Philistines, and the Aram-Zobah. His victory against the Philistines in the second year of his rule was particularly remarkable, as he led a few thousand Israelite soldiers to victory against a massive Philistine force that was about forty thousand strong.

The Philistines were a group of non-Semitic people who had settled on the southern coast of Canaan in Philistia. Their mention in the Old Testament is largely concerned with their frequent wars with the Israelites. The causes of their frequent clashes are mostly attributed to the violent lifestyle and warring tendencies of the Philistines. Their expansionist policies and differences with the Israelites, particularly with their practice of religion and social structure as a non-unified state, might have also encouraged hostilities.

The beginning of Saul's demise as ruler came after his falling-out with Samuel, who had instructed Saul to lead an army against the Amalekites and completely destroy them. While Saul did so, killing their men, women, children, and poorest livestock, he spared the king and their best livestock. When Samuel learned Saul had disobeyed him, he told Saul that God rejected him as king. When Saul seized Samuel's garments and tore them in anger, Samuel prophesized the end of Saul's rule.

Samuel then sought out David, son of Jesse and servant to Saul, and anointed him king in front of his brothers. For the remainder of Saul's rule, Saul remained distrustful of David, even attempting to have him killed on several occasions.

Saul's end came with the Battle of Gilboa, where the Philistines had gathered to launch an attack against the Israelites. Before the battle, Saul visited a witch who conjured the spirit of Samuel, who had died five years previously. He informed Saul that God had forsaken him and that he would lose both the battle and his life the next day.

While accounts vary slightly, the most common narration suggests that Saul died by suicide during battle, falling on his own sword. The Philistines took hold of the bodies of Saul and his slain brothers from the battlefield and displayed their decapitated heads on the walls of Beth-shan.

Eshbaal Takes Over

Eshbaal, or Ish-bosheth, as he is referred to in the Hebrew Bible, was the second monarch of the Kingdom of Israel, succeeding his father Saul around 1012 BCE. His two-year reign was mostly punctuated by battles and conflicts with David, who received much support. Following the death of Saul, Saul's army captain, Abner, instated Eshbaal as the new king. However, the tribe of Judah opposed this appointment, instating David as their king, which led to a war.

The war concluded in David's favor when Abner deserted Eshbaal. David's terms of peace included the return of his wife, Michal, daughter of Saul and sister of Eshbaal. Michal had been given away by Saul to another man after David was forced to flee.

Eshbaal's short-lived rule is also narrated in the Book of Samuel, which speaks of his assassination. He was killed by two of his army captains, Rechab and Baanah, who committed treason in the hopes of a reward from David. However, David refused to reward them, instead ordering their execution. He had their hands and feet cut off.

The Golden Age of Israel

The Golden Age of the Kingdom of Israel is believed to have started with the rule of David. During this time, the kingdom achieved great wealth, prosperity, and splendor. Israel's economic and religious prosperity, along with the development of effective trade relations and the wisdom of its rulers, made it a notable force in the region. Its Golden Age might have been too dependent on its rulers, though, as the end of Solomon's rule marked the decline of the period. However, Israel prospered while it lasted.

David Becomes King

David fighting Goliath.
Majumwo, CC BY-SA 4.0 <https://creativecommons.org/licenses/by-sa/4.0>, via Wikimedia Commons; https://commons.wikimedia.org/wiki/File:David_as_he_fights_Goliath.jpeg

After the death of Eshbaal, David was accepted as king of the Kingdom of Israel around 1010 BCE. According to the Bible, David would have already been a well-known figure. During the reign of Saul, David had been a favorite of the king as an accomplished harpist and the man who defeated the Philistine giant Goliath in battle. Goliath challenged the Israelites to send out a champion who would dare face him. Saul was afraid, but David volunteered, taking only a staff, a sling, and five stones with him.

It appeared to be an unfair confrontation since Goliath was many times the size of David. Goliath had armor and a javelin, while David had little to fight with other than stones. Yet David scored a victory when he slung a stone, hitting Goliath in the center of his forehead, causing him to fall to the ground. David then cut off his head, causing the Philistines to flee, with the Israelites chasing after them.

David even became close friends with Saul's son, Jonathan. However, once Samuel declared Saul was no longer in God's favor, Saul became increasingly paranoid about David stealing his throne and made multiple attempts to assassinate him.

David's most notable achievement after becoming king was his conquest of Jerusalem, which had been under the control of a Canaanite tribe called the Jebusites. He was also able to return the Ark of the Covenant to Israel, which had resided in Shiloh. The Ark was later placed in the First Temple by King Solomon. David, who already held much fame and support among the Israelites, became even more popular with his conquests over the Moabites, the Amalekites, the Philistines, the Ammonites, the Edomites, and the Aram-Zobah.

The First Book of Samuel and the Book of Chronicles narrate David's family life. While his armies laid siege to Rabbah in Ammon, David remained in Jerusalem, where he met Bathsheba, whom he impregnated. He later had her husband killed in the guise of battle. However, after acknowledging his sin to the Prophet Nathan, he was told that his child would not survive. David also faced revolts from his own sons. First, his favorite son, Absalom, rose up in vengeance against him, killing David's other son, Ammon, for raping his sister. Absalom's plans against his father might have been successful had he not been infiltrated by David's men. Absalom was caught in the Wood of Ephraim. Despite David's orders against a severe punishment, Absalom was killed for his treachery. David mourned him greatly.

On David's deathbed, David's eldest son, Adonijah, declared himself king. However, Bathsheba and the Prophet Nathan convinced David to appoint Solomon, Bathsheba's son, as king. Adonijah's revolt was quickly suppressed. Thus, Solomon became king following the death of David at the age of seventy. Solomon's rule might have been directly influenced by David, whose parting words to his son were to seek revenge on his behalf.

David plays a significant role in the biblical narrative and religious mythology. Jewish tradition represents David as the ideal king and as the ancestor to Jesus, which is mentioned in the Gospels of Matthew and Luke. Islamic tradition also shows David as both the king of Israel and a prophet of God. However, it must be remembered that the information in this chapter comes from the Old Testament; there is no firm historical evidence that David ever existed, although most scholars do agree that David and Solomon were real people. We will dive into the historicity of these rulers later in the chapter and provide some evidence for their possible existence.

Solomon Takes the Throne

A depiction of the Temple of Solomon at Jerusalem.
Wellcome Images, CC BY 4.0 <https://creativecommons.org/licenses/by/4.0>, via Wikimedia Commons; https://commons.wikimedia.org/wiki/File:The_temple_of_Solomon_at_Jerusalem._Coloured_engraving,_ca._Wellcome_L0047683.jpg

The Golden Age of Israel is said to have begun with the rule of David, but the kingdom experienced even more prosperity under Solomon. However, the end of his reign also marked the decline of the United Monarchy. Solomon is believed to have taken the throne in the year 970 BCE following his father's death. He ruled for around forty years. The First Book of Kings references Solomon's rule and his demise.

Biblical and religious references portray Solomon as a prophet and a wise ruler. His wisdom is portrayed as a gift from God, who appeared to Solomon in a dream and asked what gift he wanted, to which Solomon requested wisdom to rule his people. His wealth and power are also referenced, and the Islamic tradition portrays him as a prophet of God. Even non-religious traditions refer to Solomon as a magician, attributing many amulets recovered from the Hellenistic period to him.

Solomon's first act as king was to follow his father's instructions and purge the kingdom of usurpers and treacherous individuals, taking out those who had opposed David or plotted against him. To guard his kingship, Solomon appointed trusted friends to important administrative, civic, military, and even religious posts. According to the Bible, Solomon built the First Temple of Jerusalem, which his father had wanted to construct, to store the Ark of the Covenant. The temple was dedicated to the worship of Yahweh. Solomon also built a royal palace in Jerusalem and rebuilt many cities, which aided in Israel's trade efforts.

Under Solomon's rule, the Israelite military was strengthened, particularly with the addition of chariots and cavalry. Solomon also established many trading and military posts by founding new colonies. He followed in his father's footsteps by focusing on developing and strengthening Israel's trade relations, particularly with the Phoenicians. He also cultivated trade relationships with Tarshish and Ophir, which brought luxury products like silver, gold, sandalwood, ivory, pearls, apes, and peacocks to the kingdom. Israel's flourishing economy and Solomon's vast wealth can be attributed to these successful trade contracts.

Solomon's wisdom was highly regarded and sought after. One of the most famous examples is the judgment of Solomon. You might be familiar with the story. Two women came to Solomon, both laying claim to a child. Solomon suggested cutting the child in half and giving each woman a part. One of the women protested, choosing instead to give up her claim. Solomon gave her the child, citing that only the real mother would rather give up her child than see it die. Solomon also authored several books, including the Wisdom of Solomon, the Song of Solomon, and the Books of Proverbs and Ecclesiastes.

Solomon eventually angered God, causing the United Monarchy to split. He turned away from God and instead worshiped the false gods of his wives, even going as far as to build temples for their worship. Solomon died at the age of sixty from natural causes. Following the pattern of the hereditary monarchy that had been established in Israel, his son, Rehoboam, took the throne. The end of Solomon's rule also marked the beginning of the end of the Golden Age of Israel, as the kingdom moved from development and prosperity to conflict and unrest.

The Last Ruler of the United Monarchy: King Rehoboam

Even before Solomon's death, the kingdom had begun to disintegrate. The First Book of Kings narrates that some of the unrest might have been caused by Solomon's practices in his personal life, which did not align with the religious beliefs of the land, such as his marriage to many foreign wives and the worship of Ammonite and Moabite gods.

When Rehoboam became king, he immediately faced opposition from ten of the Israelite tribes. Rehoboam's mother was Ammonite, making her one of Solomon's foreign wives. Therefore, her son, in the eyes of the Israelites, was not fit to rule. Rehoboam's reign, which is described in the Books of Kings and the Second Chronicles, is believed to have started in 931 BCE and lasted about twenty years.

While the Israelites objected to Rehoboam's heritage, the final straw might have happened at his coronation, when the ten tribes gathered to ask for certain reforms to be passed. Instead of engaging in a civil discussion, Rehoboam imposed heavier taxation on the tribes. This, coupled with the heavier economic burden on the tribes due to Solomon's lavish lifestyle, was not well received. In addition, the Israelite and Judean regions had historically harbored animosity toward one another, which had only been quelled when David united the two with his military victories. When the ten tribes rebelled, they broke apart from the United Monarchy, establishing the Kingdom of Israel and leaving Rehoboam to be the ruler of the smaller Kingdom of Judah. The two regions remained at war with each other throughout Rehoboam's reign.

Rehoboam's fifth year of rule was marked by the invasion of King Shishak of Egypt. The fifteen fortified cities built by Rehoboam during his rule suggest he had been expecting an attack; however, whether some previous altercation had led him to believe an attack from Egypt was imminent or if he was simply preparing for the possibility of war is not clear. Shishak took all of the fortified cities, forcing Rehoboam to surrender. Rehoboam offered all the riches from the Temple as tribute. From that point forward, Judah became a vassal state to Egypt. While historical records are unclear, many historians believe this Shishak, as mentioned in the Book of Chronicles, refers to Shoshenq I. At the end of Rehoboam's reign, his son, Abijah, succeeded him.

Historicity

As mentioned, there isn't any firm evidence that the United Monarchy ever existed. Some scholars believe there is evidence that it existed, such as parts of David's palace; however, other scholars are skeptical, saying the discovery could not be that. Some archaeologists believe they have found stones and stelae with David's name on them, although other scholars believe the name might relate to someone else or is translated incorrectly.

That being said, most scholars believe that David and Solomon existed. However, they don't believe they lived as lavishly as depicted in the Bible. Although there isn't any solid proof that the Davidic kings walked the earth, it is hard to entirely discount the biblical writings, which is why archaeologists and scholars are still trying to prove their existence today.

Chapter 5: The Kingdom of Judah

The Kingdom of Judah, just like its counterpart, was descended from the Israelites who had received guidance and the blessing of God on Mount Sinai. Initially, Judah was part of the United Monarchy (at least according to biblical tradition), but the tribes later split, with two of the tribes forming the Kingdom of Judah in the south. Even if the United Monarchy existed, it likely was only superficially united.

During the kingdom's early years, it remained sparsely populated. It wasn't until much later, under foreign rule, that it began to grow and prosper. Judah plays an important role in the lives of the Jews, who are primarily descended from the people of this region.

Jeroboam's Revolt

Even before the end of the United Monarchy and the formation of the separate Kingdom of Judah, friction existed between the southern region and the northern region. One reason for the tensions was the topography. Judah (the southern region) was isolated from the other ten tribes in the north due to mountains and valleys. The seclusion of Judah from the rest of the kingdom, combined with its shared border with the Philistines, who often clashed against the United Monarchy, did not help foster friendly relations.

The true divide between the regions came with the revolt of the ten Israelite tribes. It began with the coronation ceremony of Rehoboam, the last of the kings under the United Monarchy. At the ceremony, the ten Israelite tribes, led by Jeroboam, approached the newly anointed king and asked him to grant a reduction in the heavy taxes Solomon had levied to fund his lavish lifestyle. In response, Rehoboam chose to increase the taxes, causing the ten tribes to rebel. They appointed Jeroboam as their king around 931 BCE.

While only the tribe of Judah remained loyal to Rehoboam initially, the tribe of Benjamin soon joined to form the Kingdom of Judah. Whatever tensions had existed between the north and south before the split intensified.

Jerusalem: The Judean Capital

Reconstructed model of ancient Jerusalem.
Водник at ru.wikipedia, CC BY-SA 2.5 <https://creativecommons.org/licenses/by-sa/2.5>, via Wikimedia Commons;
https://commons.wikimedia.org/wiki/File:Reconstruction_model_of_Ancient_Jerusalem_in_Museum_of_David_Castle.jpg

Jerusalem acted as the capital of Judah for around four hundred years. Before the split of the United Monarchy, it had acted as an important cultural and religious center, particularly after the construction of Solomon's Temple, which became the main center of worship. During Solomon's reign, several other important buildings were constructed in Jerusalem, such as Solomon's palace, indicating the sociopolitical significance and religious importance of the city.

After the split of the United Monarchy, Jerusalem was a politically unstable region. Throughout the Kingdom of Judah's existence, it was attacked and pillaged by the Egyptians, the Neo-Assyrians, the Philistines, the Arabs, and the Ethiopians. The presence of the Temple allowed Jerusalem to maintain its position as a religious center and a place for frequent pilgrimages. As such, it had a significant social and religious role to play until the Babylonian invasion, when the city was completely laid to waste.

Following the freedom of the Judeans from the Babylonian captivity by Cyrus the Great, the Jews were allowed to return home, and the Achaemenid king offered monetary help in rebuilding the city. The construction of the Second Temple was completed during the reign of the third emperor of the Achaemenid Empire, Darius the Great, and the walls of the city were rebuilt with the aid of Artaxerxes I, his successor. Jerusalem was restored, and its people lived in relative peace until the Greeks defeated the Achaemenids and took over the Persian Empire.

Life in Judah

After the split of the United Monarchy, Israel and Judah remained at odds with each other, and they were engaged in a civil war throughout Rehoboam's reign. Since Rehoboam had been initially appointed king of the United Monarchy, not just of Judah, he made efforts to bring Israel under his control and built many fortified cities in preparation for war. Rehoboam's son also sought to bring Israel under Judean rule.

While this civil war was going on, in the fifth year of Rehoboam's rule, Judah was invaded by Pharaoh Shoshenq I of Egypt, who brought down the fortified cities of Judah with ease. In response, Rehoboam chose to surrender rather than fight, giving Shoshenq the treasures from the Temple of Jerusalem as tribute. Having conquered the region, Shoshenq allowed the Judeans to continue living as they had, except it was now a vassal state to Egypt. The vassal state continued its efforts to bring Israel under its realm.

Battle of Mount Zemaraim

Rehoboam was prepared to go to war against the newly established Kingdom of Israel when it first split, but he was counseled to refrain from going to war against his brethren. However, his son and successor, Abijah, led a historic battle against the Israelites at Mount Zemaraim. This battle is narrated in the Book of Chronicles and is believed to have taken place around 913 BCE.

In the Bible, Abijah is said to have led an army of 400,000 men against Israel's Jeroboam, who led around 800,000 men to settle disputes between the two kingdoms, most importantly the border issue. Before the battle, the Bible narrates that Abijah attempted to encourage the Israelites to lay down their arms and return to living under a unified rule. Jeroboam ignored the invitation and instead attempted an ambush maneuver against the Judeans, with a part of his army coming up behind them. However, Abijah was able to counter this move, turning the tables on the Israelites.

The Judeans earned a decisive victory in this battle, killing some 500,000 Israelites and giving chase to the remaining men who attempted to flee the battlefield. The Judeans were able to take the Israelite cities of Ephron, Bethel, and Jeshanah. While the battle was a conclusive win for Judah, it was not sufficient enough to reunite the two kingdoms and only served to deepen the hostilities between each other, with continuous border wars between the regions occurring until the Assyrians took over the Kingdom of Israel.

Battle of Zephath

After the confrontation at Mount Zemaraim, the two kingdoms did not engage in any major battles for a while. Abijah's successor, Asa, managed to maintain relative peace during the first few years of his rule until the Ethiopians, who were backed by the Egyptians, who sought to take direct control of the region, attacked the Judeans. The Second Book of Chronicles describes the Battle of Zephath, which took place in the Valley of Zephath in modern-day Israel.

The Ethiopians, led by Zerah, were about a million men in strength, according to the Bible, which states divine intervention as the reason behind the Judeans' victory in the battle. The Judeans pursued the Ethiopians as far as Gerar, where they had to stop out of exhaustion. Asa collected a significant number of treasures as a result of his victory and was able to establish peace with the Egyptians until the mid-7th century BCE.

Shaky Alliance with Israel

King Asa was once again challenged by the Israelites, led by Basha, who forced Asa to pay a high tribute. In return, Asa bribed the Damascene king to break his treaty with the Israelites and invade the region. This attack forced the Israelites away from the Judean border. Asa's successor, Jehoshaphat, changed the Judean policy toward the Israelites, as he instead attempted to forge an alliance with them.

This alliance was initially made through marriage. As the Second Book of Chronicles states, Jehoshaphat married his son to the daughter of King Ahab of Israel. In the Battle of Ramoth-Gilead, Ahab sought to get land back from Syria, known as Aram-Damascus at the time, and he was helped by Jehoshaphat. However, the battle was lost. Syria held control of Ramoth-Gilead, and Ahab was seriously wounded in the battle and bled to death.

Jehoshaphat attempted to create an alliance with Ahab's successor, Ahaziah, to maintain trade relations and maritime commerce. Jehoshaphat later aided Jehoram of Israel against the Moabites, who had been under Israelite rule and had risen up in revolt. The rebellion was quickly suppressed but resulted in Jehoshaphat's hasty retreat from the uprising when the Moabite king offered his own son up for sacrifice.

Jehoram succeeded Jehoshaphat, and the Judean rule began to falter.[70] Though Jehoram was able to form an alliance with the Israelites by marrying Ahab's daughter, there was trouble at home. Edom, a land to the south, rebelled against Judean rule, and Jehoram was forced to declare it an independent state. Further raids and attacks by the Arabs, the Ethiopians, and the Philistines took everything from the king's wealth to his family, leaving Judah in a weakened position.

Israel Falls

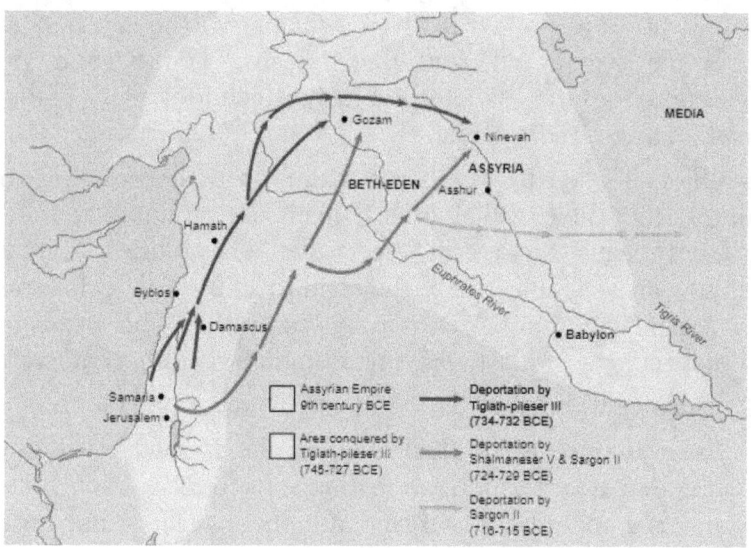

Deportations by Assyria.
Joelholdsworth, CC BY-SA 3.0 <http://creativecommons.org/licenses/by-sa/3.0/>, via Wikimedia Commons; https://commons.wikimedia.org/wiki/File:Deportation_of_Jews_by_Assyrians.svg

---

[70] Even biblical scholars are confused about who Jehoram (or Joram) was. The Bible mentions a Jehoram of Israel and a Jehoram of Judah. They reigned at the same time. So, does this mean they were the same person? Did the events get copied down incorrectly? Or was it just a coincidence that two Jehorams ruled at the same time?

Around the mid-8th century BCE, Israel was struggling against Neo-Assyrian incursions. The Book of Chronicles and the Second Book of Kings describe the relocation policy the Neo-Assyrian Empire initiated against the Israelites, which resulted in the demise of the Kingdom of Israel.

Israel was conquered by Shalmaneser V, and a period of forced removal of Israelites from their home to Assyria began. The deportations began in 732 BCE, and the Assyrians slowly conquered various Israelite cities. In 722 BCE, the city of Samaria, the capital of the Kingdom of Israel, fell to Sargon II after a three-year siege that was started by Shalmaneser V.

After hearing the news of Israel's fall, Hezekiah, King of Judah, opened up his land to the Israelites who had been left behind by the Assyrians. He wanted to hold Passover in Jerusalem. While some mocked this invitation, many Israelites who remained showed up, including those from Ephraim, Zebulun, Manasseh, and Issachar. Many historians are now of the belief that instead of the Assyrians taking all of the Israelites into their land, some of these regions were annexed by the Judeans, and the Israelites were absorbed into the Judean population following the Assyrian exile.

Unlike the Judeans, who were forced into exile by Babylonia but were able to return home generations later, the Israelites never returned. Thus, they are called the Ten Lost Tribes of Israel, and historical accounts suggest the Israelite population might have been absorbed into the Assyrian and Judean populations or among neighboring regions since history makes no mention or shows any traces of any of the ten Israelite tribes after the Assyrian exile. While the Assyrians also attacked Judah and laid siege to Jerusalem, they never took over or attempted to destroy the kingdom. Instead, the Assyrians allowed Judah to operate as a vassal state, although it had to pay much tribute to maintain its freedom.

Judah as an Assyrian Vassal

The Second Book of Kings narrates the arrival of the Assyrians to the Levant under Sennacherib, who warned the Judeans they could not withstand an Assyrian attack by just relying on their god. In 715 BCE, Hezekiah forged alliances with Egypt and Ashkelon, a Philistine region, to gather a force that would take a stand against the Assyrians by refusing to pay tribute. Sennacherib laid siege to Judah, and Hezekiah was forced to pay a high tribute, including all of the gold from the treasury of the Temple. He even stripped the gold from the doors of the Temple.

Fourteen years later, Sennacherib again laid siege to Jerusalem, but he never took the city.

Throughout the rule of Manasseh, between the early 7th century BCE to about the mid-7th century BCE, Judah remained a vassal state of the Assyrians. The tribute imposed on the Judeans included providing aid for construction projects and assisting in campaigns. In 640 BCE, Manasseh's successor, Josiah, found some leeway in self-government since the Assyrian Empire had been struggling, the Egyptians were attempting to reestablish their autonomy following Assyrian rule, and the Neo-Babylonians had not yet risen.

However, in 609 BCE, Egyptian Pharaoh Necho II aided the Assyrians in leading an army into the Levant, entering through Syria. He was blocked in the Jezreel Valley by the Judeans, who were trying to aid the Babylonians by blocking Necho's path. However, in the ensuing battle, Josiah was slain, and the Egyptian-Assyrian alliance went on to lay siege to Harran, though they failed to keep their hold on the city. Necho II retreated to Syria.

Once Necho returned to Egypt, he replaced Josiah's successor, Jehoahaz, with Jehoahaz's older brother, Jehoiakim. Jehoahaz was taken as a prisoner to Egypt. As punishment, a heavy tribute was placed on Judah, which Jehoiakim was forced to pay until the Babylonians defeated the Egyptians. In a strategic move, Jehoiakim changed his allegiance and began paying tribute to Nebuchadnezzar II of Babylonia in 605 BCE.

In 601 BCE, Nebuchadnezzar led a failed campaign to take over Egypt, which also resulted in high losses for him. After seeing this failure, many of the Babylonian vassal states rebelled, including Judah. Jehoiakim refused to pay further tribute to the Babylonians. In response, Nebuchadnezzar laid siege to Jerusalem, attempting to quash the rebellion.

Siege of Jerusalem

The Flight of the Prisoners *by James Tissot.*
https://commons.wikimedia.org/wiki/File:Tissot_The_Flight_of_the_Prisoners.jpg

The Judean revolt against Babylonia lasted from around 601 BCE to about 586 BCE when Judah was taken over by the Babylonians. In 601 BCE, Jehoiakim died and was succeeded by his son, Jeconiah. In the first siege of Jerusalem in 597 BCE, the city surrendered. Jerusalem was looted by the Babylonians, and many prominent members, including the king himself, were deported. Jeconiah's uncle, Zedekiah, was installed as a vassal king.

The Book of Kings suggests this first siege lasted three months before the city surrendered and lost many of its riches and people, most notably the royalty and many skilled craftsmen. For about ten years, Judah remained a struggling state and a vassal to the Babylonians. Around 589 BCE, against the advice of the Prophet Jeremiah, Zedekiah forged an alliance with the Egyptians and revolted against the Babylonians.

In that same year, Nebuchadnezzar returned to Jerusalem and laid siege to the city again. The siege might have lasted somewhere between eighteen to thirty months and resulted in many Judeans escaping to neighboring regions to seek refuge. Those who remained behind suffered terribly, as they were deprived of many essentials. When Nebuchadnezzar finally broke through the defenses of the city, he captured Zedekiah, who had attempted to escape with his people. After being forced to watch his sons be killed, Zedekiah was blinded and taken captive to Babylonia, where he later died.

The Babylonians then initiated the complete destruction of Jerusalem. The Temple and the city were utterly destroyed, and most of the Judean population was taken as captives to Babylon. To complete the city's destruction, it was set ablaze, as were the surrounding towns and regions. A few Judeans were left behind to tend to the lands of the province of Yehud, and Gedaliah was appointed governor of the region.

Gedaliah was a native Judean, and the news of his appointment encouraged many Judeans who had sought refuge in neighboring lands to return to Judah. However, the assassination of Gedaliah at the hands of Ishmael of the royal house of Judah did not bring about any good feelings, and many of those who had returned made a hasty escape. Many sought refuge in Egypt, settling near the Nile. Judah remained a Babylonian province until the fall of Babylonia at the hands of Cyrus the Great.

The Yehud Province

Under the Babylonians, the town of Mizpah was appointed the capital of Yehud. Jerusalem, which had been completely destroyed, had no population to speak of during this time.

The ruling elite and the people in power were immediately removed and exiled to Babylon, which was the Babylonians' standard move when taking over regions. They wanted to ensure the conquered people would not incite a rebellion. Some people were left behind to tend to the lands, and the administrative capital was shifted to remove any power, symbolic or actual, from the previous center. And this move was effective, as the Jews were unable to rise against the Babylonians.

Nothing remarkable happened in Yehud throughout the 6th century BCE. However, after the fall of the Babylonians and the return of the exiled, Yehud Medinata emerged as an active sociopolitical sphere. It operated in relative autonomy, as it was allowed to function by its own laws, although it was obligated to pay tribute to the Persians.

Chapter 6: The Persian Period

Following the fall of Babylon to the Achaemenid Empire and the liberation of the Judeans in 539 BCE, Yehud Medinata was established during the Persian period as an autonomous Jewish province. It became an important administrative center within the Persian Empire and played a significant role in the rehabilitation of the Israelites following their forced exile.

Following the death of Cyrus the Great, a period of unrest occurred under his successor and son, Cambyses. Stability returned to the region with the rule of Darius I, who introduced tighter administrative controls in all Persian-held domains, including Yehud Medinata. Such controls were tightened further when the Persians temporarily lost Egypt. During this period, distinct religious, cultural, and administrative changes took place in Judean life, which were influenced by Persian rule.

The Formation of Yehud Medinata

Yehud Medinata highlighted in pink.
https://commons.wikimedia.org/wiki/File:Palestine_under_the_Persians_Smith_1915.jpg

Yehud Medinata came into existence following Cyrus the Great's conquest of Babylon when he allowed the Israelites to return home. One of his first acts following the conquest was to commission the rebuilding of their homeland, including the destroyed Temple, which is believed to have been restored sometime around 515 BCE.

Yehud Medinata was established as a Jewish province that operated under the watchful eye of the Achaemenid Empire. Its population numbered around thirty thousand people, and it remained a relatively small region. It was not until the mid-5th century BCE that Jerusalem was restored to its former political influence. Until then, Yehud Medinata remained a theocratic state ruled by high priests and Persian-appointed Jewish governors whose job was to maintain peace in the region and ensure the collection of tribute.

The Achaemenid Empire instated a policy of religious and cultural tolerance and did not impose its own religious practices on conquered lands. In the mid-5th century BCE, during Artaxerxes I's reign, the priests Ezra and Nehemiah were sent to Jerusalem to act in a priestly capacity and as governor to oversee the restoration of Jerusalem. Yehud Medinata had been experiencing civil unrest since the return of the exiled Jews, and Nehemiah expressed sorrow over how long it was taking to restore the walls of Jerusalem.

The unrest was caused by tensions between those who had returned and those who had stayed during the Babylonian captivity. The tensions might have been caused, at least in part, by the attitude of exclusivism that the returnees adopted during their exile in Babylon, as they had set themselves apart from their captors to maintain their sense of identity and culture. Back home, this exclusivity clashed with the people who lived there, leading to frequent conflicts. The unrest also might have been caused by the redistribution of property that took place following the exile, an issue that lay in dispute now that the returnees attempted to lay claim to their former lands. The arrival of Ezra and Nehemiah was intended to resolve these conflicts, helping the returnees to reintegrate into Jewish society and return to their religious practice.

During the Babylonian exile in the early 6th century BCE, Judah experienced a steep decline. The country's elite, the royal family, and the priesthood were all forced out of Judah. As a result, the economy suffered greatly, and any progress Judah had made following the devastation of Israel was lost. Gedaliah, a native of Judah, was instated as a puppet king in what was known as Yehud. The administrative center was moved from Jerusalem to Mizpah due to the destruction of Jerusalem and to perhaps break the consolidated power that had existed there. The province of Yehud also included the towns of Bethel, Mizpah, Jericho, Beth-Zur, and En-Gedi.

The arrival of the Babylonians in Judah spurred a refugee movement in the region, with many Judeans escaping and seeking refuge in surrounding areas. When the news of Gedaliah's appointment reached them, many returned to Yehud. However, unrest soon followed when Gedaliah was assassinated. The Babylonian garrison attacked, and many of Yehud's inhabitants sought refuge in Egypt.

It is difficult to establish the exact number of people who stayed behind in Yehud, those who had been forcibly deported to Babylon, and those who escaped to Egypt and other nearby regions. In the Book of Jeremiah, it is stated that around 4,600 people were forced into exile in Babylonia. The earlier deportation of between eight thousand to ten thousand people by Nebuchadnezzar at the beginning of the 6th century adds to these figures, citing the complete destruction and alteration of the social atmosphere of Judah.

During the Persian era, between the years of 538 and 400 BCE, the unified religion that had begun to develop during the Babylonian captivity began to be practiced in Yehud Medinata. This largely happened because the Jews were given religious, social, and political independence by the Persians. This era also marked the beginning of the biblical canon. The Persian period had a profound impact on Judean life, religion, culture, and even language, and Persian policies changed the way the Judeans structured their life socially, politically, and economically. Hebrew, which had been the language of administration and the language of everyday use, was slowly replaced by Aramaic, the administrative language of the Persians, although Hebrew continued to be used in religious and social contexts.

The Organization of Yehud Medinata

Yehud Medinata developed largely under Persian influence; therefore, many Achaemenid policies determined the administrative, religious, and social organization of the region. For example, Darius I's reforms within the empire greatly influenced the writing, revisions, and organization of the Torah. Yehud Medinata consisted of the descendants from the Kingdom of Judah and the returnees liberated from the Babylonian exile.

The region also included an extensive Mesopotamian population, who joined the Jews from their much earlier exile to Samaria.

Administration in Yehud Medinata

מטבעות יהד

Yehud coinage.
https://commons.wikimedia.org/wiki/File:YHD_coins.jpg

Compared to the former Kingdom of Judah, Yehud Medinata was significantly smaller, both in terms of population and geography. It stretched from Bethel in the east to the Jordan River and the Dead Sea in the south and toward the Judean highlands and coastal plains in the west. After Jerusalem was destroyed, it could no longer function as an administrative center, so the center shifted to Mizpah, which was located in the land of Benjamin.

Benjamin had been part of the Kingdom of Israel before its destruction and served better as an administrative region compared to Jerusalem because it was more densely populated. It became an important center, considering it held the new administrative city of Mizpah, as well as the religious center of Bethel. Mizpah retained this position of importance for over a century until 445 BCE when administrative control shifted back to Jerusalem.

It is unclear what administrative role Jerusalem played while Mizpah served as the main administrative city, but Jerusalem's destruction and severely reduced population likely meant it did not serve much of a governance purpose since it lacked any administrators or priestly bodies. However, with its reestablishment, it once again became the administrative center. Cyrus the Great sent a substantial sum of money out of his own revenue to fund the reconstruction of Jerusalem. The Jews were also allowed independent governance, and the tributes stolen out of Jerusalem by the Babylonians were returned to them. In return, the Jews had to pay tribute to the Persians. Jerusalem's walls were rebuilt, and the Second Temple was constructed, measuring about ninety feet high. From the late 5th century until the early 3rd century BCE, Jerusalem even held a local mint, striking silver coins.

Even with the rebuilding of the city, Jerusalem did not grow to a great size. It held anywhere between 500 to 1,500 citizens, a shadow of the population it had boasted before the invasion. However, Jerusalem, despite its size, was the only truly urban city in Yehud Medinata, as much of the rest of the region continued to live in small, unwalled villages. The entire region of Yehud Medinata never grew beyond thirty thousand in population. And while biblical accounts narrate mass migrations of Jews from Babylonia, there is little archaeological evidence to support this.

Governance of Yehud Medinata

Under Persian rule, the governors of Yehud Medinata were appointed from among the Jews, keeping in line with the Persian tradition of preserving the cultures of conquered lands. Cyrus the Great appointed Sheshbazzar as governor of Yehud in 538 BCE. Sheshbazzar was descended from the line of David. This line of governorship continued with his successor and nephew, Zerubbabel, although it is possible that Sheshbazzar and Zerubbabel were the same person. It is believed the Davidic line continued to serve as a governor until 500 BCE. The Persians implemented similar practices in other parts of the empire, such as Phoenicia, and while it might not have represented a restoration of the Davidic line, it did serve to maintain some peace in a region that abhorred foreign rule.

Yehud Medinata was also maintained by the high priest and prophets, emulating Judean practice before the Babylonian invasion. This succession is recorded in the Hebrew Bible in the Chronicles of Ezra and Nehemiah. However, the line of the Davidic succession, as well as the prophethood, ended by 500 BCE, leaving only the high priest in charge of governance. This led to Yehud Medinata being established as a theocracy ruled by a succession of high priests.

The governor of Yehud had the dual role of implementing both Israelite and Persian policies without doing injustice to either. Jewish customs noticeably included their religious practices, on which many political matters, such as the appointment and duties of the high priest, were based. Persian policies were largely focused on the collection of tribute from Jewish subjects. Thus, the people of Yehud Medinata were largely left to manage themselves. While a governor under the Persian Empire was typically assisted by a team of officials and scribes, no such assembly has been found to have existed in Yehud Medinata, perhaps marking another way in which the Jews were allowed to live independently under Persian rule. What can be said for certain is that most, if not all, of the governors of Yehud Medinata were Jewish. Artaxerxes I also removed the tribute obligation from those working in the Temple, a move that earned him great respect among the Jews.

Evolution of Religion

During the 10th and 7th centuries BCE, the Judean religion had not yet evolved into a monotheistic belief system and, therefore, largely operated as a henotheistic religion. While it revolved around the worship of Yahweh, it did not preclude the worship of other deities. This remained a point of contention within the Kingdoms of Israel and Judah since henotheistic worship went against the Ten Commandments and supposedly led to the doom of the Israelites, who fell to the Assyrians.

Monotheism had begun to emerge as a form of rebellion against Assyrian rule before the religion more fully formed into monotheism during the Babylonian exile. The Assyrians proclaimed their king to be the "Lord of the Four Quarters," with the four quarters referring to the four corners of the world, a title that was later taken by Cyrus the Great. This title seemed to challenge the concept of Yahweh for the Jews, who embraced the worship of one god as a rebellion. Following the Babylonian exile, Yahweh emerged more distinctly as the Judean god, and the other minor gods who had been previously worshiped as the sons of Yahweh were relegated to positions of angels or demons. This religious evolution began during the Babylonian period, but it continued to develop during the Persian and Hellenistic periods.

The Persian Empire was home to a mixture of religions, customs, cultures, and traditions, owing to the different lands, regions, and even empires that were conquered by the Achaemenids. The Achaemenids practiced Zoroastrianism, and undeniable influences can be seen in the evolution of Judaism and the religious beliefs and practices of Zoroastrianism.

The Babylonian exile and the later reintegration of the Jews in Yehud Medinata played a vital role in the development of the Jewish worldview, which was especially influenced by the reconstruction of Jerusalem and the Davidic line of governors that followed in the first few years of Persian rule. During their exile, a central tenet formed within Jewish life: the idea of exclusivity, which meant the Jews used their culture and religious practices to set themselves apart from the Babylonians.

When the Jews returned to their homeland (Yehud Medinata), they spread the belief that they were set apart from others. Even though both Ezra and Nehemiah are recorded to have expressed disdain at the emerging practice of Yahweh-worshipers marrying non-believers, they still maintained cordial relations with their neighbors. The monotheistic religion was open to all twelve tribes and any foreigners who wished to convert, but the title of Jew was reserved for the tribes of Judah and Benjamin and the holy tribe of Levi. While the religion was open to anyone, it did not grant everyone the same position within the religious hierarchy.

While much evidence suggests that the Yehudi religion evolved into a largely monotheistic form of worship during the period of Persian rule, some accounts do indicate that at least some Jews remained polytheistic. This practice might have emerged from a number of sociopolitical factors, including the exile and flight of many Jewish people to escape the Assyrians and, later, the Babylonians. Some Elephantine papyri indicate that a small community of Jews, who did not return from Elephantine to Yehud following the liberation of the Jews, believed in and worshiped Yahweh while also offering praise to the Egyptian goddess Anat. They even built a temple to worship her better. Following the end of Persian rule in Egypt, the Jewish temple in Elephantine was abandoned.

There is much evidence to suggest that the Torah underwent many alterations in terms of writing and its chronology during the Persian period. Some scholars believe this was the period when the final form of the Torah was determined, although others are of the view that its composition continued until the Hellenistic period. The changes that were implemented in the Torah during this time include the revision of history, spanning from ancient Israel all the way to the Kingdom of Judah. Older prophetic books, which had formed part of the Torah up until that time, were removed.

Language in Yehud Medinata

The Torah underwent a significant transformation from earlier writings after the liberation of Jews from Babylonian rule. Older works were revised, as well as accompanying interpretations. There were also passages and books that were not part of the earlier version. The consistent references to the Hebrew Bible in this version of the Torah suggest the Jews began to develop a greater sense of their scripture and holy writing and produced the work as a religious authority in the development of a monotheistic belief system.

The development and evolution of the written Jewish religion occurred alongside the transition of the written and administrative language. This influence was expected since the Persians conducted their administrative and diplomatic business in Aramaic as a way of unifying the various regions under a single banner. Having brought Aramaic into Yehud Medinata, it became vital to translate the Torah, though the book itself remained in Hebrew at this time, into Aramaic to make them accessible to Jews and other people, although certain sections, such as the Books of Daniel and Ezra, were originally written in Aramaic.

The language shift occurred to such a drastic degree that very few, if any, written materials in Hebrew survived from the Persian period. Most epigraphic materials that have been recovered were recorded in the Aramaic language, suggesting the wider prevalence of the language in Yehud Medinata. Aramaic continued to be used in the region long after the end of the Persian period, although Hebrew would be revived much later on.

The Persian Empire played a significant, if at times indirect, role in the development of culture, religion, and language. Persian political activities in other parts of the empire also influenced the Jews in important ways. Their religious practice was influenced by many factors and took on features of Persian worship, evolving into the form of Judaism known today.

The Persians' use of Aramaic in an administrative capacity necessitated the use of Aramaic within Yehud Medinata, changing the language of the Jewish people for centuries to come. As time passed, tension grew between the Persians and the Jews. These tensions were primarily caused by the plot concocted by Haman, a governor of the Achaemenid King

Xerxes I, to murder the Jews of the Persian Empire. When Alexander the Great defeated the Achaemenids and took the Persian Empire for himself, these tensions ended, although new issues would soon arise.

Chapter 7: The Hellenistic Period (330–50 BCE)

The Achaemenid Empire lasted a little over two centuries, and in that time, it acquired and influenced many regions in the ancient Near East. The defeat of Babylonia toward the beginning of the empire allowed Cyrus the Great to liberate the Judeans held there in forced exile. He offered them the opportunity to return home, albeit under the influence of the Persian Empire. During this time, the Persian language, religion, and culture had a profound impact on Judean life.

The end of the Persian Empire came at the hands of Alexander the Great of Macedon, who faced the last Achaemenid king, Darius III, three times before gaining a sure victory over him. Alexander's rule over the Persian Empire also brought Yehud Medinata under his reign in 334 BCE. With Greek influence entering the region, the Hellenistic period began, resulting in the further evolution of Jewish thought and practice.

The Coming of the Hellenistic Period

The Hellenistic era in what had been the province of Yehud Medinata was comprised of four distinct phases. It began with the conquest of the Persian Empire and, by extension, present-day Palestine by Alexander the Great. Following his death, the Ptolemies took over at the beginning of the 3rd century BCE as an extension of the Ptolemaic rule in Egypt. At the end of the 3rd century BCE, the Seleucid rule from Mesopotamia extended to the region, lasting until the end of the 2nd century BCE. From then until the mid-1st century BCE, the Hasmoneans reigned in Judah, which came to be known as Judea in the Hellenistic period.

During the Hellenistic period, Judea was the central land between the Seleucid Empire in the west and the Ptolemaic Empire in the east. As a result, it was often caught up in the conflicts of neighboring empires, leading to a variety of rulers moving in and out of the region. However, in keeping with Persian tradition, Alexander the Great did not impose foreign rule over the Jews. Instead, Judea was ruled by the hereditary offices of the high priests, which was in line with the theocracy established in the region; however, Judea also acted as a Hellenistic vassal during this time.

Understandably, the arrival of a new people group brought new ideas and influences into Jewish lives, impacting their religion and customs. Hellenistic influences first emerged in Alexandria, Egypt, impacting the Egyptian Jews before later spreading to Judea. Most significantly, this cultural mix led to the translation of the Hebrew and Aramaic holy scripts into Greek, making it accessible to the newcomers and to the Alexandrian Jews, who could read neither Hebrew nor Aramaic.

During the Ptolemaic rule in Judea, which lasted between 301 and 198 BCE, there was relative peace in the region. A Jewish elite class emerged based on the people's involvement with the Ptolemaic Empire. They worked in administration and the military. This elite class lived under Hellenistic influence, so many Jewish practices became mixed with Hellenistic traditions. This period continued until the wars of Antiochus III, ruler of the Seleucid Empire, whose efforts led to Jerusalem falling under his rule in 198 BCE. Hellenization began during his reign, though it was mild and less enforced than compared to the rule of his successor.

Antiochus IV, his successor, did not uphold the values of religious freedom like Alexander the Great and the Ptolemies had. He looted the Temple in response to disturbances in Jerusalem, which occurred during his campaign in Egypt, causing him to divert his attention instead to the Jews. His response was to ban Jewish rites and traditions, effectively preventing the open practice of Jewish religious worship. Jewish resistance to Seleucid Hellenization led to further unrest and clashes between the Jews and the Seleucids, culminating in the Maccabean Revolt between the years 174 and 135 BCE. This led to the end of Seleucid rule over Judea, a victory marked by the celebration of Hannukah today.

This rebellion within Judean lands, other than ending foreign rule over the Jews, also led to the formation of an independent Jewish kingdom, which was headed by the Hasmonaean dynasty. This dynasty emerged in 140 BCE and lasted as long as 37 BCE. Toward the dynasty's end, it was overrun by civil wars, which were perhaps influenced by the civil wars occurring in Rome at the same time. Although the Hasmonaean Kingdom emerged out of a rebellion against the Hellenization of Judea, the dynasty became increasingly Hellenistic. The Hasmonaean dynasty was ended by Herod, leading to the start of the Herodian dynasty, with the region becoming a vassal to Rome.

Alexander the Great's Influence on Judea

Alexander the Great.
British Museum, CC BY-SA 3.0 <https://creativecommons.org/licenses/by-sa/3.0>, via Wikimedia Commons; https://commons.wikimedia.org/wiki/File:Alexander_the_Great-British_Museum.jpg

Alexander the Great's invasion of the Persian Empire in 334 BCE and its subsequent conquest in 331 BCE had profound impacts on the cultural, ethnic, linguistic, and religious makeup of the region. It introduced Greek traditions into Persian life and the various regions that had been absorbed into the Persian Empire. While no evidence indicates that Alexander's expedition took him through Yehud Medinata, his arrival still had a great influence on Jewish life and religion.

Around 332 BCE, Alexander the Great marched to Egypt, where he established Alexandria and visited the Oracle of Ammon. He was greeted by the local priest as a god, showing the acceptance of his rule by the Egyptians. Although Alexander marched through Palestine to get to Egypt, the evidence does not indicate he ever took the mountainous route that ran through Yehud Medinata to get there. Thus, there is no evidence that Alexander ever met with the Jews or had any direct interaction with them in Yehud Medinata.

Despite this, Alexander had a great impact on Jewish life. Most noticeably, he chose to leave Yehud Medinata as it was rather than imposing a new ruler on its people, which would most likely have resulted in rebellion and unrest in a region with a history of forced exile, slavery, and detestation for foreign rule. Alexander allowed the Jews to carry on as they were, simply replacing Persian officials and administrators in the region with his own. This move might have earned him great respect among the Jews, although there is little evidence that they regarded him with any particular affection while under his rule. After his death in 323 BCE, his victories and achievements began to be regarded as legendary, and he was then referred to as "the Great." At this point, the Jews sought to associate themselves with him.

Alexander in the Jewish Tradition

Jewish legends and sources began to develop accounts of a potential visit Alexander might have made to various regions of Yehud Medinata. One of the most well-known accounts is the story of Daniel's vision, which is narrated in the Book of Daniel. In the vision, Daniel sees a ram with two horns, symbolizing the kings of Media and Persia, and a goat coming from the west, which represents Alexander the Great. The goat defeats the ram, indicating the victory of the Greeks over the Persian Empire.

Other stories spawned off of this one, including one that narrates the arrival of Alexander the Great in Jerusalem. In this story, he is greeted by the high priest of Yehud Medinata, who offers his allegiance and submission to Alexander. In return, he entered the Temple and offered a sacrifice, as per Jewish tradition.

This story embeds Alexander the Great in Jewish tradition as a follower of the faith. Not only would his visit to Jerusalem have required him to take a detour on his way to Egypt, but the story also narrates that he bowed down to the high priest upon seeing him in recognition of the greatness of Yahweh. However, no other accounts of such a journey or occurrence have been found outside of the Jewish tradition.

Alexander in Samaria

While the Jews in Yehud Medinata appeared to have welcomed Alexander with reverence, the same was not the case in Samaria. Initially, Alexander had the support of the Samaritan governor, Sanballat III, and was given permission to construct a temple on Mount Gerizim. However, Sanballat III's death led to rebellions in Samaria against Alexander, resulting in rioting and the immolation of the new governor.

Alexander the Great retaliated, leading an army against the Samaritans. He destroyed the city and banished its citizens. The Samaritans exiled themselves to the fount of Mount Gerizim, where they split into two factions. One faction continued living at the foot of the sacred mountain, the city of Samaria, which became a Greek city following their banishment.

Alexander's Legacy

Following Alexander's death in 323 BCE, his vast empire could not maintain peace. His former empire was plunged into civil wars for the next two decades, and when the wars finally ceased, Alexander's once-great empire was divided into distinct sections, the most notable of which belonged to his generals Seleucus and Ptolemy.

The Seleucid Kingdom comprised most of Asia Minor, Mesopotamia, and Syria. The Ptolemaic Kingdom was based in Egypt. During the 3rd century BCE, Judea, which was nestled between the two empires, remained under Ptolemaic rule until the incursion engineered by the Seleucids, at which point it was overseen by the Seleucid Empire for around a century.

While other generals emerged victorious from the civil wars sparked by Alexander the Great's death, the bigger challenge was to legitimize their succession to the throne in the eyes of the local population. The region of the Near East, including Judea and most of the former Persian Empire, had been ruled by a monarchy, with the throne passing from father to son or another male relative. This was not a dynastic law that Alexander's successors could follow since none of his generals were related to him.

One of the ways in which the generals attempted to establish the legitimacy of their rule was to found new Greek cities and name them after themselves, similar to what Alexander had done in conquered lands, with one such example being Alexandria. These cities boasted Greek culture, religion, and art, as well as Greek-style council houses and temples. By doing this, the Greek culture spread among local populations, who appreciated the acclimatization to the Greek way of life and absorbed it into their own, thus leading to a period of Hellenization. Hellenization was a terrific tool the Greek governors used to obtain loyalty among the locals.

Ptolemaic Rule over Judea

While the Greeks kept extensive written records of their history, there is little mention of the region of Judea. Politically, geographically, and socially, this region was of little significance to the Greeks. It did not provide any important trade routes, and entry into Egypt was possible through the coastal plains of Palestine, so the Greeks did not need to go through the mountainous paths of Judea. Since the Jews also had little political involvement, they did not play a significant role in Greek history.

However, the arrival of the Greeks had a great impact on the Jews. This can be observed most noticeably in the coinage system, which changed to reflect the new rule over the region. The weight of the coinage also changed to reflect the Greek Attic weight system. However, within Judea, few political changes took place.

While other surrounding regions like Samaria and Ashdod became hyparchies (administrative units) under the Ptolemaic Empire, with the hipparchs (who managed the administration and governorship of the region) being directly instated by the Ptolemaic ruler, Judea remained relatively independent. It was answerable to the empire but was allowed to operate as a separate administrative unit governed by the high priests. This relative independence kept the peace, and life did not change significantly for the Jews.

The Seleucid Empire

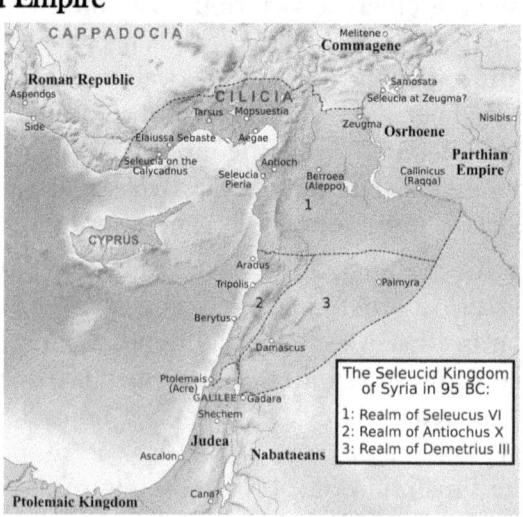

Syria in the Seleucid Empire.
Constantine Plakidas, CC BY-SA 4.0 <https://creativecommons.org/licenses/by-sa/4.0>, via Wikimedia Commons; https://commons.wikimedia.org/wiki/File:Syria_under_the_Seleucids_95_BC.svg

Seleucus, who was a senior officer in Alexander's army, established his empire in Mesopotamia. Seleucus was not happy governing a small section of the vast Macedonian Empire and engaged in a ruthless expansionist strategy, adding Anatolia, Persia, and the Levant to his territory. Eventually, Judea fell under Seleucid rule a couple of years after Antiochus III won the Battle of Panium in 200 BCE.

Under Antiochus III, Hellenization began, which involved forced conversion to the Greek religion and the practice of Greek culture among local communities. Since embracing the Greek culture brought economic benefits, many Jews accepted Hellenism. However, there were many who did not, and tensions ran high.

Antiochus III's successor, Antiochus IV, implemented a far stricter policy, attempting to convert the entire Jewish population to the Greek religion. He constructed a Greek gymnasium outside the Jewish Temple. He not only required that those who could afford it visit it but also that they remove all clothing before doing so, an act that went against Jewish law. Following a short-lived rebellion, Jewish practices like the Sabbath and circumcision were outlawed, and the worship of Greek gods was made obligatory. Refusing to do so was punishable by death.

The Maccabees, a rebel group, rose up under the leadership of Mattathias, a priest, in 167 BCE. A guerilla war began, with the Jews destroying Greek temples. They met the Seleucid army, and even though they were heavily outnumbered, they inflicted a defeat on the Seleucids and took back Jerusalem. The Jewish people ended the Seleucid rule and instated an autonomous rule.

Hellenistic Impact on the Hasmonean Dynasty

The Hasmonean dynasty emerged as a direct consequence of the Hellenistic influence experienced in Judea. Even during the rule of Alexander the Great and the Ptolemaic rule, the Jews had lived in relative harmony, undisturbed by the shifting hands of the ruling powers. The region had little to offer in the form of economic benefits or political threats.

This political scenery changed drastically with the Seleucid Empire. If the Seleucid Empire had maintained the policies of previous rulers and allowed the Jewish people to have relative autonomy in governance and religion, it is unlikely they would have made any significant contributions to the political climate of the Near East. However, the expansionist policies of Antiochus III and Antiochus IV created much friction, even before outrageous and discriminatory laws were imposed on the Jewish people.

The final straw appeared to be the imposition of the Greek religion on the Jews. The Maccabees rose up against the Seleucids and reinstated Jewish autonomy with the Hasmonean dynasty, which remained independent for over a century. However, Hellenistic influences could not be wholly removed from Judea. It continued to permeate Jewish life as remnants from the way of life in Judea under Seleucid rule. These included changes in the organization of the state and the laws of the land. It even impacted the way art was created and consumed.

Hellenistic Impact on the Herodian Dynasty

The Hasmonean dynasty was followed by the Herodian dynasty, which started under Herod, the Roman-Jewish client king of Judea. Herod the Great inherited a Hellenistic model of kingship, and he attempted to establish a sense of continuity by adopting Hasmonean practices, such as having his coinage minted with Hasmonean symbols and architectural designs. The preexisting Hellenized nature of Judean culture, politics, and social setup influenced Herod's approach to ruling. By using the same system as before, he helped establish legitimacy for his rule. However, following his death, his kingdom was divided into a tetrarchy, which was ruled by his three sons. This rule proved so ineffective that the Romans were forced to interfere in Judea.

Chapter 8: The Hasmonean Dynasty (140–37 BCE)

In 331 BCE, the Achaemenid Empire fell to Alexander the Great, and the period of the Macedonian Empire began, which gave rise to Hellenization in the lands that had been previously under the rule of the Persian Empire. The Greek takeover did not significantly change life in Yehud Medinata, as Persian officials were simply replaced with Greek administrators. Divide and conflict came with the death of Alexander the Great in 323 BCE since his kingdom lay in dispute with no legal heir to claim it.

As such, his generals broke away from the united Macedonian Empire to form their own rule over the lands, and Yehud Medinata lay determinedly in the crosshairs of the Seleucid and Ptolemaic Empires. Caught in a power struggle between the two empires, the Jews were first ruled by the Ptolemies, who gave the Jews relative autonomy, and then by the Seleucids. The Seleucid rule took away Jewish autonomy and exerted greater Hellenistic influence in the region. It also gave rise to the Maccabean Revolt and the Hasmonean dynasty.

The Rise of Jewish Hellenization

The process of Hellenization that began with the arrival of the Seleucids created significant internal conflicts within the Jewish community. Some Jews remained loyal to Ptolemaic rule and did not wish to abandon their traditional values so easily. Others, particularly those who more eagerly accepted the Hellenization process and began to conform to

Greek culture, became pro-Seleucid.

This conflict between the Jews even led to a brief civil war in 175 BCE, which pitted High Priest Onias III against his brother Jason, with the latter favoring the Seleucids and Hellenization. The high priest did not. After a period of conflict, bribery, and accusations of murder, Jason was successfully installed as the high priest, and a more widespread Hellenization process began. Onias III was killed by an official named Heliodorus, who was encouraged to do so by Jason.

Jason's accession to the role of high priest might have acted as the final determinant of Jewish Hellenization. Jerusalem became more akin to a Greek city under him, with a gymnasium that Jews would attend for the purpose of nude socialization after undergoing non-surgical restoration of the foreskin. This was to avoid the stigma of circumcision, a practice the Greeks considered barbaric and unacceptable.

Unrest in Judea

The Hellenization of the Jews was not the only reason for the Jewish uprising against the Seleucid rule. Jason's success in establishing himself as high priest and in promoting the Hellenization process, as well as many Jews' eager acceptance of this new culture, indicates that dislike of the Greeks and their culture was not the primary factor.

Antiochus IV's excessive and, at times, barbaric policies toward Jerusalem helped lead to a rebellion. Antiochus had been asked to withdraw from Egypt in 168 BCE by the Romans in the middle of a successful campaign in the region. In his absence, rumors of his death spread among the Jews. Menelaus, Jason's younger brother, was acting as high priest after undermining Jason in front of Antiochus and convincing him to depose Jason. Jason took the news of Antiochus's presumed death as a sign and attacked Jerusalem, driving Menelaus to take refuge in a Seleucid fortress.

Antiochus returned to Judea upon hearing this news. He drove Jason out and proceeded to impose excessive policies on the Jews, presumably to prevent any further actions like what Jason had done. The Jews were required to pay heavy taxes, and their rights to practice their religion were almost completely taken away. Antiochus attempted to suppress all observances of the Jewish religion and customs. He even desecrated the Temple Mount by establishing an idol of Zeus there. The practice of Jewish customs, such as sacrifices, circumcision, and even the Sabbath, was punishable by death. These actions appeared to be the last straw for the Jews, especially those who were already opposed to Hellenization.

The Maccabean Revolt

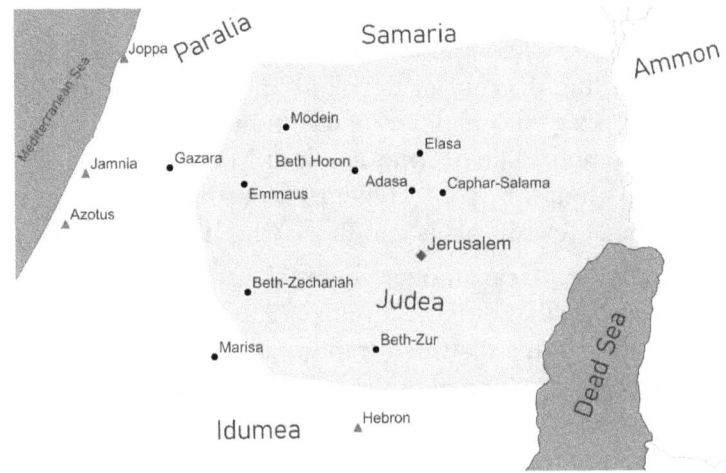

Region of the Maccabean Revolt.
SnowFire, CC BY 4.0 <https://creativecommons.org/licenses/by/4.0>, via Wikimedia Commons; https://commons.wikimedia.org/wiki/File:Judea-Maccabees-Battles.png

The Maccabean Revolt was led by Mattathias, who was part of a priestly family that came to be known as Jewish rebels, the Maccabees, in 167 BCE. The name Maccabee was a title of honor originally given to a son of Mattathias, Judas, in recognition of the role he played in the revolt, and the title was eventually extended to include his whole family. Mattathias encouraged the Jewish people to gather for a holy war against the foreign rulers and began to gather men for a military campaign, which was led by Mattathias's sons Judas, Simon, and Jonathan.

This initial attempt at an uprising was largely unsuccessful and cost the Jews, primarily because the Jews refused to fight or engage in any kind of violence on the Sabbath. It wasn't until one thousand Jewish men, women, and children were killed at the hands of the Seleucids that some Jews reasoned it would be acceptable to fight back. Seven years of warfare ensued, and Judas's guerilla warfare techniques proved successful in securing a victory against the Seleucids.

The Jews had few weapons to speak of; they mainly used modified farm tools in their attacks. Judas's initial tactic was to move slowly and use a hit-and-run approach, lying in ambush for small bands of Seleucid forces. Meanwhile, he slowly increased the number of his own men and added what he had obtained from attacking Seleucid forces to the Jewish arsenal.

Scholars disagree on the immediate causes behind the rise of the Maccabees. It might have been a combination of factors, including the opposition of traditional Jews against the reformists, who had accepted a different culture and religion and abandoned their roots. The First Book of Maccabees cite the Maccabean Revolt as an uprising of Jews against the barbaric Seleucid king who had attempted to eradicate their religion and, therefore, their identity. The Second Book of Maccabees calls the revolt a conflict between Judaism and Hellenization—that is, those who still practiced traditional Jewish values and those who had abandoned them.

Since there is no clear motive behind Antiochus IV's actions in banning the Jewish faith, some historians argue this might have been his attempt to end the conflict between traditional and Hellenized Jews. The rising unrest between traditional and Hellenized Jews could have pushed Antiochus to instate extreme measures to maintain peace in the region, as the practice of banning local religions was rare and against Seleucid tradition. Eventually, both the Hellenization and the actions of the king pushed the traditional Jews to take a stand to gain back their religion and customs.

The Battle of Beth Horon

The Syrians marched with two thousand men in 167 BCE, and Judas's men lay in wait along a narrow pass near Nahal el-Haramiah. Unprepared for the ambush, the Syrian army was completely destroyed, and Seron, a general in Antiochus's army, led the charge against the Jews. Their victory over the Syrian band gave the Jews a much-needed boost in morale and weapons.

In the hopes of avoiding detection and ambushes, the Seleucids took an alternate route to Jerusalem in 166 BCE, which led over wide coastal plains and through the pass at Beth Horon. However, Jewish lookouts saw the approaching Seleucid army and prepared a thousand-man force to meet the Seleucids. Once again, the advancing army was forced into a narrow passage, which Seron dealt with more carefully than the Syrian army had. He had his army proceed through the passage with gaps among individual units, making it impossible to trap the entire army in the event of an ambush.

The Jews, led by Judas, led an attack against the vanguard, immediately killing Seron, with archers simultaneously launching an attack on either side of the Seleucid army. The Seleucids were then attacked from behind by the Jews with the swords they had won from the Syrians. The Seleucids fled, leaving much equipment behind, and were chased back to the coastal plain, where many were killed. Following this victory, the Jewish army grew to more than six thousand in number and came to be reckoned as a formidable force by the Seleucid army.

The Death of Judas

Statue of Judas Maccabeus, Milan.

Yair Haklai, CC BY-SA 4.0 <https://creativecommons.org/licenses/by-sa/4.0>, via Wikimedia Commons; https://commons.wikimedia.org/wiki/File:Statue_of_Judas_Maccabeus_at_exterior_of_the_Duomo_(Milan).jpg

The Jewish army defeated another Seleucid army under Nicanor at the Battle of Adasa. Following this, a Seleucid army numbering nearly twenty-two thousand men was sent to fight the Jews at the Battle of Elasa. Before the confrontation, Bacchides, who led the Seleucids, marched to Galilee and massacred a large number of Jews and then marched to Judea, forcing Judas to meet him in open battle.

The two forces met between the plains of Elasa and Berea in an open land that favored the Seleucids, as it was not suited to the Jews' tactics of ambush. The Jews' initial attack made the Seleucids retreat, with the Jews chasing after them. This might have been a purposeful maneuver to draw the Jews into a position where they could be surrounded with no means of retreat. The Seleucids were able to regain their positions and trapped Judas's army. He was killed, and those who survived fled the battle.

Bacchides' victory and the death of Judas reestablished Seleucid authority over the region, and Bacchides went about fortifying major cities. He also took hostages from prominent Jewish families to ensure they would not join the rebellion. Judas was replaced by his brother Jonathan as leader of the Maccabees, though his encounters with the Seleucids did not achieve much.

The Hasmonean Dynasty Is Formed

While the Maccabees rose up in rebellion against the Seleucid Empire, King Demetrius I Soter of the Seleucid Empire, who had taken over for Antiochus IV nearly five years after the beginning of the Maccabean Revolt, was struggling against the Greek king of Pergamon and the king and queen of Egypt, Ptolemy VI and Cleopatra II. The Seleucid king's relations were deteriorating with these rulers so much that they withdrew their support from Demetrius and instead supported Alexander Balas, who laid claim to the throne as the supposed son of Antiochus IV.

This put Demetrius in a difficult position, and he was forced to recall his troops from around Judea to strengthen his forces. In a strategic move, he offered Jonathan lucrative terms to earn his loyalty and diffuse the situation to fortify his position as king. Jonathan moved to Jerusalem in acceptance of these terms in 153 BCE. The terms allowed him to continue building up his army and released hostages in Acre. Once Jonathan was in Jerusalem, he began working on fortifying the city.

Alexander Balas offered Jonathan even better terms, which included appointing him as high priest. Though Demetrius immediately tried to rectify the situation, writing Jonathan a letter that made promises that he could not hope to fulfill, his efforts were in vain. Jonathan accepted Balas's terms and declared allegiance to him. As high priest, Jonathan held an important office, and as a result, so did the Hasmoneans, which protected them from attacks by the Seleucids or supporters of Hellenism. From 153 BCE to 37 BCE, the Hasmoneans held the influential position of high priest in Judea.

The alliance between Balas and Jonathan appeared more than just a strategic move. In 150 BCE, Demetrius lost the throne and was killed by Balas, who became king and married Ptolemy's daughter. Given Jonathan's allegiance to Balas, the former was invited to the ceremony and arrived with many presents, sitting among the kings as an equal. Balas also offered Jonathan royal garments, appointed him *meridarch* (governor), and sent him back to Jerusalem in honor, despite the complaints of the Jewish Hellenists.

The Rule of the Hasmoneans

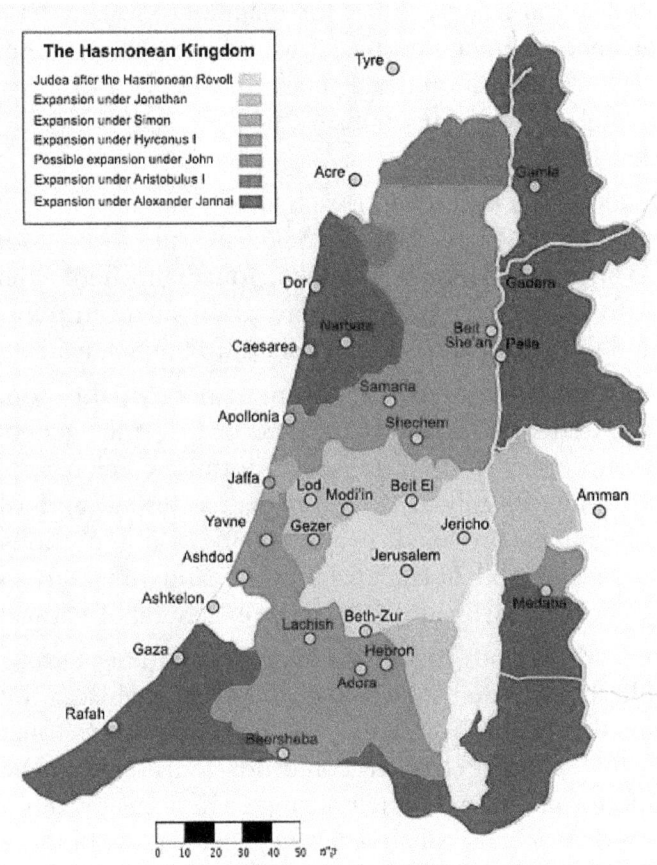

The Hasmonean dynasty.
Effib, CC BY-SA 4.0 <https://creativecommons.org/licenses/by-sa/4.0>, via Wikimedia Commons; https://commons.wikimedia.org/wiki/File:Hasmonean_kingdom.jpg

The beginning of the Hasmonean rule is marked by bids for the throne between various members of the Seleucid Empire, among whom the Hasmoneans often switched allegiances. In 147 BCE, while Demetrius II laid claim to Balas's throne, Jonathan was challenged to a battle by Apollonius, the governor of Coele-Syria. Jonathan and his brother Simon led a force of ten thousand men against Apollonius and attacked the Syrian force unexpectedly in Jaffa, which was forced to surrender quickly.

However, Apollonius was not as quick to accept defeat. He gathered reinforcements from the city of Azotus and met Jonathan's army again in the plains. Jonathan was able to capture Azotus and burn the city, along with its temple and the surrounding regions.

Balas honored Jonathan for his victory, but Ptolemy VI, his son-in-law, marched to make war against Balas. Jonathan met Ptolemy VI at Jaffa and forged an alliance, maintaining peace with Egypt, despite their differing support for who should sit on the Seleucid throne. In 145 BCE, Balas was defeated by Ptolemy VI, who himself died in battle, and Demetrius II took the Seleucid throne.

Jonathan adopted a unique approach against the new king, laying siege to the city of Acre, a symbol of Seleucid rule over Judea. When Demetrius II marched to meet Jonathan, Jonathan offered him gifts. An alliance was formed, and the Jews were given an exemption on taxes. Jonathan lifted the siege and returned the city to the Seleucids.

When a new claimant to the throne emerged, the son of Balas, Antiochus VI, under the helpful guidance of a former general of Balas named Diodotus, Demetrius promised to withdraw Seleucid forces from Acre. In return, he officially instated Jonathan as his ally and asked for his aid, which Jonathan provided in the form of three thousand men. However, Demetrius did not keep his word, and Jonathan switched his allegiance to Diodotus, who appointed Simon general of Paralia.

Jonathan and Simon made successful conquests, such as Gaza, Ashkelon, Hazar, and Beth-Zur. Jonathan was also able to form friendly relations with the Romans and the Spartans. However, Jonathan's new alliance with the Seleucid claimant could not be trusted, as Diodotus had no plans to honor the terms of their alliance. Diodotus invited Jonathan to Scythopolis under the guise of a conference, persuading him to dismiss his army of forty thousand men. Not sensing a trap, Jonathan's remaining one thousand men were killed at Ptolemais, and he was taken prisoner by Diodotus in 142 BCE. He was succeeded as high priest by his brother Simon.

Simon Thassi Becomes High Priest

Simon became the high priest and the prince of Israel, the first to hold this title, following his brother's capture. His army blocked Diodotus's entry into Judea, and Diodotus demanded Jonathan's two sons as hostages in exchange for Jonathan's release. Despite not trusting Diodotus, Simon complied to show the people he had done everything possible to save his brother. However, Diodotus was frustrated by the lack of progress he made in Judea, as Simon's army blocked his passage. He executed Jonathan and kept his sons hostage.

Following Simon's election to office by a priestly assembly, which is narrated in the First Book of Maccabees, his first order of business was to fortify Jerusalem and secure the port of Joppa. Simon then forged an alliance with Demetrius II and asked for tax exemptions for the country, which were granted. Simon is recognized as the first leader of the Hasmonean dynasty since the nation became independent of Seleucid rule under his guidance. The dynasty was declared in the same resolution that declared Simon king of the Hasmoneans, which was adopted in 141 BCE.

For the duration of his kingship, Simon ruled in relative peace. His end came at the hands of his son-in-law Ptolemy, who killed him and his two sons, Judah and Mattathias, at a banquet. Simon was succeeded by his remaining son, John Hyrcanus, in 135 BCE. However, he was unable to avenge his father and brothers.

John Hyrcanus

The sudden death of John Hyrcanus's father and brothers created a precarious political situation. Antiochus VII, who succeeded Demetrius following the latter's capture by the Parthians, entered Judea and laid siege to Jerusalem. The siege stretched on for a year, and Hyrcanus's attempts to evacuate the people who could not fight were in vain, as they were unable to pass through Antiochus's army. Finally, when food supplies began to run short, Hyrcanus negotiated peace with Antiochus.

The truce between the two parties required tribute to be paid to Antiochus, the Jews' aid in the Seleucid campaign against the Parthians, and the unequivocal acceptance of Seleucid rule. Under the rule of Hyrcanus, the Hasmonean dynasty faced immense struggles but also one of the greatest periods of its rule, given the expansion of the dynasty to Idumea (Edom) and Samaria. Under the Seleucids, the Hasmonean dynasty and the Jews under its rule struggled economically, a situation made worse by the high taxes levied on them by Antiochus VII.

In addition, Hyrcanus lost much support and became the reason for dissatisfaction and unrest among the population. Since he was forced to aid Antiochus's military campaigns, he was an absent ruler. His raid of the Tomb of David to pay tribute to Antiochus to end his siege of Jerusalem and his attempt to drive out the civilians of Jerusalem during the siege did not earn him any favors. It was not until Antiochus's death in 129 BCE that Hyrcanus emerged as a powerful leader.

Hyrcanus took advantage of the unrest in the Seleucid Empire and gathered a mercenary force, declaring Judea an independent state. By the time Demetrius II returned from exile in 130 BCE to take control of his empire once again, the power dynamic had shifted too greatly for him to make much headway.

Following Antiochus VII's death in 129 BCE, a period of unrest began in the Seleucid Empire. His death resulted in a victory for the Parthians, ending Seleucid rule over them. In 116 BCE, Antiochus VIII and Antiochus XI, who were half-brothers of Antiochus VII, broke out in a civil war, leading to the further disintegration of the empire.

In 113 BCE, Hyrcanus began extensive military operations. He was able to take Samaria after a difficult year-long siege, with the Samaritans being aided by Antiochus VIII.

Hyrcanus also invaded Transjordan in 110 BCE and laid a six-month siege to Medeba, after which he moved on to Mount Gerizim and Shechem. He was also able to conquer the Edomite towns of Maresha and Adora, among others. With every conquest, Hyrcanus forced the non-Jewish population to accept and observe Jewish customs, a first for any Hasmonean ruler. Before he died, he called for a separation of the office of civil authority between the offices of the king and high priest. He appointed his wife as the civil administrator and his son, Judah Aristobulus, as high priest. He died in 104 BCE, leaving the Hasmonean dynasty to his wife and son.

Alexander Jannaeus

Aristobulus rightfully came into the office of high priest but did not approve of his father's decision to split authority. So, he imprisoned his mother and three brothers and took on the title of king. During his short-lived rule, he was able to conquer Galilee, but he died of an illness in 103 BCE after having ruled for hardly a year. His widow released his brothers from prison; his mother had died of starvation before Aristobulus's death. One of the brothers, Alexander Jannaeus, took the throne.

Hyrcanus's reign was marked by successful expansion, and Alexander Jannaeus adopted much the same approach; however, his rule is regarded as much more violent and stuck in a never-ending cycle of conflict. Alexander began his rule with an attack on Ptolemais at the same time Zoilus of the city of Dora attempted to take the city. Zoilus was defeated by the Hasmoneans. The city of Ptolemais requested the aid of Ptolemy IX before realizing this would unintentionally declare war against Ptolemy's mother, Cleopatra III, who had banished her son. Alexander did not wish to become trapped in a civil war, so he abandoned the campaign. Instead, he secretly forged an alliance with Cleopatra and then offered Ptolemy tribute so he could continue his campaign without direct involvement.

After learning of Alexander's betrayal, Ptolemy laid siege to Ptolemais and pursued Alexander, destroying much of Galilee in the process. At the Battle of Asophon, Alexander's armies were defeated by Ptolemy, who had amassed a formidable force and went on to conquer much of the regions ruled by the Hasmonean dynasty. It wasn't until Cleopatra interfered that Ptolemy withdrew to Cyprus. Alexander bowed before Cleopatra, and she allowed him to retain his rule.

Alexander's successes could not satisfy the Jews at home. The Judean civil war was primarily invoked during an incident at the Feast of Tabernacles, which Alexander presided over as high priest. During the libation ceremony, he threw water over his feet rather than pouring it over the altar, a move that upset the Pharisees. The Pharisees were a group that strictly followed traditional laws and customs. Alexander's display of frustration against the Pharisees earned him the wrath of the people, who began to insult and throw citrons at him. In response, he killed some six thousand Jews and built wooden barriers around the altar to prevent people from coming near him.

While Alexander was at first victorious in the civil conflicts that started around 92 BCE, he began to struggle when the Jews sought the aid of the Seleucids. Demetrius III provided aid and defeated Alexander at Shechem, where he was forced to withdraw into the mountains. In sympathy, around six thousand rebel Jews returned to Alexander, and he launched further attacks until Demetrius was forced to withdraw. Alexander was able to quash the rebellion and had about eight hundred Jews executed after they were forced to watch their wives and children be executed.

Alexander's reign continued, expanding the Hasmonean Kingdom into Gaulanitis and Galaaditis, as well as Transjordan. He died of an illness caused by a combination of alcoholism and malaria. He died in 76 BCE and was succeeded by his wife, Alexandra. Their son, Hyrcanus II, was named high priest.

Hyrcanus II

Alexandra was the only Jewish queen in the era of the Second Temple (the era of Jewish autonomy after the end of the Babylonian exile), and she named Hyrcanus II her successor, a role he took over after his mother's death in 67 BCE. Within three months of his ascension, Hyrcanus II's rule was challenged by his brother, Aristobulus II. The two met with their forces near Jericho, where many men abandoned Hyrcanus to join Aristobulus, giving him the victory. Hyrcanus fled to Jerusalem and sought refuge in the Second Temple, which was then besieged by his brother. A truce was reached. Hyrcanus had to relinquish the office he held, but he could continue receiving revenue.

However, the truce could not last. Hyrcanus feared his brother would kill him, a fear that was encouraged by Antipater, the general and satrap of Idumea and father to Herod the Great. Antipater wished to control the region through Hyrcanus. Bribed by Antipater, the Nabataeans offered Hyrcanus sanctuary and took Jerusalem, besieging the Temple where Aristobulus had taken refuge. At the same time, Pompey of the Roman Empire had been gaining power after defeating the Seleucids. Since the Romans had been allies of the Hasmoneans since the rule of Judas, both Hyrcanus and Aristobulus asked for aid through Pompey's deputy, Scaurus, who chose to help Aristobulus.

The matter was brought before Pompey, who favored Hyrcanus and chose to help him. Aristobulus then fortified himself in the Temple of Alexandria but surrendered when Pompey's army approached. However, his followers did not, forcing Pompey to lay siege and destroy much of the city and the Temple in the process. Hyrcanus was restored to the office of the high priest, but political authority lay with the Romans. In effect, the actual power lay with Antipater, to whom Hyrcanus deferred all matters.

In 40 BCE, at the instigation of Antigonus, Aristobulus's son, Hyrcanus, was captured by the Parthians. His ears were mutilated, making him ineligible for the high priesthood, thus taking care of the threat he posed. He was then taken to Babylonia, where he lived among the Babylonian Jews. In 36 BCE, Herod I, son of Antipater, defeated Antigonus and had Hyrcanus return to Judea, as he feared that Hyrcanus might encourage the Parthians to fight for the throne alongside him. Six years later, Herod had Hyrcanus executed under the charge of treachery. This was the end of the Hasmonean dynasty, and Herod began the Roman Herodian dynasty.

Chapter 9: The Herodian Dynasty (37 BCE–100 CE)

The foundation of the Herodian dynasty began with Antipater, who exerted great influence over Hyrcanus II and attempted to establish him on the throne as his puppet king. Antipater was able to establish better relations with the Romans, which placed him in a favorable position after Pompey ended Aristobulus's last stand in Jerusalem and established Judea as a Roman vassal state.

Julius Caesar of Rome had initially supported Aristobulus in the Hasmonean conflict, deeming him the stronger of the two candidates. Aristobulus ended up a prisoner in Rome, and Caesar could have used him to take control of Judea were it not for a clever move from Antipater, who was able to secure the favor of Caesar and ensure that Hasmonean rule belonged to Hyrcanus. It was because of Antipater that his sons were able to establish the Herodian dynasty.

Antipater and the Romans

Around 50 BCE, it appeared that Caesar might attempt to use Aristobulus to regain control of Judea. This did not work for Pompey, who had forged an alliance with Antipater and Hyrcanus. Therefore, his supporters had Aristobulus poisoned. Tensions had already been building up from Caesar's ten-year invasion of Gaul. And eventually, those tensions sparked a civil war between Pompey and Caesar. Initially, Hyrcanus, at Antipater's urging, led a force to aid Pompey. When Pompey was murdered in 48 BCE, Antipater turned the Jewish forces to help Caesar.

The Judeans were rewarded for their aid since the Romans lifted their tax obligations. Hyrcanus was reinstated as the ethnarch, or governor, though that position held little actual power, and Antipater ruled over Palestine in 47 BCE. Antipater was also appointed as the Roman procurator, an imperial governor, of Judea. As a result, Antipater was able to further his own cause, appointing his sons to positions of power. After Antipater's assassination in 43 BCE at the hands of the Nabatean king, his sons were able to maintain control of Judea and its puppet king Hyrcanus.

Rise of the Herodians: Herod the Great

Herod the Great.
https://commons.wikimedia.org/wiki/File:HerodtheGreat2.jpg

Herod the Great, son of Antipater, held much of his initial power and influence because of his father. He was made provincial governor of Galilee in 47 BCE, where he managed the taxation system and resolved the region's corruption. In this position, he cultivated a close relationship with the governor of Syria, Sextus Caesar, cousin to Julius Caesar, which secured him the position of general of Coele-Syria. In 41 BCE, Mark Antony, a Roman leader, appointed Herod and his brother Phasael as tetrarchs to serve under Hyrcanus II.

When Antigonus, son of Aristobulus, forcibly took the throne from Hyrcanus in 40 BCE, Herod escaped to Rome and begged the Romans to take a stand against Antigonus and reinstate Hyrcanus. While there, he was unexpectedly named king of the Jews by the Romans and received their aid to help him defeat Antigonus. Herod returned to Judea to win what he saw as his rightful throne from Antigonus. In an attempt to secure his claim to the throne and earn the favor of the Jews, he married Hyrcanus's daughter, Mariamne, banishing his first wife and son in the process.

In 37 BCE, Herod was able to establish himself as the sole ruler of Judea. He led an army and captured Jerusalem, taking Antigonus prisoner and sending him to Mark Antony for execution. Herod's rule might not have been welcomed by all since many Judeans were suspicious of his religious practices and did not believe him to be a true Jew. His involvement with and attempts to appease the Romans, along with his hostile behavior toward the Jewish priestly class, made Judeans less than eager to accept him as one of their own.

Judea under Herod

Herod's thirty-three-year rule over Judea helped him establish the Herodian dynasty. In effect, he was a vassal king to the Romans. However, Herod faced threats to his rule immediately after coming to the throne. His mother-in-law, Alexandra of the Hasmonean dynasty, sought to reestablish Hasmonean rule by having Aristobulus III instated as high priest.

To do this, she sought the help of Cleopatra, who was married to Mark Antony and held some influence over him. Though Cleopatra agreed to help, she also encouraged Alexandra to leave Judea with Aristobulus III to meet Antony. Herod ordered the assassination of Aristobulus III when he heard of the plot. He feared the potential meeting between Antony and Aristobulus, worrying that Aristobulus might be granted the position of high priest. Aristobulus III's assassination removed that threat to Herod's power.

A second threat to Herod's rule emerged when a power struggle began in Rome between Antony and Augustus. Herod, as a Roman vassal, was forced to pick sides. He decided to support Antony. However, Antony was defeated in 31 BCE, and Herod feared his support of Antony might result in him losing the throne. As a result, he was forced to convince Augustus of his loyalty. Herod offered the Romans passage to Syria and

Egypt, as well as tribute, and Augustus accepted. While Herod was allowed to rule Judea with autonomy, restrictions were placed on his relationships and dealings with other regions.

Much of Herd's rule was punctuated by distrust and his fear of losing the throne, which drove him to take extreme measures against potential opponents and those who could challenge his rule. Many historians suggest that Herod was not a popular ruler and that the Roman support he received was a major factor in helping him maintain power over Judea, which might have otherwise been crippled under the opposition.

Herod is reported to have taken extreme measures to assuage his fears, including deploying secret police whose job was to gather and report the feelings and attitudes of the Judean population. He acted in secret to prevent any opposition to his rule and made use of force to take down opposers and protestors. Herod also had a bodyguard made up of two thousand men, indicating he constantly feared an attack.

In addition, the lack of Jewishness in his lifestyle remained a major point of contention among the populace. He introduced foreign entertainment in Judea, which was seen as an attempt to promote Roman culture over Jewish culture. The Roman taxes the Judeans were required to pay, combined with the lavish spending by Herod, who constantly prepared excessively valuable gifts in fear of losing his popularity or support among the nobility and the Romans, further angered the Judeans.

At the time of Herod's rule, two major sects lived in Judea: the Pharisees and the Sadducees, the latter belonging to the political elite who shared similar views as the Pharisees. Both groups were unhappy with Herod's rule. The Pharisees had cause for complaint because Herod would not listen to them on matters regarding the construction and restoration of the Temple. The Sadducees were dissatisfied with his rule because Herod had handed their responsibilities for priestly duties in the Temple to Babylonian and Alexandrian outsiders. This move had been made to gain support from the Jewish diaspora living outside of Judea but earned him little favor among the Jewish community.

Architectural Achievements

While Herod did not achieve much in his efforts to be a beloved or even liked ruler, much of his rule focused on architectural projects in Judea. He undertook the reconstruction of the Second Temple, expanding the platform on which it stood to almost twice its original size and fully restoring the structure. He also began a project to expand the

Temple Mount in 19 BCE and used the latest underwater construction and hydraulic techniques to build the Caesarea Maritima. His projects also focused on building several fortresses.

However, these construction projects, much like many other administrative decisions made by Herod, served a selfish purpose. For example, the fortresses were primarily built for him and his family to take refuge in case of an attack. Other construction projects, such as those for the Temple, were intended to appease the Jewish population. Herod also built several cities for pagans to gain their support.

While these projects created substantial employment opportunities for the population, they also burdened the Jews. Herod's projects were funded by taxes, adding to the financial cost of the Judeans since they already had to pay Roman taxes. However, Herod is known to have personally provided for his people during times of crises, such as during a famine in 25 BCE.

The End of Herod

Herod's rule was punctuated by a desire to appease the various factions who were stakeholders in his rule, including the Jews, the non-Jews, and the Romans. As such, his religious policies were designed to cater to all three groups, which produced mixed results in terms of his popularity. His lavish spending was a matter of contention to his Jewish and non-Jewish subjects alike since it added a great financial burden on them. On the other hand, projects like the expansion of the Second Temple might have gained him some favor from the Jews.

Since Herod was proclaimed to be the ruler of all of the Judeans, Jews or otherwise, his policies also catered to the non-Jewish population, which might not have been well received by the Jews. His loyalty to Jewish customs and religion was often questioned because of his heritage, his non-religious practices (such as building temples for the non-Jewish populations), and the murder of his own family members, which he had done to neutralize threats to his throne.

However, some evidence suggests that Herod maintained some degree of Jewish practices in his personal life. While he might have often mixed these practices with Roman and non-Jewish traditions, he did observe some Jewish customs, which is indicated by the construction of mikvehs (baths used to achieve purity) in many of his palaces. And his efforts in building pagan cities for the non-Jewish populations should be praised since they mark the actions of a more accepting ruler than many of the later Hasmonean kings.

Herod died sometime between 5 BCE and 1 CE. The exact date of his death is disputed, though most historians agree it happened in 4 BCE. The cause of his death was an unknown and severe illness dubbed "Herod's Evil." Some narratives claim the illness was so painful that Herod attempted to end his life but was stopped by his cousin, while others suggest his attempt was successful. Regardless, the dissatisfaction with Herod's rule sparked protests and unrest after his death, and the Herodian dynasty changed following the passing of its founder.

The Tetrarchy

Before Herod's death, he created a will. He wanted his kingdom to be divided between his sons. Augustus, the Roman emperor, respected his wishes and split the kingdom in three, with a third going to each son. Herod Archelaus became the ethnarch of the regions of Samaria, Judea, and Idumea (also known as Edom). Philip was made tetrarch of the northern and eastern regions of Jordan, and Antipas was given Galilee and Perea. Of the three, Philip might have ruled with the least amount of trouble, while Archelaus faced harder challenges during his rule.

Herod Archelaus

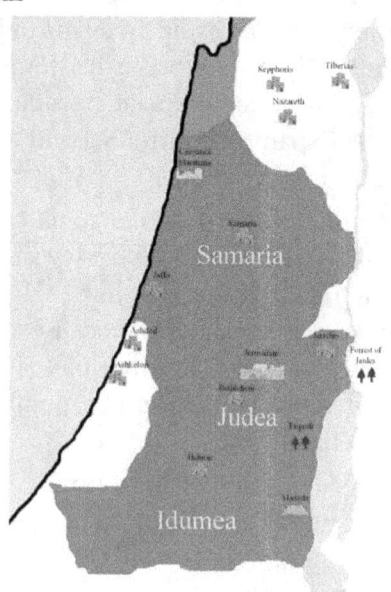

Archelaus's ethnarchy.
Rh0809, CC BY-SA 4.0 <https://creativecommons.org/licenses/by-sa/4.0>, via Wikimedia Commons; https://commons.wikimedia.org/wiki/File:Archelaus_Ethnarchy.jpg

Following his father's illness but before he had officially been declared king or tetrarch, Archelaus attempted to appease the Judean population to secure support for his rule. The protests that had broken out following Herod's death needed to be dealt with immediately to maintain peace in the region. The Judeans demanded lower taxes and the release of political prisoners. Archelaus accepted these terms to show his kindness to the people.

However, the demands of the Judeans did not end there. Herod had erected the statue of a golden eagle over the Temple, which was seen as blasphemous. In the days just before his death, the statue had been cut down, and two teachers and forty students were burned to death as punishment. The people of Judea now demanded punishment for those who had ordered and carried out the immolation of the teachers and youths.

The Jewish population also demanded that the Herod-appointed high priest be deposed and replaced with someone who was more pious. The people's non-stop demands irritated Archelaus, who asked them to be patient and wait for Augustus to officially appoint him king. However, the people did not take kindly to being told to wait, and at night, they began a mourning protest at the Temple for the executed teachers and youths. Archelaus sent several men to ask the mourners to wait until Archelaus had visited Augustus. These soldiers were stoned to death by the mourners, who then returned to their protests.

This incident was the last straw for Archelaus. He ordered the army into the Temple, and a massacre ensued, resulting in the death of some three thousand people. Finding the situation precarious, Archelaus immediately set out for Rome to meet with Augustus, where he was confronted by Antipas, his younger brother. Antipas argued that not only had Archelaus faked his grief for their father's death, but he had also produced a phony will, which gave Archelaus lands that had been intended for Antipas. He also attempted to use the massacre of the three thousand Jews against Archelaus, stating that he had acted inappropriately since he had acted like a king even though he had not yet been appointed as such.

However, the philosopher Nicolaus of Damascus came to Archelaus's aid, stating that he had acted appropriately in his capacity and in accordance with a valid will. The will was verified as having been written by Herod while of sound mind and attested by the keeper of Herod's seal.

Whether this was truly the case or if Nicolaus was serving some ulterior motive is unclear. He had been a confidant of Herod during his time, and the keeper of his seal, Ptolemy, was his cousin. After hearing this evidence, Augustus declared Archelaus the ethnarch of Judea, Samaria, and Idumea.

Opposition to Archelaus

Archelaus's rule had many problems from the start. The tensions had begun with the killing of three thousand Jews, but his rule continued to draw ire. For one, it was opposed by his brother, who believed that Archelaus had modified the will and taken the throne that was rightfully his. In addition, Archelaus divorced his first wife, Mariamne III, to marry Glaphyra, the widow of his brother Alexander, even though her second husband was still alive. The marriage went against the Mosaic Law and contributed to Archelaus's rising unpopularity.

Unrest, protests, and general unhappiness and dissatisfaction were rife during Archelaus's rule. As a result, he was unable to manage the lands he was responsible for or the people, as he could not maintain any measure of stability. Complaints of Archelaus's rule reached Augustus, who deposed the former of his rule in 6 CE. Archelaus was exiled to Vienna. The regions of Samaria, Judea, and Idumea became a Roman province. Archelaus never regained his lost throne and died around 18 CE while still in exile.

Philip

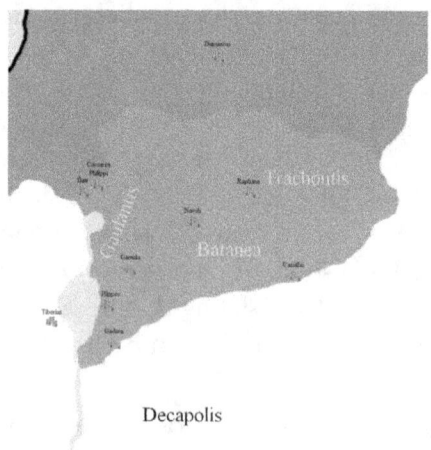

Philip's tetrarchy.
Rh0809, CC BY-SA 4.0 <https://creativecommons.org/licenses/by-sa/4.0>, via Wikimedia Commons; https://commons.wikimedia.org/wiki/File:Herod_Philip_Tetrarchy.png

The second tetrarch of the Herodians was Philip, the half-brother of Antipas and Archelaus. He ruled over regions of Jordan that included Iturea, Trachonitis, Gaulanitis, Paneas, Batanea, and Auranitis. He rebuilt the city of Caesarea Philippa during his rule, which served as the capital of his tetrarchy. Little is known of Philip's reign since most of it was uneventful. Unlike his brothers, Philip ruled in relative peace. He had few Jewish subjects to speak of, so he did not impose any significant Jewish practices on his subjects.

His ruling policy leaned more toward Hellenization. He founded the towns of Bethsaida and another along the Jordan River, which were given large degrees of self-governance in accordance with Roman practice. He was also less extravagant in his rule than his brothers, avoiding long trips to Rome and instead devoting time to his subjects and the tetrarchy. Philip ruled until his death in 34 CE.

Herod Antipas

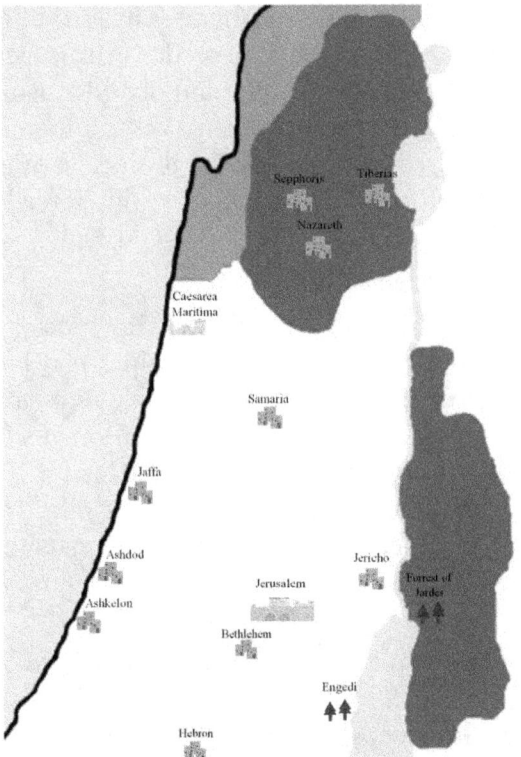

Antipas's tetrarchy.
Rh0809, CC BY-SA 4.0 <https://creativecommons.org/licenses/by-sa/4.0>, via Wikimedia Commons; https://commons.wikimedia.org/wiki/File:Antipas_Tetrarchy.jpg

While Herod Antipas laid claim to the territory that had gone to Archelaus, he was later recognized as a tetrarch by his brother and Augustus, who gave him Galilee and Perea to rule. Antipas had originally argued he should inherit the whole of Judea and rule it as its only king; however, Augustus decided to honor Herod's will. Antipas became ruler of his designated regions in 4 BCE and was immediately faced with unrest.

Just before Antipas assumed office, Judas, son of Hezekiah, attacked the palace at Sepphoris in Galilee, wreaking havoc in the region by looting it and threatening its people. In response, the governor of Syria led an attack in which Sepphoris was destroyed and the inhabitants were enslaved. The borders of Perea were home to constant skirmishes since they connected with the borders of Nabatea.

Antipas's attempts to restore order to these regions included financing construction works. He rebuilt Sepphoris and walled the city of Betharamphtha. He also built his capital city, Tiberias, to the west of the Galilee Sea in honor of Tiberius, who succeeded Augustus in 14 CE. The city held a stadium and a prayer sanctuary and played a significant role as a center of learning during the Jewish-Roman Wars. It was not a successful project at first, as Jews refused to live in it since it was built over a graveyard. Antipas was forced to populate it with forced migrants and slaves.

Contention with John the Baptist

Antipas's conflict with John the Baptist, a Judean prophet and missionary, began over Antipas's marriage. Antipas had been married to the daughter of King Aretas of Nabatea, probably as a strategic move to improve relations between the Nabateans and the Romans. While Antipas was visiting his half-brother, Herod II, he fell for his wife, Herodias, and the two agreed to marry after Antipas divorced his wife. His former wife chose to return to her father, and after having her safely in his custody, Aretas declared war, which might have occurred sometime around 36 CE, two years after Herodias and Antipas were married.

Antipas also faced opposition at home. John the Baptist began preaching between 28 and 29 CE near the Jordan River on the edge of Perea. As related in the Gospel of Mark, he used Antipas's marriage to criticize an incestuous practice, as Herodias was also Antipas's niece and had been his brother's wife. John also encouraged the widespread belief that the two had married while Herodias's first husband still lived, although the two were divorced before her second marriage. Given John's influence, Antipas feared a rebellion since many Jews did not approve of his union with his second wife. John was arrested and imprisoned in the fortress of Machaerus and was executed when Herodias urged her daughter to ask for John's head.

The Execution of Jesus of Nazareth

When Jesus of Nazareth began preaching in Galilee, Antipas feared it was John risen from the dead. Fearful of what might happen, Antipas plotted the execution of Jesus. Jesus was reportedly warned of such a plot and declared that he, as a prophet, was not vulnerable to such schemes. Antipas might have also played a role in his trial. Pontius Pilate, the governor of Judea who presided over the trial of Jesus, sent him to Antipas since Jesus was from Galilee and, therefore, under Antipas's jurisdiction.

Antipas hoped to see Jesus perform a miracle, for which he was known, and was reportedly pleased to see him. But Jesus refused to perform one. Antipas mocked him and sent him back to Pilate, where he was crucified on the charge of blasphemy. Pilate's actions served to improve relations between the two rulers, as Jesus had posed a threat to Antipas's rule and had caused much unrest, thus pacifying the earlier enmity between Pilate and Antipas. It is not known why the two were upset with each other, but many historians believe it may have had something to do with the massacre of some Galileans.

End of Antipas

The hostilities with the Nabatean king turned into an all-out war in 36 CE. After suffering humiliating defeats at the hands of the Nabateans, who were joined by deserters from Antipas's brother, Philip's, armies, Antipas turned to Roman Emperor Tiberius for help. Tiberius ordered the governor of Syria, Vitellius, to provide aid. Vitellius prepared two forces, which were instructed to march around Judea while he attended a festival in Jerusalem, where Antipas was also in attendance. There, news reached Vitellius of Tiberius's death. He stated he no longer held the authority to carry out the attack and recalled his troops, although some sources suggest that an argument between Vitellius and Antipas caused the former to use Tiberius's death as an excuse to withdraw his support.

Antipas's end came at the hands of his nephew, Agrippa, who had turned to his uncle for help when he found himself struggling with much debt. Antipas refused to provide any money. Agrippa was later imprisoned when he was heard telling his friend Caligula that he could not wait for

Tiberius to die and for Caligula, Augustus's great-grandson, to become ruler. After Caligula became emperor in 37 CE, he had Agrippa released and gave him Philip's tetrarchy following his death.

Agrippa then set about seeking his revenge and accused Antipas of plotting against the emperor and of stocking up weaponry to lead an assault. Since Antipas had a store of weapons that he could not deny, Caligula believed Agrippa's other accusations and exiled Antipas to an undetermined location, where he died.

The End of the Herodian Dynasty

Agrippa's close friendship with Caligula secured him the position of tetrarch, and he was given Philip's territories in 37 CE. In 40 CE, after Antipas had been exiled, his territories were given to Agrippa. In the following year, Agrippa was also given the territories that had once been governed by Archelaus. Thus, Agrippa reunited the Herodian dynasty as it had once existed under Herod I and became its sole ruler under the Romans.

Agrippa died in 44 CE and was succeeded by his son, Agrippa II. He did not inherit all of his father's territories, nor was he given a rule anywhere as vast as Agrippa I. Instead, he was given the tetrarchy of Chalcis, to which were later added the territories that had once been ruled by Philip. When the first revolt began in the Jewish-Roman Wars, which broke out in response to Roman oppression, heavy taxation, and religious conflicts between the Romans and the Jews, Agrippa II was an active participant on the side of the Romans.

Agrippa had initially attempted to avoid a war with Rome altogether. The Jews refused to pay taxes that were owed to the Romans, and Agrippa desperately tried to pacify the situation by encouraging the people to withstand some of the injustices and accept Roman rule. He failed to suppress the rebellion and was driven out of Jerusalem, along with his sister, Bernice, in 66 CE. He also provided aid to the Roman forces in the form of archers and cavalry units to show his support to the emperor. He even accompanied the Romans on some campaigns. After the capture of Jerusalem, Agrippa II returned to Rome, where he was designated praetor and given additional territories to rule.

With the death of Agrippa II, sometime between 92 and 100 CE, the Herodian dynasty came to an end. The lands ruled by Agrippa as a tetrarch were incorporated into the Roman Empire.

Conclusion

The role ancient Israel played in the formation of religious history and in the current religious landscape cannot be doubted. In the present day, many of the currently practiced religions find their bases in ancient Israel, making its study vital to understand the ways in which these ancient peoples and regions continue to affect modern life.

To begin with, the ancient Israelites introduced one of the world's first monotheistic religions. Before this, most religious practices were polytheistic or, at best, henotheistic, such as during the rule of the Persian Empire. Idol worshiping and the worship of multiple gods and deities were common, and the concept of worshiping a single god was new and unprecedented at the time.

The basis of the Israelite religion, the Ten Commandments, played an important role in the foundations of other religions. The Hebrew scriptures lay the basis of Judaism. The appointment of the Israelites as God's chosen people at Mount Sinai forms an integral part of the Jewish belief system, with Jews having to set an example to the world of righteous behavior.

Moreover, the Israelite religion forms the basis of Christianity, with the Hebrew scriptures forming part of the Old Testament. Christianity also recognizes many prominent Israelite figures, such as David and Abraham. The religion of Islam also recognizes the prophethood of these figures and acknowledges Hebrew scriptures as divine revelations. So, two of the world's largest and most widely practiced religions are derived from Judaism, which itself is an extension of the religion of the ancient

Israelites.

Ancient Israelite history began with the Iron Age, and archaeological discoveries have attested to the period with the findings of iron tools in the region. Given that the Bible and the Hebrew scriptures provide an extensive history of the region, archaeological efforts have been focused on making discoveries that can verify or further expand on events related to the Bible. However, in most instances, the religious scriptures offer the only evidence of some events.

The main focus of archaeologists in Israel has always been to explain, expand, or illustrate religious passages through discoveries. Such evidence aids in the interpretation of the Bible. For example, many historians once believed that Jesus might not have been real. Today, enough evidence has been uncovered to attest that he did exist. Thus, it stands to reason that events without significant archaeological evidence might have at least some basis in fact.

The influence of the Israelites persists today in more ways than one. The history of the region, as it transformed from an independent state to being ruled by foreigners to then being granted relative autonomy under the rule of foreign nations, narrates the progress of a nation that survives to this day, with its religious system intact, despite the enmeshment of different cultures and religions throughout the later parts of its existence.

In addition, the architectural feats of the Jews, even during the period of vassal rule, hold great value today. The remains of the Second Temple, which was destroyed by the Romans (only the western wall remains), is a sacred site to Jews today and is a reminder of their plight. However, even though the Jews suffered under foreign religious influences and rulers, they persevered and did not allow their beliefs to fail or be lost to time.

Here's another book by Enthralling History that you might like

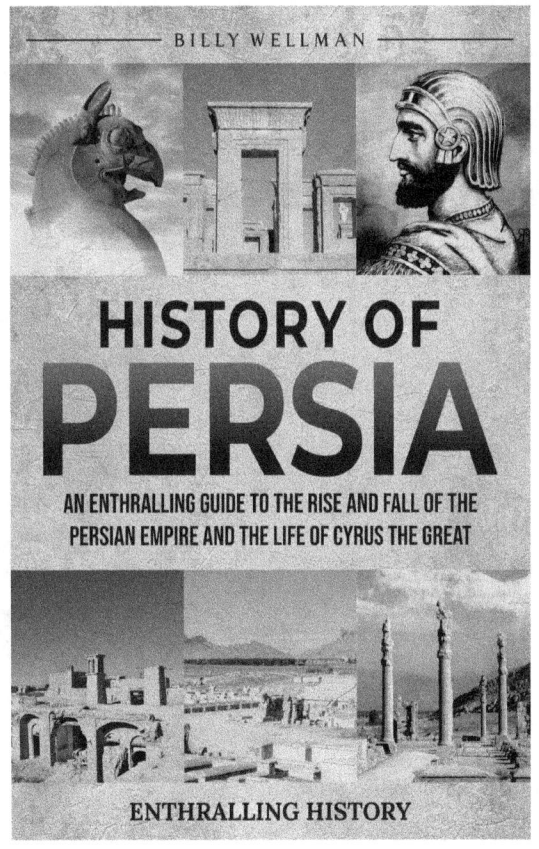

Free limited time bonus

Stop for a moment. We have a free bonus set up for you. The problem is this: we forget 90% of everything that we read after 7 days. Crazy fact, right? Here's the solution: we've created a printable, 1-page pdf summary for this book that you're reading now. All you have to do to get your free pdf summary is to go to the following website:

https://livetolearn.lpages.co/enthrallinghistory/

Once you do, it will be intuitive. Enjoy, and thank you!

Bibliography

Alstola, Tero. "Judean Merchants in Babylonia and Their Participation in Long-Distance Trade." *Die Welt Des Orients* 47, no. 1 (2017): 25-51. http://www.jstor.org/stable/26384887.

Baker, Luke. "Ancient Tablets Reveal Life of Jews in Nebuchadnezzar's Babylon." *Reuters*,

Bareket, Elinoar. "The Head of the Jews (Ra'is al-Yahud) in Fatimid Egypt: A Re-Evaluation." *Bulletin of the School of Oriental and African Studies, University of London* 67, no. 2 (2004): 185-97. http://www.jstor.org/stable/4145978.

Baron, Salo W. *A Social and Religious History of the Jews*. New York: Columbia University Press, 1957.

Baskin, Judith R. ed. and Kenneth Seeskin, ed. *The Cambridge Guide to Jewish History, Religion, and Culture*. New York: Cambridge University Press, 2012.

Bertman, Stephen. *Handbook to Life in Ancient Mesopotamia*. Oxford: Oxford University Press, 2005.

Brenner, Michael. *After the Holocaust: Rebuilding Jewish Lives in Postwar Germany*. Translated by Barbara Harshav. Princeton: Princeton University Press, 1997.

Brook, Kevin Alan. *The Jews of Khazaria*. Lanham, Maryland: Rowman & Littlefield, 2018.

Cohen, Mark R. "Jews in the Mamlūk Environment: The Crisis of 1442 (A Geniza Study)." *Bulletin of the School of Oriental and African Studies, University of London* 47, no. 3 (1984): 425-48. http://www.jstor.org/stable/618879.

Cohn-Sherbok, Dan. *Judaism: History, Belief and Practice.* New York: Routledge, 2017.

Cohn-Wein, Eli. *The Golden Age of Jewish Philosophy.* Sefaria. https://www.sefaria.org/sheets/327268?lang=bi

Dalley, Stephanie. *Myths from Mesopotamia Creation, the Flood, Gilgamesh, and Others.* Oxford: Oxford University Press, 2008.

Delorme, Jean-Philippe. "בת דוד in the Mesha Stele: A Defense of André Lemaire's Reading and Its Historical Implications." *SBL and AAR New England and Eastern Canada Region Annual Meeting.* Tufts University, Massachusetts, March 22, 2019.

"Einstein's Deeply Held Political Beliefs." *American Museum of Natural History.* https://www.amnh.org/exhibitions/einstein/global-citizen#:~:text=Although%20Einstein%20did%20not%20observe,that%20I%20belong%20to%20it.%22

Enuma Elish: The Seven Tablets of Creation. Translated by Leonard William King. London: Luzac, 1902. https://www.sacred-texts.com/ane/enuma.htm

Eridu Genesis. Translated by Thorkild Jacobson. Livius, accessed October 18, 2021. https://www.livius.org/sources/content/oriental-varia/eridu-genesis/

Gibb, H. A. R. The Damascus Chronicle of the Crusades: Extracted and Translated from the Chronicle of Ibn Al-Qalanisi. Mineola, New York: Dover Publications, 2003.

Haas, Richard N. "Israel at 75." *The Strategist: Australian Strategic Policy Institute.* May 23, 2023. https://www.aspistrategist.org.au/israel-at-75/

Herodotus. *Capture of Babylon.* Livius. https://www.livius.org/articles/person/darius-the-great/sources/capture-of-babylon-herodotus/

"Immigration to Israel: The First Aliyah (1882-1903)." *Jewish Virtual Library.*

Jacob, Walter, ed. The Pittsburgh Platform in Retrospect: The Changing World of Reform Judaism. Pittsburgh: Rodef Shalom Congregation Press, 1985.

Johnson, Paul. *A History of the Jews.* New York: Harper & Row, 1987.

Josephus, Flavius. *The Antiquities of the Jews.* Translated by William Whiston. Project Gutenberg EBook. https://www.gutenberg.org/files/2848/2848-h/2848-h.htm

Josephus, Flavius. *The Wars of the Jews.* Translated by William Whiston. Project Gutenberg EBook. https://www.gutenberg.org/files/2850/2850-h/2850-h.htm

Lenin, Theodore I., et al. *Associates, Rabbi and Synagogue in Reform Judaism.* West Harford: Central Conference of American Rabbis, 1972, 98-99.

Marcus, Jacob. *The Jew in the Medieval World: A Sourcebook, 315-1791.* New York: Jewish Publication Society, 1938.

Meyer, Michael A. Response to Modernity: A History of the Reform Movement in Judaism. New York: Oxford University Press, 1988.

Minsky, Michael G. *Agobard and His Relations with the Jews.* Amherst: University of Massachusetts, 1971.

Na'aman, Nadav. "Three Notes on the Aramaic Inscription from Tel Dan." *Israel Exploration Journal* 50, no. ½ (2000): 92–104. http://www.jstor.org/stable/27926919.

Nebel, Almut, Dvora Filon, Deborah A. Weiss, Michael Weale, Marina Faerman, Ariella Oppenheim, Mark G. Thomas. "High-resolution Y Chromosome Haplotypes of Israeli and Palestinian Arabs Reveal Geographic Substructure and Substantial Overlap with Haplotypes of Jews." *Human Genetics.* 107, no. 6 (December 2000): 630–641. doi:10.1007/s004390000426.

Pollock, Susan. *Ancient Mesopotamia.* Cambridge: Cambridge University Press, 1999.

Rohl, John C. G. The Kaiser and His Court: Wilhelm II and the Government of Germany. Cambridge: Cambridge University Press, 1995.

"S/Agenda/58." *Security Council Official Records.* (April 16, 1948), 19.

Shagrir, Iris, and Netta Amir. "The Persecution of the Jews in the First Crusade: Liturgy, Memory, and Nineteenth-Century Visual Culture." *Speculum* 92, no. 2 (2017): 405–28. http://www.jstor.org/stable/26340194.

Shaus, Arie, Yana Gerber, Shira Faigenbaum-Golovin, Barak Sober, Eli Piasetzky, and Israel Finkelstein. "Forensic Document Examination and Algorithmic Handwriting Analysis of Judahite Biblical Period Inscriptions Reveal Significant Literacy Level." *PLOS One.* September 9, 2020. https://doi.org/10.1371/journal.pone.0237962 S

Stub, Sara Toth. "Letter from Ethiopia: Exploring a Forgotten Jewish Land." *Archaeology.* January/February 2023. https://www.archaeology.org/issues/498-2301/letter-from/11057-ethiopia-beta-israel

Talmud. The William Davidson Edition. Sefaria. https://www.sefaria.org/texts/Talmud

The Book of Maccabees II. Second Temple. Sefaria. https://www.sefaria.org/The_Book_of_Maccabees_II?tab=contents

"The Code of Hammurabi." Translated by L.W. King. In *The Avalon Project: Documents in Law, History, and Diplomacy.* Yale Law School: Lillian Goldman Law Library. https://avalon.law.yale.edu/ancient/hamframe.asp

The Complete Tanakh: The Jewish Bible with a Modern English Translation and Rashi's Commentary.

https://www.chabad.org/library/bible_cdo/aid/63255/jewish/The-Bible-with-Rashi.htm

"The Program of the National-Socialist German Workers' Party, February 24, 1920." *Jewish Virtual Library.* https://www.jewishvirtuallibrary.org/platform-of-the-national-socialist-german-workers-rsquo-party

"The Question of Palestine." *United Nations.* https://www.un.org/unispal/history/#:~:text=After%20looking%20at%20alternatives%2C%20the,(II)%20of%201947).

"The Suez Crisis, 1956." *Office of the Historian.* Foreign Service Institute: United States Department of State. https://history.state.gov/milestones/1953-1960/suez#:~:text=On%20July%2026%2C%201956%2C%20Egyptian,since%20its%20construction%20in%201869.

Van De Mieroop, Marc. *A History of the Ancient Near East ca. 3000 - 323 BC.* Hoboken: Blackwell Publishing, 2006.

Van Maaren, John. *The Boundaries of Jewishness in the Southern Levant 200 BCE–132 CE.* 43-108. Boston: De Gruyter, 2022. https://doi.org/10.1515/9783110787450-002

Ballentine, Debra Scoggins. "The Kingdom of Judah." *Bible Odyssey,* 2009, https://www.bibleodyssey.org/places/main-articles/the-kingdom-of-judah/.

Bell, Kelly. "Judas Maccabeus, Hammer of the Jews." *Warfare History Network,* 2009, https://warfarehistorynetwork.com/article/judas-maccabeus-hammer-of-the-jews/.

BibleToday. "WHY IS THE BIBLE GOD'S WORD?" *BibleToday,* 2020, https://www.bibletoday.com/?gclid=Cj0KCQjwt_qgBhDFARIsABcDjOfmwnQ38bDtShSe0SDZZ-3GSLAl-AtwE23EAHE-n1J2Xf0qJkovWdEaAkqZEALw_wcB.

Boston University. "First Temple Period: Jerusalem as the Capital of Judahite Kingdom (930-722)." *Capital of Judah I (930-722),* 2020, https://www.bu.edu/mzank/Jerusalem/p/period2-2-1.htm.

Britannica, Editors of Encyclopedia. "Biblical literature | Definition, Types, Significance, Survey, & Development." *Encyclopedia Britannica,* 30 March 2023, https://www.britannica.com/topic/biblical-literature.

Britannica, The Editors of Encyclopedia. "Hasmonean dynasty." *Encyclopedia Britannica,* 2021, https://www.britannica.com/topic/Hasmonean-dynasty.

Britannica, The Editors of Encyclopedia. "Israelite." *Encyclopedia Britannica,* 2022, https://www.britannica.com/topic/Israelite.

Britannica, The Editors of Encyclopedia. "Judah | Hebrew tribe | Britannica." *Encyclopedia Britannica,* 2023, https://www.britannica.com/topic/Judah-Hebrew-tribe.

Brown, William. "Ancient Israelite & Judean Religion." *World History Encyclopedia*, 13 July 2017, https://www.worldhistory.org/article/1097/ancient-israelite--judean-religion/.

Cataliotti, Joseph, and Christopher Sailus. "Israelites History, Timeline & Religion | Who were the Israelites? - Video & Lesson Transcript." *Study.com*, 7 October 2022, https://study.com/learn/lesson/israelites-history-timeline-religion-who-were-the-israelites.html.

The Church of Jesus Christ. "The Assyrian Conquest and the Lost Tribes." *The Church of Jesus Christ of Latter-day Saints*, 2022, https://www.churchofjesuschrist.org/study/manual/old-testament-student-manual-kings-malachi/enrichment-d?lang=eng.

Claudia, F. "King Saul of Israel: History & Timeline | Who Was the First King of Israel? - Video & Lesson Transcript." *Study.com*, 21 October 2021, https://study.com/academy/lesson/king-saul-of-israel-history-timeline-quiz.html.

Cornerstone Connections. "The Golden Age of Israel." *Cornerstone Connections*, 2015, https://www.cornerstoneconnections.net/assets/teens/Lessons/2015/Q4/English/TEACHER/CC-15-Q4-L11-T.pdf.

Cundall, Arthur E. "The United Monarchy: Fact or Fiction?" *Vox Evangelica*, vol. 8, 1973, pp. 33-39, https://biblicalstudies.org.uk/pdf/vox/vol08/monarchy_cundall.pdf.

Encyclopedia Judaica. "Antigonus II." *Encyclopedia.com*, 2023, https://www.encyclopedia.com/religion/encyclopedias-almanacs-transcripts-and-maps/antigonus-ii.

Encyclopedia.com. "Hasmoneans." *Encyclopedia.com*, 2018, https://www.encyclopedia.com/people/philosophy-and-religion/judaism-biographies/hasmoneans.

Facts and Details. "MOSES, MT. SINAI, THE TEN COMMANDMENTS, THE GOLDEN CALF AND HIS DEATH JUST SHORT OF THE PROMISED LAND." *Facts and Details*, 2018, https://factsanddetails.com/world/cat55/3sub1/entry-5698.html.

Faust, A. "Cities and Towns in Ancient Israel (Bronze and Iron Ages)." *Encyclopedia of the History of Science, Technology, and Medicine in Non-Western Cultures*, edited by Helaine Selin, Springer, 2008.

Ferguson, John. "Hellenistic age | History, Characteristics, Art, Philosophy, Religion, & Facts." *Encyclopedia Britannica*, 17 March 2023, https://www.britannica.com/event/Hellenistic-Age.

Finkelstein, Israel. "The Campaign of Shoshenq I to Palestine: A Guide to the 10th Century BCE Polity." *eitschrift Des Deutschen Palästina-Vereins*, vol. 118, no. 2, 2002, pp. 109-135. *JSTOR*, https://www.jstor.org/stable/27931693.

Finkelstein, Louis, and W. D. Davies, editors. *The Cambridge History of Judaism: Volume 2, The Hellenistic Age.* Cambridge University Press, 2008.

Fraser, Peter Marshall, et al. "Palestine." *Encyclopedia Britannica,* 21 March 2023, https://www.britannica.com/place/Palestine.

Gier, Nicholas F. "Hebrew Henotheism." *University of Idaho,* 2020, https://www.webpages.uidaho.edu/ngier/henotheism.htm.

Gilad, Elon. "Meet the Hasmoneans: A Brief History of a Violent Epoch - Jewish World." *Haaretz,* 23 December 2014, https://www.haaretz.com/jewish/2014-12-23/ty-article/meet-the-hasmoneans/0000017f-e30d-d75c-a7ff-ff8d7cdd0000.

Gottheil, Richard, and Samuel Krauss. "PTOLEMY I - JewishEncyclopedia.com." *Jewish Encyclopedia,* 2021, https://www.jewishencyclopedia.com/articles/12420-ptolemy-i.

Grabbe, L. L. "The History of Israel: The Persian and Hellenistic Periods." *Text in Context: Essays by Members of the Society for Old Testament Study,* edited by A. D. H. Mayes, OUP Oxford, 2000. Accessed 3 April 2023.

Harris, Raphael. "The Golden Age of Israel." *The Jewish Magazine,* 1999, http://www.jewishmag.com/18mag/golden/golden.htm.

The Hebrew University of Jerusalem. "Hellenistic Period." *Tel Dor,* 2014, http://dor.huji.ac.il/periods_HL.html.

Herron, Dustin. "Israel and Judah: Difference Between the Two Kingdoms." *The Fellowship of Israel Related Ministries,* 2 June 2021, https://firmisrael.org/learn/israel-and-judah-two-kingdoms-and-their-differences/.

Higgins, William. "Dangerous Partnerships: The story of Jehoshaphat & Ahab." *Christian teaching,* 1 March 2008, https://williamshiggins.net/2008/03/01/dangerous-partnerships-the-story-of-jehoshaphat-ahab/.

HISTORY Editors. "Hellenistic Greece." *HISTORY.com,* 4 February 2010, https://www.history.com/topics/ancient-greece/hellenistic-greece.

HISTORY Editors. "Iron Age." *HISTORY,* 3 January 2018, https://www.history.com/topics/pre-history/iron-age.

Horwitz, Aharon. "A Brief History of Ancient Jerusalem | The Jerusalem to do guide - AAJ." *Jerusalem*

Hunt, Robert D. "Herod and Augustus: A Look at Patron-Client Relationships." *BYU ScholarsArchive,* 2002, https://scholarsarchive.byu.edu/cgi/viewcontent.cgi?article=1013&context=studiaantiqua.

Israel Antiquities Authority. "The Archaeological Periods in Israel." *Antiquities.org,* 2022, https://www.antiquities.org.il/t/PeriodSub_en.aspx?id=3.

Israel Embassy. "History: Second Temple." *Israeli Missions Around the World*, 2018, https://embassies.gov.il/baku/AboutIsrael/history/Pages/History-Second-Temple.aspx.

Jarus, Owen. "Ancient Israel: History of the kingdoms and dynasties formed by ancient Jewish people." *Live Science*, 22 September 2022, https://www.livescience.com/55774-ancient-israel.html.

Jewish History. "Alexander the Great." *Jewish History*, 2020, https://www.jewishhistory.org/alexander-the-great/.

King, James, and Frank W. Walbank. "Saul | king of Israel | Britannica." *Encyclopedia Britannica*, 7 March 2023, https://www.britannica.com/biography/Saul-king-of-Israel.

Kunst Historisches Museum Wein. "Judah after Alexander the Great." *Kunst Historisches Museum Wein*, 2020, https://data1.geo.univie.ac.at/projects/muenzeundmacht/showcases/showcase2%3Flanguage=en.html.

Laie, Benjamin T., and Osama Shukir. "Mesopotamian Effects on Israel During the Iron Age." *World History Encyclopedia*, 23 December 2015, https://www.worldhistory.org/article/850/mesopotamian-effects-on-israel-during-the-iron-age/.

Lendering, Jona. "Herod Antipas." *Livius.org*, 4 August 2020, https://www.livius.org/articles/person/herod-antipas/.

Lendering, Jona. "Herod Archelaus." *Livius.org*, 23 April 2020, https://www.livius.org/articles/person/herod-archelaus/.

Lendering, Jona. "Philip." *Livius.org*, 21 April 2020, https://www.livius.org/articles/person/herod-philip/.

Lipschits, Oded, and Manfred Oeming. *Judah and the Judeans in the Persian Period*. Penn State University Press, 2006.

Mark, Joshua J. "Kingdom of Israel." *World History Encyclopedia*, 26 October 2018, https://www.worldhistory.org/Kingdom_of_Israel/.

Maxine Grossman. "Legacy of Ancient Israel - Legacy of Ancient Israel Ancient Israel - "Israel" was first." *University of Maryland*, 2020, https://www.studocu.com/en-us/document/university-of-maryland/introduction-to-the-hebrew-bible/engl262-legacy-of-ancient-israel/40401708.

Miller, Charlotte. "The Importance of the Israelites and Ancient Israel." *LibreTexts*, 2020, https://human.libretexts.org/Bookshelves/History/World_History/Book%3A_World_History_-_Cultures_States_and_Societies_to_1500_(Berger_et_al.)/02%3A_Early_Middle_Eastern_and_Northeast_African_Civilizations/2.12%3A_The_Importance_of_the_Israelites_and_Ancient_Israel

Moulton, Sunday. "Iron Age: Timeline & Facts." *Study.com*, 2023, https://study.com/academy/lesson/iron-age-timeline-facts.html.

Muscato, Christopher. "Kingdom of Judea: History & Explanation - Video & Lesson Transcript." *Study.com*, 2020, https://study.com/academy/lesson/kingdom-of-judea-history-lesson-quiz.html.

Nenner, Ravit, and Noa Evron. "Ancient Jerusalem: The Village, the Town, the City." *Biblical Archaeology Society*, 2022, https://www.biblicalarchaeology.org/daily/biblical-sites-places/jerusalem/ancient-jerusalem/.

New World Encyclopedia. "Henotheism." *New World Encyclopedia*, 2021, https://www.newworldencyclopedia.org/entry/Henotheism.

New World Encyclopedia. "Kingdom of Judah." *New World Encyclopedia*, 2018, https://www.newworldencyclopedia.org/entry/Kingdom_of_Judah.

Oates, Harry. "The Maccabean Revolt." *World History Encyclopedia*, 29 October 2015, https://www.worldhistory.org/article/827/the-maccabean-revolt/.

O'Connor, David, and Stephen Quirke. "Why Were the Philistines and Israelites Enemies." *DailyHistory.org*, 2018, https://dailyhistory.org/Why_Were_the_Philistines_and_Israelites_Enemies.

Penn Museum. "IRON AGE I - Canaan & Ancient Israel @ University of Pennsylvania Museum of Archaeology and Anthropology." *Penn Museum*, 2016, https://www.penn.museum/sites/Canaan/IronAgeI.html.

Prabhat, S. "Israel and Judah." *Difference Between*, 2021, http://www.differencebetween.net/miscellaneous/culture-miscellaneous/difference-between-israel-and-judah/.

Profilbaru. "Yehud (Babylonian province)." *PROFILBARU.COM*, 2023, https://profilbaru.com/article/Yehud_(Babylonian_province).

Rice, Damien, and Matt Galbraith. "Biblical Israel: The Land of Kush." *The Curse of Ham*, Princeton University Press, 2003, https://www.degruyter.com/document/doi/10.1515/9781400828548.17/pdf.

Rice, Damien, and Matt Galbraith. "The Persian Period and the Origins of Israel: Beyond the "Myths."" *Critical Issues in Early Israelite History*, 16 November 2008, https://www.degruyter.com/document/doi/10.1515/9781575065984-007/html.

Ritenbaugh, Richard T. "What the Bible says about Israel's Golden Age." *Bible Tools*, 2013, https://www.bibletools.org/index.cfm/fuseaction/Topical.show/RTD/cgg/ID/17709/Israels-Golden-Age.htm.

Rogerson, J. W. "Israel to the End of the Persian Period: History, Social, Political, and Economic background." *The Oxford Handbook of Biblical Studies*, edited by Judith M. Lieu and J. W. Rogerson, OUP Oxford, 2008.

Rolling, C. "Henotheism in the Bible - 807 Words | 123 Help Me." *123HelpMe.com*, 2020, https://www.123helpme.com/essay/Henotheism-In-The-Bible-526821.

Rooke, Deborah W. *Zadok's Heirs: The Role and Development of the High Priesthood in Ancient Israel.* Clarendon Press, 2000.

Rose, Jenny. "The "Persian" Period - Biblical Studies." *Oxford Bibliographies*, 2020, https://www.oxfordbibliographies.com/display/document/obo-9780195393361/obo-9780195393361-0194.xml.

Ross, Lesli Koppelman. "The Hasmonean Dynasty." *My Jewish Learning*, 2015, https://www.myjewishlearning.com/article/the-hasmonean-dynasty/.

Rubel, Ahsan, and JE Wright. "The Campaign of Pharaoh Shoshenq I in Palestine | Bible Interp." *Bible Interpretation*, 2004, https://bibleinterp.arizona.edu/articles/Wilson-Campaign_of_Shoshenq_I_1.

Schäfer, Peter. "History of the Ptolemies." *Boston University*, 2009, https://www.bu.edu/mzank/Jerusalem/cp/ptolemies.htm.

Shapira, Dan. "Who Were the Hasmoneans?" *Tablet Magazine*, 30 November 2021, https://www.tabletmag.com/sections/history/articles/who-were-the-hasmoneans.

Thomas, Brian C. "Significance of Israel in Bible Prophecy." *God 1st Bible Fellowship*, 2020, https://www.god1st.org/Signficance-of-Israel-in-Prophecy.

TimeMaps. "Ancient Israel: Religion, Culture and History." *TimeMaps*, 2011, https://timemaps.com/civilizations/ancient-israel/.

Trentin, Summer, and Debby Sneed. "The Hellenistic Period-Cultural & Historical Overview | Department of Classics." *University of Colorado Boulder*, 14 June 2018, https://www.colorado.edu/classics/2018/06/14/hellenistic-period-cultural-historical-overview.

United Church of God. "Israel's Golden Age." *United Church of God*, 16 February 2011, https://www.ucg.org/bible-study-tools/booklets/the-united-states-and-britain-in-bible-prophecy/israels-golden-age.

United Church of God. "Israel's Golden Age." *United Church of God*, 16 February 2011, https://www.ucg.org/bible-study-tools/booklets/the-united-states-and-britain-in-bible-prophecy/israels-golden-age.

Velázquez, Efraín, and JE Wright. "The Persian Period and the Origins of Israel: Beyond the "Myths" | Bible Interp." *Bible Interpretation*, 2009, https://bibleinterp.arizona.edu/articles/persian.

World History. "The legacy of ancient Israel." *World history*, 3 September 2015, https://www.worldhistory.biz/ancient-history/70552-the-legacy-of-ancient-israel.html.

Zhakevich, Philip, and Ben Noonan. "From Texts to Scribes: Evidence for Writing in Ancient Israel." *American Society of Overseas Research (ASOR)*, 2021, https://www.asor.org/anetoday/2021/08/writing-in-ancient-israel.

www.ingramcontent.com/pod-product-compliance
Lightning Source LLC
Chambersburg PA
CBHW070327010526
44107CB00004B/441